Ultimate Glory

Also by David Gessner

All the Wild That Remains

The Tarball Chronicles

My Green Manifesto

Soaring with Fidel

The Prophet of Dry Hill

Sick of Nature

Return of the Osprey

Under the Devil's Thumb

A Wild, Rank Place

Ultimate Glory

Frisbee, Obsession, and My Wild Youth

DAVID GESSNER

RIVERHEAD BOOKS

NEW YORK

2017

RIVERHEAD BOOKS
An imprint of Penguin Random House LLC
375 Hudson Street
New York, New York 10014

The author gratefully acknowledges permission to quote from the following:

Excerpt from "To My Twenties" from *The Collected Poems of Kenneth Koch* by Kenneth Koch, copyright © 2005 by the Kenneth Koch Literary Estate. Used by permission of Alfred A. Knopf, an imprint of the Knopf Doubleday Publishing Group, a division of Penguin Random House LLC. All rights reserved.

Excerpt from "East Coker" from *Four Quartets* by T. S. Eliot. Copyright © 1940 by T. S. Eliot. Copyright © renewed 1968 by Esme Valerie Eliot. Reprinted in the United States by permission of Houghton Mifflin Harcourt Publishing Company. Reprinted outside the United States by permission of Faber and Faber Ltd. All rights reserved.

Lines from "Brandy (You're a Fine Girl)." Words and music by Elliot Lurie © 1971 (renewed) WB Music Corp. and Braided Chain Music in the United States. All rights outside the United States administered by Chappell & Co., Inc. All rights reserved. Used by permission of Alfred Publishing, LLC.

PHOTOGRAPH CREDITS
Pages xiii, 73, 105, 136, 155, 157, 164, 180: © 2016 Stuart S. Beringer. Page 4: Used by permission of Ellise Fuchs. Pages 9, 249: Photo © Dan Hyslop. Page 35: Used by permission of Mark Epstein. Page 41: Photo courtesy of the author. Page 70: Used by permission of Tom Kennedy. This picture was originally published in *Ultimate: Fundamentals of the Sport* and is used by permission of the authors. Page 90: Used by permission of Robert Richardson. Pages 128, 258: © Karl Cook. Page 176: Used by permission of Ken Dobyns. Page 192: Used by permission of Toby Green. Pages 199, 223: Used by permission of Mark Honerkamp. Page 296: Photo courtesy of *Rocky Mountain News*. Pages 301, 312, 328: Photographer unknown. Page 308: © Rick Collins. Page 325: Photo by Paul Andris/UltiPhotos.

ISBN 9780735210561

Printed in the United States of America
1 3 5 7 9 10 8 6 4 2

BOOK DESIGN BY AMANDA DEWEY

Some names and identifying characteristics have been changed to protect the privacy of the individuals involved.

Penguin is committed to publishing works of quality and integrity. In that spirit, we are proud to offer this book to our readers; however, the story, the experiences, and the words are the author's alone.

To Jeff Sandler, Jim Levine, Paul Turner, Neal Lischner, Roger Gallagher, Steve Gustafson, David Barkan, Bill McAvoy, Craig MacNaughton, Matt Fogarty, "Rasta" Bill Newman, Steve Smith, Roger Geller, Adam "Mada" Phillips, Chris Phillips, Matt Williamson, Mike Becker, Ted Roach, Tommy Conlon, Bob Harding, Hank Miller, and Mark Honerkamp. In other words, to the Hostages.

CONTENTS

To the Reader

first set out to write this book almost twenty years ago. It came close to being published, but in the end the editors and marketers didn't know what to make of this thing called Ultimate Frisbee. I was used to that. As you will see in these pages it isn't always easy to commit fully to something that many regard as ridiculous. Frustrated, I turned parts of the book into an essay called "Ultimate Glory" and focused my energies on writing other books. But, to my surprise, the essay found its way into the world on its own, with little help from its maker, and, in the end, insisted that I return to it. It is only now, all these years later, that I am reclaiming those sentences and returning them to their rightful place.

If you have never played the sport, consider this an invitation to a party, a wild party of course, and one where you can spend some time inside a world you never knew existed. As for my fellow Ultimate players, you will likely not find yourself in here. Or maybe you will, but not by name. My goal was never to write a comprehensive history of the sport. There is one of those already.

Instead I wanted to tell the story of my oft-deluded youth, the story of a strange but tight community, and the story, most of all, of our shared obsession.

The following events are true, though a name or two have been changed.

The author, wallowing

Who so should be a man must be a nonconformist.

—*Ralph Waldo Emerson*

And the ultimate reward for their time, money, and effort? Nothing.

—*Howard Cosell*

Ultimate Preamble

That Primal Feeling

I t is a hot November day in southern Florida in 1987 and Frisbees fill the air. People driving by the Miami Dade College athletic fields stare out their car windows, not quite able to figure out what is going on. At first glance the fields look like they have been taken over by an alien culture. Those drivers who remember the '60s slow down to scratch their heads and wonder if the Summer of Love has returned. The place does seem caught in a time warp: music occasionally blares from huge speakers, men wear longish hair and beards, and both men and women run around in strange bright-colored costumes. Groups cluster to smoke pot, others drink beer and urinate on trees, and, at one point, a half dozen young women sprint naked across the fields.

But while a carnival atmosphere pervades, it becomes clear, upon closer inspection, that this isn't exactly Woodstock. First, these hippies seem exceedingly fit. Second, they sport a surprising number of bloody knees and elbows, as if they had just emerged not from a love-in but from some primitive form of battle. What originally looked like costumes turn out to be uniforms. Tattered unconventional uniforms but uniforms all the same that, combined with all the blood, leave the men and women looking less like Deadheads than like extras from the movie *Braveheart*. Finally, there is what these ragged people are doing with all the Frisbees. They are throwing them, sure, but not in the way Uncle Joe throws Frisbees at your backyard barbecue. In fact, not in the way you've ever seen people throw anything. Plastic discs fly through the air, flicked with a rolling dice motion or thrown upside down like spears. These discs can travel over 80 yards, hovering, bending around objects, some slicing like knives, others describing absurd parabolas.

A curious woman, out for a stroll, walks over to one of these Frisbee people, a man who is sitting on the ground lacing up his cleats. He's a young guy with thick veined legs and long, dark hair like Samson's. She asks him what exactly it is he is doing.

"Playing Ultimate," he says.

She scrunches her face as if trying to place this. Then her eyes brighten with recognition.

"Isn't that the thing you do with dogs?" she asks.

The man smiles, resisting rolling his eyes, as if he's heard this question a hundred times before.

"No, it's played with *human beings*," he says in a patient if slightly put-upon voice. "It's a serious field sport like soccer or football."

The woman takes a closer look out at the fields and begins to notice some order within the seeming chaos. She considers the possibility that the young man is not entirely wrong. Perhaps a serious sport *is* being played.

Certainly the people playing it take it seriously. Players run at full speed up and down lined fields the same size as those used for football. They wear intense looks and the atmosphere is more competitive than communal. They root and heckle and scream and argue. What's more, both men and women throw their bodies through the air and crash to the dirt as they try to catch hovering Frisbees, and some even spike the discs when they score. Clearly this is no hippie nirvana. In fact, hippies would frown on how much these people appear to care about *points*. About *winning*. Despite the colorful outfits and occasional whiff of cannabis, it is very much the 1980s and these people seem very much concerned with what concerns so many people in this less groovy decade. They want to be the best.

O ver on field seven, the team I play for is one of four left in contention to win the National Championships. Our team from Boston, ominously named Titanic, is playing Windy City, the Chicago team, in the semifinals. We are the top seed in the tournament but have gotten off to a rocky start. We drop passes we usually catch and our throws are lazy and off-target.

Out of sync, we search for guidance. In doing so, our eyes turn naturally upward toward the same man that top Boston Ultimate players have been looking to for almost a decade. They turn to Steve Mooney. Moons, as he is known, is a giant in the Ultimate world. In a sport without coaches and full of egos, he has the rare gift of being able to lead those who often don't want to be led. At 6'7" with no more body fat than a greyhound, he is also one of the game's best players. A taller and finely coordinated Ichabod Crane, he plays the game with the control of a much smaller man. He tends to keep his head up, even slightly tilted back at a patrician angle, and excels at graceful throws that, with his impressive wingspan, prove impossible to block. Moons also has an all-American apple pie personality, Andy Hardy in cleats, though there are those who feel that the good-guy image is an act, that

Steve Mooney and his wingspan

Moons's goodness sometimes treads close to sanctimoniousness, and that something ruthless lurks just below.

Moons stalks our sidelines like a heron, a full head above the other players, and watches as our offense betrays us. It is a single elimination game, and if we lose, all the work and commitment of the last year will be for naught. One of our players who does not usually handle the disc in these big-game situations has had two or three drops, and we find ourselves in a deep hole. I am not much help. At twenty-six years old, I am in the best shape of my life and this should be *my* tournament. I have been training hard not just by playing and sprinting with the team but with my own track and weight workouts, and have not had a drop of alcohol for over a month. But last night I slept poorly. It wasn't just that I was nervous. I also spent the night in the same bed as my grandfather, Earl, a man I had not seen for over a decade, until he suddenly appeared on the fields yesterday and started cheering my name.

How had I come to be sleeping in my grandfather's bed? The first day of the tournament I'd done an interview about Ultimate with a local Miami TV station and though I didn't know it at the time, the interview was seen by Earl, inspiring him to come out to the fields. Earl divorced my mother's mother when my mother was a baby. That side of the family was full of great jocks, and he was the greatest jock of all. He had played pro baseball for the Yankees, with the distinct misfortune of playing first base behind Lou Gehrig. But while his baseball career had sputtered, his golfing career had thrived. For a while he was known throughout Florida as the Golfing Cop, a motorcycle policeman who won the Florida State Amateur as well as several pro tournaments, and he played in exhibitions with Sam Snead and Bobby Jones. He was once the low-scoring professional at a tournament in Ohio, but was beaten by a sixteen-year-old amateur named Jack Nicklaus. As an amateur, of course, Nicklaus couldn't collect the pot. This delighted Earl. When asked about it by reporters, he cracked, "Jack, you may have the trophy, but I have the money."

After watching me play on Saturday, Earl invited me and my girlfriend, Stephanie, to have dinner and to sleep over at his home in Miami. He struck me as both strange and intimidating, and referred to me not by my name but as "Pard," which I assumed was short for "Partner." Like most Ultimate players I, having devoted my life to a sport that paid nothing, had little money and so took him up on his offer. The night quickly turned weird. His was an odd ranch-style home filled with three miniature Schnauzers and with dozens of little porcelain statuettes of the same dogs that his nutty wife, Betty, collected. She was his fourth or fifth wife, I think, a woman with frizzy Collete hair, pointy Far Side glasses, and a peculiar distant look. When we asked her about the tiny jewel-encrusted vases on the mantel we learned that these were urns filled with the ashes of Schnauzers past. Tacky glass chandeliers hung from the ceilings and black velvet paintings adorned the walls, and the dog statuettes were everywhere, giving the place the feel of an upscale miniature golf course. Later Stephanie would compare the evening to being trapped inside an existential play. Betty spent the better part of the night kissing and baby-talking with the little yapping dogs, until, after we'd all had a couple of nightcaps, she suddenly pulled a small pistol from her purse and proceeded to wave it around. We were surprised, to say the least, though not scared as it was a cute little gun with embedded jewels and it was clear she had it out not to shoot us but to show off. Over dinner Earl had mentioned how dangerous Miami was becoming, but as a liberal antigun sort, I couldn't help asking the crazy woman why she kept it in her purse. In reply she stared at me with a fierce and protective intensity.

"For the coloreds," she said. "If they come."

If possible, the night got even stranger after that.

"You're in here, Pard," Earl said when it was time for bed.

He pointed toward his little bedroom while Betty ushered Stephanie toward the guest room. Earl, I learned, would be sleeping in the same bed with me. He had me sleep on the inside, away from the door, and then showed me his own gun, a larger and decidedly less cute weapon that he kept under his mattress. He flicked off the light before I could really fathom the implications of my elderly bedmate packing heat. I knew that the next day I would play in the semifinals of the National Championships for which I'd trained all year, but I would barely sleep a wink. I lay there stiff and terrified, vowing that, no matter what, I wouldn't get up and go to the bathroom during the night. It wouldn't be wise to startle my armed grandfather.

"This is going to be your coming-out party," Moons had said to me on the flight down to Miami. "This is when you are going to let them all know who you are."

Certainly that was what I hoped for.

Instead I find myself sleep-walking through the semifinals. I feel like I am playing underwater or in a dream, and while my overall sense is one of numbness, that numbness is occasionally punctuated by spikes of panic as I realize I'm letting my chance for glory slip away. And I am not alone: my teammates, too, are playing like zombies. It is starting to look like Titanic will live up to its name.

It takes a little while for a new spectator to get a sense of the sport. Things move fast. A hybrid of hockey, soccer, basketball, and football, Ultimate was invented at Columbia High School in Maplewood, New Jersey, in 1968, and played on a parking lot there during its first years. The object of Ultimate, which is played seven men or women to a side, on fields 70 yards long with 25-yard end zones, is to advance the disc across a goal line in the air before it is caught on the other side of the line by a teammate, and that is how a point is scored. Instead of running with the disc, however, players must stop, establish a pivot foot, and throw it within ten seconds. If the disc is dropped or knocked down, play instantly changes direction, offense becoming defense and defense offense. There are no stoppages of play until a goal is scored. Then the Ultimate equivalent of a kickoff occurs; the scoring team throws or "pulls" the disc to the receiving team, which waits to receive on its own goal line.

The sport is filled with running, jumping, and diving, but has the unfortunate distinction of being played with an object universally considered a child's toy. In fact, cardiovascular studies have shown Ultimate, with its nonstop running, to be more than a match for soccer, but though teams often share the fields with— and often practice harder than—rugby squads, they can never quite escape the taint of the whimsical. For those who devote their lives to the sport, it's a little more serious. For instance, the throws used to advance the disc are hardly the casual from-behind-the-hip flips made by old guys at picnics. Long passes, called "hucks," occasionally carry the full distance from end zone to end zone. Players uncurl traditional backhands or flick forehands, but they also employ a varied arsenal of nonfloating passes. These include the spearlike "overhead," where the disc is hurled in football style and can travel 50 yards upside down before dropping into a receiver's hands, and the "blade," a knifing pass that describes great arcs, and that the very best players slice surgically around the field.

When watching Ultimate the first thing that strikes the uninitiated is the way men and women throw their bodies around. Often they do this on fields only a little more forgiving than the parking lot where the sport evolved. And if Ultimate is a game of moments—of improbable dives and acrobatic catches—then these moments are heightened by two physical facts: (1) a disc is a hell of a lot easier to catch than a football or basketball, and (2) a disc hovers. On the back of a van in the Miami soccer fields parking lot is a bumper sticker that reads, "When a ball dreams, it dreams it's a Frisbee." Players make wild stabs or catch the trailing plastic edge, the disc seeming to stick to their hands. Throws curve 20 yards out of bounds and then boomerang back in, and there are times the disc actually seems to *wait* for players to catch it.

It is our defense that starts to bring us back.

In the past Titanic had just been a collection of the best players from the Boston area but earlier in the year we began to feel more like a unified group. Our most obvious stars are Moons and Jeremy Seeger, a long-limbed nephew of the folksinger Pete Seeger,

Titanic, with Moons dead center and the author raising a leg

who is so good he earned the nickname "God." But we also have less-heralded players like Scott Conrad, whose nickname "Turbo" is still cool, not yet having been usurped by the TV show *American Gladiators*. Turbo seems the very definition of hardiness, and he flies around the field on both offense and defense without a care for the harm it will do his body. Other defensive stalwarts on that team are Jeffy Williams, Adam Phillips, and Joel Mallet. Now, when it looks like we are dead in the water, the iceberg struck, our defensive players start making diving blocks.

The Ultimate term for diving horizontally through the air is "laying out." It may be that this moment of trust and uncertainty, of leaving your feet and not knowing where or how you will land, is as close as you can get to the wild essence of the sport. And laying out may be what truly separates Ultimate from other sports, thanks to the physics of a spinning disc, the way a disc hovers.

While layout catches are exciting, nothing galvanizes a team like a layout defensive block. Suddenly, sensing the desperation of the situation, our defensive players are laying out everywhere, and slowly, gradually, we are edging our way back into the game. Watching our team wake is a rousing thing, and soon we are all getting caught up in the energy of the comeback. There is something almost primal about the sort of game when all is lost and then it isn't. You have been left for dead, and then suddenly you are alive again. Life comes coursing back. Already our brains had been writing off the season but then a block here by Turbo, a tip by Jeff Williams. Could it be that we might yet live?

After another Titanic score, the Frisbee is lying on the ground, and someone asks, "Who is going to pull it?" It's a good question. Pulling the disc is an act of specialization and our best puller, Buzz Ellsworth, is out with an injury. When there is a pause Turbo blurts out, "I'll fucking pull it!" and while making that sort of long throw is not in his job description, adrenaline helps him get the disc into the opposite end zone.

I am slower to wake than others but then, as I am cutting across the middle of the field, something good happens. The catch I make isn't spectacular, just the usual two-handed clamp-down chest catch, but as I am making the catch I collide with two Chicago players. I taste a little blood in my mouth. As a player I sometimes excel in big moments but I also have a tendency to think too much. There is nothing better for subverting the Gessnerian brain, however, than hard physical contact. When I get hit, or when I hit others, the animal in me tends to elbow out the self-conscious overthinker. The next thing I know I have the disc at half field and there is Chris Phillips, who I have played with for many years, standing in the middle of the end zone with his defender to my right and his left. A quick tilt of my head to direct him and he is sprinting toward the left corner and I am ripping an overhead, thrown like a football, for a goal. And just like that I am *in* it.

A transformation comes over me. I feel stronger, more awake

and alive. Though I have a good first step, I am relatively slow for an Ultimate player, and over the years it has gotten harder and harder to play defense, once my bread and butter. But when one of my teammates turns the disc over, I stick to my man. Newly roused, I can suddenly hear the breathing of the player I am defending and know where that man will cut before he does. The game is turning primal in the way I love: life reduced to running, skying, diving, hucking. Sweating out all nagging thought and caution. In my normal life I might be an occasionally employed framing carpenter and unpublished writer, but at the moment I am feeling a confidence that can't be contained.

And as great—as absorbing and enlivening—as this feeling is, it is made better because I am part of a *team*. An individual athlete may experience a similar indomitable feeling, but he will never quite have what we have now. The psychedelic drug user or ecstatic naturally wants to share his vision with others, with the world, and so does the athlete in this state. For me it isn't hard to see a physical manifestation of the feeling that is welling up in my chest. I only have to look at the faces of my teammates, faces that have begun to shine with joyous savagery. The modern and antiseptic cliché "in the zone" doesn't do this feeling justice. It would be better to say that I am experiencing one of Abraham Maslow's "peak experiences," but that doesn't quite do it either. What is really happening to us is more a tribal thing. We move with one surging purpose, trusting our teammates as we trust our own muscles, judgment, and skills.

It should be noted that no one is filming the game and that there are few fans other than players from other teams watching on the sidelines. When the game ends the score will be 25–24, the longest game, in terms of points, in the history of Nationals. But if this game is going to be remembered, it will be in the manner that almost all Ultimate games are remembered at this point. Not by instant replay but through the retelling of great plays and heroic feats. So it isn't fame, at least fame of the usual modern sort, that motivates an Ultimate player.

During my years playing I was driven by a complicated mix of motives that included ambition, whimsy, love, and vanity, but it wouldn't be until many years later, when I had hung up my cleats, that I would start to recognize what I missed most about the game. What I missed most was not just camaraderie but camaraderie with a purpose. I missed all the moments like those in the Chicago game, few and far between, when I lost myself completely in the game, when pestering thought disappeared and was replaced by a joyful thoughtfulness and a sense of being a strong animal.

Over the years I became interested in players who seemed in the throes of what I called "going animal," and began to collect examples—stories—of these transformations. More than once I saw a wild glimmer in the eyes of Turbo, for instance, and there were times when he could appear almost feral. But Turbo was naturally pretty wild and the story that most intrigued me was one involving Jim Parinella, who was a more unlikely, quieter Wildman.

It wasn't until a decade after the Miami game, my last year of playing, that I would come to hear Parinella's story. It happened while a later Boston team called DoG (an acronym for Death or Glory) was playing a North Carolina team, Ring of Fire, in the semifinals of the National Championships exactly ten years after my own semifinals experience, and by then I had long since moved away from Boston. DoG was in disarray, down 6 to 1 in a game to 18, and after winning three championships in a row it looked like their dynasty was over.

Moons was still playing, and he was the likely person to lead them out of the hole they had dug, but instead it was Parinella who took over the game. Of average height with a slightly exotic blur to his eyes and black curly hair, Parinella was a tireless runner and one of the game's best players. He was also a self-admitted engineering geek, who could look at his own game as disinterestedly as a computer program that needed debugging. In fact, he worked for Raytheon, where he studied their enterprise systems with an eye toward creating efficiency. Earlier in the tournament, after dropping a pass, he'd considered changing his receiving style and actually said these words out loud: "I will probably adjust my pass-catching algorithm to incorporate this new information." It wasn't particularly surprising that Parinella would be a factor in Boston's comeback. What would surprise everyone is the manner in which he did this.

The first signs came after he scored a goal to close the gap to 7–3. When he caught the goal he became wildly excited, screaming uncontrollably and exhorting the Boston players.

"Come on, we're still in it!" he yelled. "We're not going to lose this thing! Come on!"

Later, Parinella would recall this as perhaps the most emotional moment of his entire life, and for a second his teammates didn't know what to make of him. They were shocked. It was like watching the episode of *Star Trek* where Spock finally finds passion. But as Parinella continued, his face uncharacteristically animated, they got swept up in his emotion. *That's right, we're not going to lose this thing, we've worked too fucking hard!* The Boston sideline suddenly came alive, players pumping their fists and yelling encouragement.

And then things did start to turn. Momentum is often called an intangible, but anyone who has ever played in this type of game knows that it is something that can be smelled, tasted, and touched. And suddenly Boston had it. White-shirted DoG players swarmed over their black-shirted opponents. Soon Boston was in a kind of place where even bad plays turn good. Parinella, perhaps overamped by the endorphins pumping through him, put a little too much mustard on a throw to Chris Corcoran and the Frisbee sailed past him down the field. But Mike Cooper, a long-limbed man who was built to run, anticipated the screwup and caught up to the disc for a 40-yard gain. Jeff Brown, who was running the team's substitutions, began to criticize Parinella's throw, but Parinella uncharacteristically turned on him.

"Don't even fucking think of pulling me," Parinella snapped, and Brown stepped back, slightly amused but also intimidated by this new creature. Parinella, meanwhile, was caught up in whatever it was he was becoming. He wouldn't stop to put it into words— what he felt was not about words—but the feeling surging up in him may be the real reason that people put so much into a sport that seems to give back so little of what's usually considered important. This wasn't about money or trophies or reputation, or even about that satisfying afterglow that will come once the game is won. Right then it was about *feeling*. A feeling inside Parinella that he was—*at that second, right at that time*—unstoppable. Indomitable. And don't even fucking think of pulling him out of the game. When he caught a goal to pull Boston closer, he felt something he'd never felt on an Ultimate field before. Tears welled up in his eyes.

"I felt I wasn't going to let the team lose," he'd say later. He made several mistakes that on a usual day might have left him doubting. But this was not a usual day. Ring of Fire remained ahead by 2, but Boston would win this game; Parinella was certain of that now.

Jeff Brown didn't quite know how to put words to what was

going on, but he understood it was something special, something to be savored. Hurt the day before, he would never set foot on the field, but, making the substitutions and cheering on the team, he still felt part of this upwelling of emotion. "There was a level of focus in everyone's eyes that I've never seen before," he would say. "And a trust that everyone else was in the same place." Months later, he would still only be able to talk about the comeback in the most dramatic, perhaps melodramatic, of terms. But melodrama fit the situation. It wasn't often in people's complicated lives that the world got simplified to terms of utter defeat or glorious victory.

Brown had a good vantage point to watch the continuing transformation of Jim Parinella. It looked to Brown as if Parinella was going primitive, working his way back to a more primal self like the character William Hurt played in *Altered States*. But if there was a sense of regression, of sinking into the past in this behavior, there was also a feeling of movement toward the future, toward, perhaps, a larger self.

"Jim used to have a tendency to get real down on himself," Brown would say. "If he made a mistake, he sometimes went into a shell. That day he lifted us up on his back and took a real leadership role." Others would concur. If some looked back amused at the spectacle of the mild-mannered engineer gone feral, they admitted he was a changed man. It was as if he, at that moment, was coming into himself, a self not necessarily better, but certainly larger and more powerful.

For Ring of Fire, the goals were getting harder and harder to come by. What had been flow was now a trickle. It was gradually dawning on the Ring players that their little dreamtime was over. Before they knew it Boston had caught and passed them and was up by 2, needing only one goal to win. Then the inexplicable happened. Closing in on the win, Parinella failed to catch a throw from Jeremy Seeger that would have ended the game. It was a play that, in the past, might have brought him down. But one or two mistakes could no longer send Parinella into a funk. He had become a different player, a sloppier player perhaps, but a better one.

Parinella's miscue was soon rendered moot. A Ring player dropped a difficult pass thrown in perpendicular blade fashion, and DoG quickly converted for the winning goal. Parinella felt his chest starting to heave. They had won, despite his fucking up, and part of what he felt was relief. But it wasn't *all* relief. His emotional high had been tailing off, but now the whole surge of it came back strong again, washing over him. The rest of his teammates raced onto the field, losing themselves in an orgy of high fives, hugs, and victory hoots. After calming down a little, they went through the ritual of shaking hands with the vanquished Ring of Fire players, before setting to the serious business of beer drinking, reliving great plays, and basking.

The next day, after Boston had won the finals and been crowned a four-time champ, the DoG players celebrated again. In Ultimate, there is no locker room to which players retire, so the celebration occurs right on the field. This tradition, which is known as the "milling period," or simply the "mill," can last as long as two or three hours after the games end. Most of the fans are usually players from other teams, and, drinking beer, they try to forget about their team's losses or their own poor plays, and join in the carnival spirit of the mill. For Boston, it was time for pure revelry, with no need to forget. DoG players sought out friends from other teams who had watched the game, basking in praise (while occasionally fishing for a few more compliments) and beginning the endless process of reliving their greatest plays and gravest errors.

Despite the fact that the game had not been televised, and that few people outside the Ultimate world cared, Jim Parinella was as happy as any Super Bowl champion. We may live in a country where it's hard for people to imagine the concept of glory and achievement without national television or magazine coverage, but right then, as he lay back on the grass and sipped a beer, you couldn't convince Jim Parinella that what he had gone through over the last two days had been anything short of glorious. For five seconds after winning the championship, he felt nothing. Then a huge wave of elation swept over him. That lasted about fifteen minutes before the next wave came—a deeper, quieter feeling of calm and contentment.

When he got back home he would start nitpicking over the mistakes he'd made during the weekend, but for the moment the win seemed perfect. Perfect, not in a perfectionist's sense, or even in the engineering sense, but more a kind of sloppy, emotional, unkempt perfection. The fact of the matter was that over the previous two days, playing the two most important games of the season, Parinella had been involved in more errors, more turn-overs, than in any two-game stretch he could remember. But that wasn't the feeling that lingered.

"I wish I could describe exactly what was going through my head," he would say, thinking back to that surge during the semi-finals comeback. "But I can't . . . I can barely remember it. At the time, though, every action looked perfectly clear, every motion was exaggerated. I have never before in my life been in such a heightened state of awareness."

Sometime during the mill, a player from another team, who had been eliminated early in the tournament, teased Parinella about having dropped what could have been the final pass the day before. At first, Parinella felt tempted to rush to his own defense. But, in his state of near blissful calm, he stopped. He could handle the teasing. Let the snickerers snicker, the hecklers heckle, the nit-pickers pick nits. The appropriate attitude toward those who had merely watched, Parinella decided as he sipped his beer, was not defensiveness, but pity. Pity the poor observers. After all, they had not been *in* it. They hadn't experienced that overwhelming tribal sensation that Parinella would always remember. They had no way to comprehend what it was like to be part of that surging whole.

Back on field seven in Miami Titanic's own surging momentum is brought to a brief halt. People are no longer running but standing still. What has stopped the game is that someone on our team has called a foul, and now the players involved are trying to hash out what happened. Though Ultimate players dedicate their lives to the sport and spend months training and thousands of their own dollars to make it through the season, the sport still resembles a casual pickup basketball game in this respect: there are no referees. This is not due to lack of finances, but to philosophy, and perhaps nothing brings out the mixed feelings of the players like the subject of referees. For some it's a matter of pride that Ultimate players police themselves, and there's even a clause in the rules regarding this: it's called the "Spirit of the Game" and asks each player to perform honestly and do what's right. It's a noble concept, a concept left over from the sport's hippie roots, but one wonders how it translates to the modern game.

It does seem asking a bit much of human nature. Imagine the NBA finals with players calling their own fouls. Then imagine one long argument occasionally interrupted by play. While the ideas behind the Spirit of the Game are indeed noble, the reality on the field here in Miami turns ugly. Tempers grow hot and players snarl at each other. There is too much at stake. Ultimate is a game of movement but the thrilling moments—the throwing and diving and skying—are counterbalanced by the not-so-thrilling arguments that sometimes lead to long stoppages of play. Finally, the disc is returned to us and the game resumes.

As the afternoon lengthens another factor begins to change the game. Wind affects the flight of a Frisbee more than that of a ball, and wind can play havoc with the best-laid Ultimate plans. We switch to a zone defense, and now I am in on D, one of the deeps in the zone. I am starting to feel like I can do anything and then a cold moment of reality intrudes. The disc goes up in the air and while I get a great jump my hand only reaches the elbow of the guy who catches the disc for Chicago, Joey Giampino. I will come to regard Joey, who will tragically die before his fiftieth birthday, as the greatest receiver I've ever played against.

Other than that one blip, the game is so far an almost perfect Ultimate fantasy. Titanic is rising up at last, looking like a real team. But the Chicago team doesn't wilt. The wind picks up more but they throw both into the wind and with it with seeming ease. The players who spend the most time around the disc are called handlers, and Chicago's best handlers, Mike Glass and Michael O'Dowd and Chris Van Holmes, are creative throwers, slicing blades and overheads around the field. They also have a receiver in Joey G., who seems to be able to shoot up one hand and catch everything. Jeremy is doing a good job covering him, but still Joey keeps making his nearly impossible catches.

My best throw of the game, and possibly of my life, comes after we get a block deep in our own end zone. The defender leaves the disc for someone else to pick up, and that someone is me. Usually this is a moment for regrouping, and I march slowly to the disc, pick it up, and begin to walk up to the goal line, the picture of composure. Until I see Moons. Moons is a finesse player despite his great height, and apparently his defender knows this since he is guarding him to keep him from coming back to the disc. But then I notice that this leaves Moons as the deepest man on the field. You would think that Moons would always be running long, catching deep throws over shorter players, and he occasionally does. But he is at heart a handler, staying close to the disc and controlling the flow.

While Moons might be a finesse player, he is also almost seven feet tall. My eyes become laser beams and then I do away with all subtlety and mouth the word "Go!" I no longer walk up to the goal line, where play will officially become live again, but sprint. My defender moves to guard my backhand, the more common deep throw, and that is his mistake. All I can see is Moons and I let my forehand rip. It is a big floating throw with the wind behind it and Moons catches it deep in the opposite end zone.

Our hungry defense takes the field again and gets another stop. Improbably we are really back in it now. Other players, better players, future hall-of-famers, might regularly have games like this. But for me this is the pinnacle. I am peaking, the team is peaking, and all we have to do is keep this train rolling and we will be in the finals of Nationals.

I s that the thing you do with dogs?"

The woman who strolled up to the fields in Miami is not the only person who has ever asked some variant of that question. In fact, the sport has always had a Rodney Dangerfield aspect to it, getting no respect. If you play Ultimate, you quickly get used to people misunderstanding or even laughing outright when you tell them what you do. It is tantamount to claiming you are a professional tiddlywinks player.

Out on the fields, running and diving, you can feel like a superhero, wearing your uniform—your *costume*—and embracing your alter ego as a Frisbee player. But in real life it is different.

Pat King, one of the stars of the great New York Ultimate teams, would come back from winning Nationals and never say a word about it to his coworkers in the law office.

"I just don't mention it to people at work," he said. "Because they can't understand. You can't really explain it. Because you've got to start by saying, 'I play Ultimate.' 'Ultimate *Frisbee*.' And then right there you're pretty much a big loser."

Pat King was Clark Kent, but for a different reason. Not because he was worried that revealing his true identity might expose those close to him to danger. But because he was embarrassed about being Frisbee Man.

But, King went on to say, this might be what made the bonds between teammates, and to some degree among all Ultimate players, even tighter. They are the only ones who understand, the only ones who share this seemingly insane obsession.

We are tied up with Chicago when the game is time-capped by one of the tournament directors who knows they need to get the next game, the finals, started on time. This means the next point wins. While there are still relatively few fans, the players from all the other teams now ring our field, right on the sidelines in a way they never could be in pro sports, and we can feel their energy fueling ours. We have the disc to score but are headed upwind when Chicago gets a block and starts moving it the other way. If they score, they win and our season is over and a depressing winter of second-guessing lies ahead. But then we get a turnover and once again the game is ours to win.

This is the moment that will seal my Ultimate fate. The second the disc is turned over I start sprinting deep for the end zone. I immediately notice that I am not alone. Ten yards in front of me Jeremy Seeger is sprinting in the same direction. Better yet it is Bobby Harding who has run to pick up the disc. Bobby, who has been my teammate since well before Titanic was formed, has our team's best long backhand—his special weapon—and he has never been shy about throwing that backhand deep. As I run I have no doubt what he is about to do. Not only does Bobby have the arm for it, he has a target, or rather, two targets. Jeremy, our best receiver, is now in the end zone, and I, Bobby's favorite receiver, am not too far behind, ready to play mop-up man should anything go wrong. There are no Chicago players with us. All Bobby has to do is grip it and rip it. If by some freak chance Jeremy doesn't catch the disc, I sure as fuck will.

And then Bobby does something extraordinary. Something that years of good athletic training, and watching a whole lot of TV sports, have taught him is the right and sensible thing to do. Something that all coaches would nod sagely about, and that Moons likely also feels is wise. Bobby Harding calls a time-out.

As we huddle up for the time-out I try to keep a new less-animal sensation in check. But it is lurking there somewhere, nibbling away at the feeling of invincibility that had, until a few seconds before, been waxing in my personal universe.

When we return to the field Bobby starts with the disc. The rest of us line up in the middle of the field in a stack, getting ready to cut for him. There are fourteen players on an Ultimate field at a time, seven on a side, and when you stack up in the middle of the field it is fairly easy to hide. The easiest kind of choking is the choke of omission. You simply keep away from the action and don't get involved because then you can't personally fail and be held responsible. You hide, cower a little, so you can't be blamed when it's over. You don't have the courage to step up and possibly really fail—right there in front of everyone.

My feeling of invulnerability has faded but it doesn't matter: I have made a pact with myself. While I can't control the chemicals in my brain, I am sure of one thing. Mine will not be a choke of omission. It will be a full-on choke of failure or it will be nothing, which is to say *everything*. After all, that is Bobby Harding, good friend and longtime teammate, with the disc.

Though Bobby's brain might be generally a little better suited for moments like these, he has to be a little nervous too, particularly since he called the goddamn time-out.

Moons makes the first cut. He is always the best target; there is nothing like having that seven-foot wingspan to give you a feeling of safety. But he is well covered and Bobby can't hit him and a few seconds tick off of the ten allotted for Bobby to throw: five, six, seven. . . . At ten the defender will call "Stall" and the disc will be turned over.

I figure it is up to me. Do or die, rah-rah. All that. I cut directly toward Bobby but he doesn't throw it yet. We know each other well. Just when it looks like I am going to keep coming toward him, I flare out to my left, where I have the whole field in front of me and to myself. Bobby floats out a beautiful forehand, a tiny bit high but that's how I like it. I jump in the air and slap down on the disc, two-handed and emphatic, pulling it into my chest. When I land I am about 30 yards from the goal.

And there is someone streaking toward me down the line. And not just someone, but Jeremy. *Jeremy Seeger.* If you can't have the security of throwing to Moons, here is the next best thing. Joey G.

is right on his tail but there is a window. Better yet my forehand is unguarded.

At this moment in time my future is still unscripted. Things can go in any direction. Possibilities abound. If I am not aware of all the implications as I get ready to throw, I know this moment is packed with meaning. While it may sound melodramatic, I have a funny feeling that it isn't just a 175-gram plastic disc, but my fate, that I hold in my hands.

I pull back, cock the disc, and let it rip.

I

Fair Harvard

What you gave me you gave whole
But as for telling
Me how to best use it
You weren't a genius at that.
Twenties, my soul
Is yours for the asking
You know that, if you ever come back.

—Kenneth Koch, "To My Twenties"

1.

Origin Stories

We labor over our big decisions and big dreams, but sometimes it's the small things that change our lives forever. What could be smaller than this: It is the first week of my freshman year of college and I, looking for a sport to play, am walking down to the boathouse to sign up for crew, resigning myself to four years of servitude as a galley slave, when I see a Frisbee flying across the street. The Frisbee, tossed from one long-haired boy to another, looks like freedom to me. Then I notice that there are several Frisbees flying back and forth between a band of young men, all wearing shorts, with cleats hanging over their shoulders. At the time I am quite shy but, uncharacteristically, I cross the street and ask them where they are going. To Ultimate Frisbee practice, it turns out, and I am going with them.

It is my first practice, and almost my last. The college I am attending is Harvard but if I thought there would be plenty of snobbery at the boathouse, I didn't expect it out on an open field tossing Frisbees around with a bunch of semi-athletic half-hippies. But it's here all right, mostly in the form of a tall, skinny preppy-nosed boy named Paul Edwards. I'm not yet aware of the castelike layers of the sport, not aware that Edwards has spent the last season playing for the soon-to-be national finalist Boston Aerodisc and considers himself laughably above practicing with a bunch of beginners (some, like me, who can't even throw fore-hands!). But if I am shy during that first practice, it isn't because I'm naturally passive or subdued. I might not say much to other people, but inside my head plans already roil, slights are carefully noted, and words wait to pour out. Right from the start I love chasing down the Frisbee as it soars and curves, but by the third time Edwards criticizes the way I cut for the disc I am ready to storm off. Who does this skinny prick think he is? I played high school football and tennis and am a decent basketball player, and though I might not know how to make the fancy little throws he can, I know right off that I'm a better athlete. It's true he can do almost anything with a Frisbee—on the sideline he very seriously sprays silicone on the disc (with the air of a doctor starting an IV) so that he can spin it on his well-trimmed nails—but does that give him the right to criticize me? The next time he opens his mouth I storm off. Fuck this, I think, and start walking back toward the boathouse. Full of righteous indigna-tion, huffing and puffing, I make it about 50 yards before one of the team's captains catches up with me. He is a small energetic man named Stuart and he gives me a pat on the back, acknowl-edging that Edwards can sometimes be hard to play with. He talks me into staying. As it turns out, he knows the right way to win me over.

"You're going to be great at this," he says. Music to my young ears.

. . .

That was the beginning of almost twenty years lost in the world of Ultimate. If that first long-ago Frisbee looked like freedom to me, it would lead to a kind of servitude, two decades in lockstep with the growing sport.

Why did I keep coming back? I think that chasing down a disc, diving or jumping for it, is at the core of the game's appeal. For many people, myself included, all this action proves addictive. The Ultimate world is full of young people who, for reasons they can never quite explain, have given up the normal benefits of life to chase plastic, men and women brimming with the passion and impracticality of the clichéd artist, a band of jock Van Goghs, painting on and on without the faintest hope of a sale.

Whatever the mysterious motivation, each year more innocents are drawn into the Ultimate underworld, often leaving behind mystified parents wondering exactly where they went wrong. After graduating from some of the country's best schools, their minds are subtly warped, and, instead of putting their energies into sensible pursuits like law or medicine, they throw themselves into this ridiculous sport. During my time it was like a new LSD in this way: turn on and drop out. Suddenly Ivy League graduates were working at warehouses so that they could have time to pile in a van— stuffed in with ten rank-smelling teammates—to drive to a tournament in Texas. Meanwhile, they lived in warrens filled with other players, and drank beer and talked incessantly of Ultimate. It was enough to make parents want to call in the deprogrammers.

In the early twenty-first century the sport has changed, exploding with millions of people playing around the world in competitive and corporate leagues, pro leagues sprouting up in a dozen

American cities, frequent appearances on the top ten lists of *SportsCenter*, and, most recently, official recognition from the International Olympic Committee as a contender sport for the Olympics. What was long considered preposterous now appears to be coming true: in an age of concussions and corruption in pro sports, this untainted game, filled with wild and beautiful moments that are aided by the physics of a thrown, hovering disc, seems to be realizing its dream of becoming a "real" sport. But what does this mean? Some longtime players argue that the sport has become too tame and that its success will corrupt it. The argument is that if money comes pouring in, then Ultimate will lose its purity, including the Spirit of the Game.

I'm not sure where the sport is heading, but I know one thing: in my day we didn't worry too much about selling out. It wasn't even a possibility. We didn't know it but what we really were back then were pioneers. Ultimate was barely ten years old when I started playing, just emerging from its tangled countercultural roots, with the rules, and even the types of discs we used, still in flux. It never occurred to me as I ran around the fields in my too-short shorts and my too-long hair that I was part of history. It is only now that I understand that I am like one of those mustached men you see in the black-and-white pictures of the early football teams. One of the men in the leather helmets.

My immersion in the sport began on that same field during my freshman year. Thanks to Stuart, I came back to the next practice. And the next. Then, before I knew it, I was in a van full of teammates on the Maine Turnpike headed to an Ultimate tournament at Bates College in Lewiston. The tournament, for me the first of hundreds, had a carnival atmosphere as a dozen or so teams spread out over several fields. My memories of that trip are vague but I know I played barefoot, as did more than a few players on other teams. And I know there was a keg in the middle of the fields that I suckled on between and sometimes during games. It was after drinking that I loosened up, on the field at least since off it I was still too shy to talk to my teammates. But with the beer in me I did something that came naturally: I ran deep toward the end zone. We were going up against a team where no one played barefoot and where, unlike ours, there were no women on the roster. The players seemed tall and collegiate and unhippieish and athletic, and they were thrashing us. At the time I had no way of knowing that Ultimate was in a kind of nether region, a place in between. The days of the long-hairs and barefoot players and informally coed teams were at that moment dying and something more serious and competitive and cleat-wearing was emerging.

But I was still barefoot and now I was running toward the end zone and one of my teammates was throwing it—*what the hell?* he must have thought, since we were getting creamed by these jocks anyway. The next thing I knew the disc was floating up there lost in the sun and two of the jocky cleated guys were closing in on me and they were sure they had it and you could almost see them snickering but suddenly I wasn't thinking or worrying like I did back in my normal life at school and instead I was seeing the Frisbee clearly, or rather seeing the spinning edge of the Frisbee, and I was jumping and going after it and grabbing it tight and then I had it in one hand and I was landing with my bare feet in the end zone and my teammates were rushing down the field and out from the sidelines and slapping me on the back and hooting and congratulating me.

How did I feel? I felt excited, I felt proud. Maybe I even felt a little *loved.*

And that moment, that catch, was it. The exact second my addiction began.

For me and my generation it seemed as if Frisbees had been around forever, thrown on the beach or stuffed in our summer closets. But, in fact, the thing itself was still relatively new in 1979. That is not to say that things the shape of Frisbees, or things that flew like Frisbees—cake pans or plates or oil can lids—were new. It didn't take much of an eye or imagination to see that anything round and flat and spinable was fun to throw. Myth has it that it was students on the Yale campus who first started throwing the metal pie tins from the nearby Frisbie Pie Company, yelling out the word "Frisbie!" to alert bystanders if a tin was flying toward them. Aerodynamically, the pie tins weren't much, and it would take the invention of plastic, and an inventor named Fred Morrison, to create a disc originally called the Pluto Platter. Those first discs were produced by Wham-O on January 13, 1957, though it wasn't until seven years later, with the closing of the old pie company and the dwindling possibility of lawsuits, that the name "Frisbee" was imprinted on the discs. It was a fateful moment for what would become the sport of Ultimate, since the word *Frisbee*, like *boing* or *zowie*, is a hard one to take seriously, and the future sport's lifelong inferiority complex likely started right then and there.

From the very beginning people created games for the Frisbee. In fact, for a long time those very words—PLAY CATCH, INVENT GAMES—were printed along with the name right on the disc. One of those games was a form of Frisbee football that sprung up spontaneously at colleges around the country, and one of those colleges was Amherst. Then, in the summer of 1968, an Amherst student named Jared Kass took the game to Mount Hermon, a prep school in western Massachusetts where he was teaching in a summer program. The game was a hit, played on the large lawn behind the Crossley Dorm where Kass was staying, but it likely would have remained a quickly forgotten summer diversion if not for the fact that one of the players who learned the game from Kass was a brash, somewhat loudmouthed but charismatic high school student from New Jersey named Joel Silver. Later in life, Silver would become famous as the producer of movies like *Lethal Weapon* and *The Matrix*. But what most people don't know is that he was also the individual most responsible for the invention of Ultimate Frisbee.

The game that Silver and his good friends Johnny Hines and Bernard "Buzzy" Hellring would codify as much as create was essentially the same game that I would start playing ten years later.

It is important to remember that Ultimate, which is poised, as I type these words, on the threshold of being played in the Olympics, began its life as a kind of inside joke. When the man who would become the sport's James Naismith stood up one day in the Columbia High School student council after the meeting was almost over and the call for "New Business" went out, he was not acting unironically. After getting the attention of the council, Joel Silver made a fateful motion.

"I move that Columbia High School create a varsity Frisbee team," he announced. There were snickers and a little laughter, but there was also a crucial seconding of the motion. And so Ultimate was born, appropriately, as part farce, part performance art.

Later Silver would become known not just as a famous producer of action films but also as an exemplar of excess, a modern-day King Henry the VIII who blew through money, owned multimillion-dollar homes (one designed by Frank Lloyd Wright), rode waves of debt and extreme wealth, and, according to the *Hollywood Reporter,* "indulged in an annual tradition: shipping the staff of the Venice trattoria Vini Da Arturo from Italy to Los Angeles for eleven days to cook such favorites as *scaloppine senape e panna* (veal with mustard and cream) and spaghetti al gorgonzola for him and his guests."

Silver has earned a reputation as a prototypical producer, with a temper and temperament that have been frequently satirized in print and film. Almost everyone who remembers him paints a similar portrait: opinionated, rude, smart, loud, but funny, too. This last descriptive is important. Because if he was brash and often got his way, he also had a sense of humor, or, at least, a sense of fun. And gusto, of course. The game that Silver brought back from his summer stint at Mount Hermon in the fall of 1968 may or may not have already been referred to as "Ultimate" by Jared Kass, who taught Silver to play, but that hardly matters. It was Silver who taught it to his friends, Silver who pushed it as a varsity sport, Silver who organized a game between the student council and newspaper (he was a member of both) in the spring of '69 and Silver who no doubt talked the most shit as the game approached.

There are Frisbee scholars who, deep within their monastery walls, quibble over who really deserves the credit for inventing Ultimate, and many of them claim that Silver has been given too much credit. But whatever else you want to say about Joel Silver, one thing is clear: he was the type of person who could get excited about an idea and then carry that idea to its conclusion. Even then he was a *producer.* People had been throwing pie tins and then plastic around forever by that point but there was a need for a prime mover, and as it turned out, that prime mover was the man who would later bring us *Lethal Weapon* and *Xanadu.*

Mock-proud Joel Silver (at left) with his Columbia High School team in 1969

Leave it to others to work out the details and spread the sport. He was the fountainhead.

He was also an underaverage athlete, who never particularly excelled at the game he invented. No matter. In P. T. Barnum fashion he talked up the game between the student council and the school newspaper, the *Columbian*, and would later rightly call the paper's team, which he captained, "undefeated," after its 11–7 win. The game itself only vaguely resembled what Ultimate would become, with amorphous blobs of players gathering around the disc, crowding the thrower, but there were hints of grace, mostly in the way the Frisbee flew. This was the first officially recorded game of Ultimate and it was trumpeted in the *Columbian* with this headline: "Paper Snatches Frisbee Title."

Members of both the paper and student council would go on to form the first official Ultimate team, Columbia High School Varsity Frisbee. There is a photo from that time that perfectly captures the spirit of the team. The players all wear their Columbia High School Varsity Frisbee shirts and at first glance it looks like a normal photo of a normal sports team. But if you take a closer look, you can see something in Silver's posture. With his chest puffed out and head thrown back he is a parody of athletic victor. This is more a satire of glory than glory celebrated, with Silver as Teddy Roosevelt standing with his Rough Riders, smiling broadly, but this Teddy, if proud, is also aware of the absurdity of a Frisbee victory, of Frisbee *glory*. The players, after all, were from the paper and the student council, geeks not jocks, and they, like their whole generation, were more under the spell of *Mad* magazine than *Sports Illustrated*.

Look even closer and you'll see that Silver is holding a kind of top-secret briefcase/notebook with the words "International Frisbee Association" printed in a circle on it and that he has his arm around an older man, decidedly not a high school student. This is the school's janitor, Cono Pavone, who Silver has listed as the coach. At the other end of the line is the school's septuagenarian security guard, Alexander Osinski, who is listed as the team's "general manager."

"We saw it as an anti-sport," Silver would later say. "We loved the idea of this structured game all based on what was essentially a gag."

Others, however, began to take the new game a little more seriously. Buzzy Hellring bugged Silver and told him they needed to write up the rules. Silver was reluctant—why if the game was a joke?—but gave in. Together with Johnny Hines they wrote up a set of rules that would be reverently referred to by later players as "the first edition." While these would establish many of the rules that are still used, sometimes in modified form, today, they were also suffused with a sense of humor.

"The game is played until one of the players dies," the rules read, "or one team gives up."

The copyright is held by Silver, Johnny Hines, and Richard Denberg, with Denberg listed only because his father owned the printing business that printed up the rules. On the second edition of the rules there was a picture of Michelangelo's David with Silver's face superimposed and mention of the year 1898, when politicians met to throw out the historic first Frisbee.

There were cinematic as well as ironic touches to the early rules. For instance, the Ultimate equivalent of a kickoff occurs when the team that has just scored throws the disc to the receiving team, which waits to receive on its own goal line. This would become known as the "pull," a name coined by Silver, who lifted it from the skeet-shooting scene in the James Bond movie *Thunderball*. A decade later, when I waited to catch the pull, I had no idea of the name's filmic aspect or origin.

There was some debate over who deserves the credit, or, depending on your point of view, blame for burdening the sport with the pretentious adjective *Ultimate*. Silver says that Hellring wanted to call it *Speed Frisbee* and that he told him it wasn't cool enough. Silver suggested *Ultimate*. It is also possible that the sport was called that by some as far back as the Amherst–Mount Hermon days, when Jared Kass—who, remember, taught Silver the game—declared after making a great catch that "This is the ultimate game." Future Frisbee scholars will no doubt argue endlessly over this matter of origin but the point is that, for better or worse, the name stuck.

Silver himself graduated in 1969 and stopped playing, except in a few alumni games back in the Columbia High School parking lot, and he would soon head to Hollywood for more lucrative, and gaudier, pursuits. But there was no question he had started something.

"Someday they're going to be playing this game all over the world," he said to a friend during one of the very first pickup games.

I knew none of this when I started. Of course I sensed that throwing so much energy into a game played with a toy, and not, say, studying hard or starting the novel I dreamed of writing, was kind of absurd, and so I made self-deprecating jokes about my growing obsession with this nonsport. There were plenty of people, my father included, who I simply decided not to tell what I was spending so much time doing.

I remained shy throughout most of my freshman year. I still didn't talk a lot, unless I drank enough beer, but I gradually became friends with two of my fellow rookie teammates, Jon Epstein and Simon Long, and when the upperclassmen put us on the field together they called us the "Freshman Death Squad." Both Epstein and Long had attended Brookline High School, a progressive public school in the Boston area that had its own tradition of Ultimate, and they came into the college game as full-blown players, complete with forehands (or, in Long's case, an ugly but effective throw called the "thumber," in which the disc was launched from closer into the body with the thumb, not the fingers). While I lacked their skills, I made up for it through a kind of brutal effort, playing defense for the whole season in about the same mood I'd been in when I stormed away from Paul Edwards, and running deep to catch the passes Epstein and Long threw.

After practice I would often head back to Simon's room and drink beer, smoke pot, listen to music, and talk Ultimate. Like many people who go to Harvard, I was, after the initial intimidation, unimpressed with my classmates as a whole. I'd expected to be in the presence of "genius" and though they were a lively group, with varied talents and interests, I wasn't nearly as dazzled by their intelligence as I'd imagined I'd be. But Simon was smart. Perhaps a little too delighted by his own raconteur's wit, but smart.

After we partied for a while we would invariably head out to the Yard to throw. Hours and hours spent curving discs around trees and streetlights and racing and diving after discs in a manner I was sure the statue of John Harvard had never witnessed before. It's amazing how long you can throw a Frisbee while stoned and amazing how *interesting* the act seems, the way it bends and arcs and turns. We would keep throwing when we walked across Mass. Ave. for munchies at Store 24, floating Frisbees over traffic and zipping them between pedestrians. I was working hard on my forehand and if I hit an occasional car or human it seemed a small price to pay for mastery.

My throws were still just developing, but it was my hands that were my real strength as a player. During my freshman year I became obsessed with catching—"You are what you catch," read a note on my wall over my desk—and this obsession, like most of mine, ran like a parent stream back to my father. When I was eight or nine I loved nothing more than playing football with him on the front lawn of our house in Worcester, Massachusetts. He had been a scrappy high school athlete himself and would line up at quarterback, taking the imaginary snap, while I'd run patterns: buttonhooks and down-and-outs and square-outs. I remember the square-outs best because they sent me directly into the front hedges. He threw tight mean lefty spirals and if they were out of my reach, I would dive for them, often ending up sprawled and cut in the bushes. If the ball tipped off my fingertips, he always said the same thing: "If you can touch it, you can catch it." This was a phrase that stayed with me, sometimes resurfacing in my dreams. Playing Ultimate at eighteen, I felt I could catch anything, however poorly thrown.

My father loomed over my athletic life, and I suppose he still does. He is long gone, dead almost twenty years now, but he lives on in me in middle age whenever I bitterly lose a Ping-Pong game or fret to myself, the next day, over not having tossed a bocce ball better. His peculiar brand of competitiveness—cocksure, slightly crazed, nearly constant—marked my childhood in a thousand ways. From the rounds of "duck-duck goose," where if you dared tag him goose, he would tag you right back (without once in recorded family history leaving his own seat), to the games of Hearts where I would run bawling from the room after he had stuck me, once again, with the deadly queen of spades.

He had gone to Harvard, too, and was a snob about it, though in his own unique and boisterous way. No Thurston Howell the Third, he had grown up in less-than-opulent surroundings in Worcester, and was as much street urchin as patrician. The main thing he seemed to like about Harvard was that he could use it as a cudgel to bludgeon those of his friends who had gone to what he liked to refer to as "lesser" schools. He did this in an arrogant chortling manner that he thought funny. And it wasn't just his buddies whom he liked to tease and pick and prod. For the longest time he beat me in tennis, even though I was the better player. Since I was more athletic than he was, he worked on my weakness: my young mind. Many of us hear little whispers of doubt when we shoot a foul shot late in the game or serve on match point, but unlike most I have no problem putting a face to that whisper.

My father gradually learned that my less-competitive brother was better left unteased, and he also went a little easier on my two sisters. So I, the firstborn male, bore the brunt, which in retrospect I don't really mind.

I do regret, however, that I never won our family's coveted annual award, KID OF THE YEAR. My father gave the award at random

The author's father, David Gessner, Sr.

times (often it seemed to me, more than once a year) and made quite a ceremony out of it for a few years running until my mother finally made him stop. During the peak years of the award he actually, to my mother's chagrin, had trophies made up at Olympic Sports in downtown Worcester. They were just like the trophies you won at junior tennis or swimming competitions, but these little people, instead of serving or diving into the pool, just stood there doing nothing. KID OF THE YEAR was engraved on one trophy, and on another KID OF THE YEAR—RUNNER UP. I was never quite sure what the criteria for KID OF THE YEAR was, but as I got older I began to suspect that it was based on varying parts pity, whim, and perceived need. Whatever the case, the best I ever did was runner-up, and I began to understand that this was because it was assumed that I could take it, which by then I could. During one of the final years of the tournament, my mother insisted that, if he was going to give out the damn trophies, he better at least give *everyone* a trophy. This was much more in the spirit of equality popular in today's schools, grating against my father's child-rearing philosophy, which was equal parts Darwin and Teddy Roosevelt, but he relented and bought four trophies. At that year's ceremony he made his usual speech before announcing the results and handing out the trophies in reverse order in the manner of beauty contests. It was a while ago and I don't remember all the specifics, but I'm pretty sure my brother won and that I was handed either the first or second trophy. What I do know for certain is what it says on my trophy, because it sits here in front of me like a muse as I type. It reads:

KID OF THE YEAR: PARTICIPANT.

Joel Silver saw Frisbee as a "way to make fun of the establishment" and claimed he and his friends "never took it seriously."

But a strange thing started to happen during the fall after the student council–newspaper game. That summer the high school built an overflow parking lot, across the street and down the hill from the school. It's a safe bet that none of the construction workers building the lot knew that what they were creating would one day be regarded as the Frisbee equivalent of Lourdes. But it was on that parking lot, equipped with lights, that the earliest games of Ultimate were played and that the earliest of the game's best players were formed. And it is there also that we can see the earliest documented instances of the sport's addictive nature.

While its function was to serve as a home for parked cars, the lot made a surprisingly good field, a nice wide, flat surface with a humped gravel hill topped with train tracks on one side and a creek on the other. Since it was an overflow lot, and the teachers and students just used it in the day, it was empty at night, and it was there in 1969 and 1970 that something began to happen. For the earliest players, those from Silver's class, playing Ultimate in the lot was primarily a social event, coed not incidentally, something they did often, almost every night, until quite late or at least until the police came when residents of the nearby housing complex called to complain about the noise. It became a major hangout for Ultimate geeks, and geeks they were for the most part: sometimes members of the football team drove by and threw eggs at them. The games themselves could go on for hours, and often no one kept score.

But somewhere along the line the scene changed and something close to real Ultimate broke out. A few players began to fall in love with making cool throws and with jumping in the air to catch the hovering discs. (Of course players never dove for the disc at this point, since they were playing on concrete, though occasionally someone did slide down into the creek or hit the ground, and there was at least one collision that led to broken ribs.)

A kind of succession, the process of the more athletic players deposing the less, would become the rule of Ultimate over the next decades, and the first time this would happen was right there in the Columbia H.S. lot. Among the earliest players, Johnny Hines had been the most athletic, but along came David Leiwant, who would become captain of Columbia's track team and MVP of the football team, and who started to show what happened when someone who could really run and jump played the sport. It was an exciting moment: Jesus, look at the way the disc just sits up there and can be snatched out of the sky by a real jock, or look at the way you can make a deep throw bend up toward the train tracks and then back into the end zone.

Among this second wave of players, the ones with skills and some athleticism, no one would be more important to the developing sport than Irv Kalb, who would become known as "Dr. I." You would have a hard time creating two more opposite personalities than Joel Silver and Irv Kalb, and it all came out in their attitude toward Ultimate. For Silver it had begun as a joke and to a certain extent always remained one. He had a creator's vision, lacquered with a *Mad* magazine glaze, of what the game was. Later, as Ultimate became established, he began to like the fact that, along with his other accomplishments and awards, *he had created a sport.* Who outside of Naismith or Walter Camp could say that? He even, in the days after he left school but before movie success, was known to gripe that the game hadn't proved profitable yet.

Irv Kalb, by contrast, is a serious man who even back then was a serious boy. In the earliest pictures he is a tall and upright-looking fellow with the stern but benevolent face of a parish priest. Though Jewish, there is something in the early pictures, his sideburns perhaps, that could have landed him a role as a preacher, the town's stern conscience, in an old Western. From the start the serious Mr. Kalb saw Ultimate as a real sport worth dedicating himself to—it wasn't a joke, not at all—and he looked down his nose, or at least askance, at the frivolous attitude of Silver and his gang. It wasn't all that surprising that Kalb was a dedicated Boy Scout, a fact that does not have small significance in the spreading of the sport since, after a year of playing almost daily, Kalb got in touch with his old Boy Scout pals, now attending different New Jersey high schools, and told them about a game called Ultimate, urging them to start teams, too. This would lead to teams forming beyond Columbia H.S. and to the first Ultimate league, a group of eight to ten schools known as the New Jersey Frisbee Conference.

Kalb's seriousness showed itself not just in his commitment to the sport itself, and in helping start a league, but in his dedication, along with that of other second-generation Columbia High School players like Larry Schindel, to spreading the game throughout the country. Johnny Hines, from the first group of players at CHS, had already started a team at Princeton with classmate Buzzy Hellring, and now Kalb would do the same at Rutgers while classmate Ed Summers, along with New Jersey Frisbee Conference alumni Jim Pistrang, would form a team at Tufts. This small group, and a few others, would later be dubbed by Silver "the Johnny Appleseeds of Ultimate," and they approached their mission with the zeal of proselytizers. Irv Kalb's Rutgers team would dominate the earliest years of the sport, and over the next three years more than twenty college Ultimate teams were founded, many of them by the original players from Maplewood.

"We knew early on that this was something we would take outside," said Kalb. "It was kind of like a religion. It was our mission to take the sport far beyond Columbia High School."

It was perfect, really; it's how a lot of things got started, Christianity for one. First came the prime mover with the vision and next came the ranks of disciples, the true believers eager to spread the word. Maybe it is too crazy to see Joel Silver as Frisbee Jesus, and his apostles led by Kalb as spreading Christianity throughout the known world (or at least the Northeast), but we can at least admit that those earliest players were sort of like missionaries, or at the very least that they saw themselves that way. They had found something they loved and that filled them with passion and joy, and they wanted others to know this thing, too. They wanted to share and to spread.

Looking back, the truly crazy thing was how quickly they succeeded. By 1972, just four years after Silver had brought the sacred flame back from Mount Hermon to CHS, teams had been started at not just Princeton and Rutgers and Tufts, but at Hampshire College, University of New Hampshire, University of North Carolina, Clark, and Rensselaer Polytechnic Institute. The next year Columbia, Yale, and Cornell were among those to join the fray. A year later over thirty college teams were playing; two years after that, over sixty.

And Ultimate, despite its ironic roots, was up and running.

Y ou're playing what?" my father asked when I first told him what I was doing.

He must have had hopes that I would follow in his footsteps at the textile company he ran, or at least become something accept-able like a lawyer. Until then I had been good at school, athletic, borderline normal. But if he still held any illusions that his son would excel in sports and business as a kind of latter-day Frank Merriwell, this did them in. Frisbee of all things. Clearly a sport for long-hairs and druggies.

As well as laughing at Frisbee, however, my father would feel its sting. During my sophomore year he drove to Cambridge to tail-gate at a football game. The Ultimate team was playing in a tour-nament on a nearby field and so he decided to drop by to take a look at his son's eccentric preoccupation. I can see him chortling with the friends he dragged along, amused that such a foolish game existed (as he waited to get into a stadium where he could watch a sport played with an oblong ball made from a pig) while concerned that the wayward son sounded a wee bit too passionate about his strange new obsession. It was nice of my father to come watch, but he was standing too close to the field, sipping drinks with his friends, and not really paying attention.

He should have been paying attention, if for no other reason than that my teammate Nathan was roaming the field. With Na-than around, there was always potential for danger. Nate was a physics genius who dropped in and out of Harvard, taking a half dozen years to get his degree. But while Nate's mind could soar and dance subtly among quasars and string theory, he played Ulti-mate like the classic wild man. He had thick-veined plowman's legs, a squat powerful torso, and wore his wild red hair long, with a frayed red beard and mustache. When he tore around the field you could squint and imagine, without much of a stretch, that this was how Neanderthals looked chasing after deer. Nathan was an "impact player"; he played passionate defense, dove at the slightest provocation, and could run all day, but he also could make an impact in a less positive way. His throws weren't quite as developed or accurate as he imagined they were. And his first instinct was to make the most difficult and, if possible, longest throw. This in-stinct to punt the disc deep, an instinct that apparently could not be controlled, would cause his teammates to sometimes cringe and mutter when Nathan got the disc. "No, Nate, no . . ." they would plead. But the answer was always yes. Nathan saw things that were sometimes there, sometimes not, and then he wound up and let 'er rip. As Simon liked to say, Nathan "had a notion."

Nathan's forehand flew like a dying quail. Sometimes when he launched it Simon would look at me and say, "Duck full of buck-shot" and then, after mimicking the motion of pumping a shot-gun, would pretend to point his imaginary gun and shoot the wavering disc out of the air. But Nate's backhand was raw power. He would curl around the disc and then uncoil, launching it with a fury, sometimes heaving it right out of the end zone.

When he caught the disc around half field, on the sideline where my father stood, his defender left Nate's ferocious backhand open. Someone was streaking deep and Nate's eyes lit up and we all knew what would happen next. Nate had a notion and if my father had been paying closer attention, he would have had a no-tion, too. Something, some atavistic, primal instinct would have tingled and warned him that this was a dangerous man nearby, a hunter from another clan, a clan not like his own. But at that moment my father, inebriated, oblivious, imagining himself safe watching a mere "Frisbee" game, foolishly ignored whatever subtle signals his brain or body was sending. He stood there smiling, barely an arm's length away from this wild red-headed troglodyte, as Nathan wound up, virtually coiling around his backhand, and then, his eyes glinting with notions, unwound himself in a violent, powerful jerk.

The disc traveled barely three feet. It caught my father on the side of the head and knocked him to the ground. The game stopped. My father instantly went from one of the spectators to the main attraction. A crowd gathered around him.

My father and I would joke about it later. As would my teammates. And it was funny, a comic moment. But there was something else there, too. Looking back, my symbol-making imagination can't help but mold the incident into personal myth. If I had more Robert Bly in me, I might be inclined to explore the idea of my father, authority figure and businessman, knocked to the ground by the team's wild man, Id flooring Superego.

"Are you all right, man?" Nathan asked. There was a cut and some blood, but my father was just dazed.

An old athlete himself, he tried to make light of what had happened, gesturing for us to back away. Then, after gathering himself for a minute, he gamely climbed to his feet.

2.

Arête, and the Dawn of
the Barbarians

Most people would be surprised to know that Ultimate began on the East Coast. In the popular imagination all Frisbee games were born in California and played on a sunny day at the beach, or, perhaps, on a grassy bluff above the beach. This vision would soon enough come true in places like Santa Barbara and Santa Cruz. But the early days of Ultimate were all Jersey.

The first intercollegiate game in history was played on November 6, 1972, between Rutgers and Princeton, on the 103rd anniversary of the first football game between those two schools, widely regarded as the first official intercollegiate football game ever. In fact, the game was played on the exact same spot where those first footballers had played, though that spot was now a parking lot and therefore covered with asphalt.

It seemed like this would be the day the world would discover the new sport. The founders of Ultimate showed a gift for marketing that later players would lack, and both *Sports Illustrated* and the *New York Times* took note of that first game, which was also covered by a local ABC affiliate with Jim Bouton of *Ball Four* fame as the correspondent. It was played in front of a packed house, a big, raucous crowd, more than 1,500 spectators, ten deep on the sidelines in spots.

"It was one of the best experiences of my life," Irv Kalb would remember. "It was clear from the response of the crowd that it really could be a great spectator sport. We felt that the sport had arrived on that day."

Not quite. Ultimate would have to wait a long time for a comparable crowd and in some ways, almost fifty years later, it is still waiting.

And while Ultimate would later become known for not having referees, this first high-profile game had one, striped shirt and all. David Leiwant, ex–Columbia High School jock (and former Boy Scout tent-mate of Irv Kalb), filled the role, though he made very few, if any, calls that day.

Kalb described the game as "fairly high-level competition" with fans *ooh*ing and *ahh*ing when people made deep throws or skyed for discs. The fact that the game was on concrete didn't bother the players much—most of them were used to it and had honed their games on the same surface. The star was Dan Roddick, a 6'6" Rutgers undergrad who would go on to become a spokesman for the sport and whose name, for many years after, was imprinted on the front of Frisbees. He had great throws and used his height to catch the disc over other players and the crowd zoned in on him. In particular, a bunch of frat boys began to chant, semi-sarcastically perhaps, "Stork, Stork, Stork!" a nickname that would stick to him for the rest of his life. As it turned out Stork's would be a life in Frisbee, and he would be the only Ultimate pioneer actually hired by Wham-O to promote its disc sports. From that perch, Stork would start the first newsletters and nurture the growing game.

But that day, back in the parking lot, his impact was more direct, physical, and immediate. With Stork leading the way, Rutgers won 29–27. The *Times* concluded its article, "'This game is going to catch on,' said one member of the crowd, which clearly outnumbered the few spectators at that historic game 103 years ago, which Rutgers also won. 'The Rutgers football team is dead.'"

If Ultimate did not gloriously ascend after that first game, as Kalb and others dreamed it would, it still had come a long way in just four years. Two years later *Time* magazine devoted a full-page article to the emerging sport, and while, in the spirit of Joel Silver, they referred to it as a "spoof on big-time sports," Ultimate was now on the map. During that era, the Rutgers team, with "Dr. I" and Stork, not to mention numbered shirts, a team bus, and a huge wooden scoreboard, won three straight National Championships, though "national" at the time essentially meant the northeast and mid-Atlantic. Joel Silver, meanwhile, had moved to Hollywood and had begun wondering just when he was going to cash in on his creation. "When am I going to make some money off this thing?" he griped to a fellow Columbia High School grad.

A decade that would begin with Jersey's dominance would end with the same. Glassboro State College, known in the Ultimate world as the 'Boro, would win what was by then a true National Championship in 1979 and repeat in 1980. Glassboro was a New Jersey college that focused on education and their team was made up of would-be teachers who played a zone defense, just like Rutgers, and ran something like basketball's four corners offense to stall out the play clock after they got ahead.

The heart and soul of the 'Boro was Tom D'Urso, known to all as Timba. Timba, a skinny kid with a white man's afro, had transferred to Glassboro as a sophomore and spent his first fall redshirting for the cross-country team. While he waited to begin cross-country he was nagged by his roommate to come out to try a game called Ultimate that a bunch of guys were all playing on the quad. That spring he finally gave in to the cajoling and within a week of his first practice his life was changed forever. It's a familiar Ultimate story, but what distinguishes it is the sheer passion of both Timba and his team.

"If Springsteen were an Ultimate player, he'd have played for the 'Boro," Timba, who would eventually see the Boss in concert more than seventy times, would say, and it's hard to deny.

It wasn't just the fact that another of the team's stars, Frankie Bono, was Timba's cousin that gave the team the feel of a family. They practiced every day on the sloped lawn below the president's house and while they never did sprints or officially trained they felt they didn't need to. "We played for two and a half hours every day and basically sprinted the whole time," said Timba. For him it was good-bye to cross-country and hello to a group of guys he would stay close to for the next forty years: "We always gave each other shit, but I loved those guys then and I love them now. I made my closest friends out on that field." This closeness translated almost immediately into wins. In 1979 the 'Boro won the National Championships by upsetting a Santa Barbara Condors team that had smoked them in round-robin pool play. Before that game they spent forty-five minutes dancing and singing, and blowing trumpets, and building themselves into a froth. In Pasquale Anthony Leonardo and Adam Zagoria's comprehensive history, *Ultimate—The First Four Decades*, a Glassboro player describes the team's method of warming up:

> Our pre-game rituals evolved into a 30-minute psych-up rant, involving calisthenics, songs (with guitar accompaniment) and, finally, the Balok chant. "Balok" was a rubber dinosaur attached to a long pole. The name originated from a "Star Trek" episode

featuring a character of that name. We started whispering "Balok" over and over again, slowly increasing the volume until everyone was screaming at the top of his lungs. . . . In addition, team players wore different outfits, including bathrobes, capes and helmets, cre-ating an atmosphere that combined Mardi Gras and Halloween.

The frenzy spilled over onto the field and the 'Boro beat the Condors to win it all in 1979, following it up with a win over Bos-ton Aerodisc the next year. Both games were decided by one goal.

"I was so ready to play," said Timba of the first Nationals. "I knew we were going to win that day. We all had each others' back. No one could have beaten us that day."

After winning their second Nationals the 'Boro team was pre-sented with a trophy, a large cup that rivaled Lord Stanley's in size, and that cup would become an important part of Glassboro lore. They took the cup out to a bar and drank from it for hours, telling the bartender, "Just keep filling it up and let us know how much it costs." Over the next decades that same cup would be passed from player to player and would attend countless weddings and several births, and even make it to the hospital room of one dying team-mate, Dave Flood. Timba himself drank out of it the night before his wedding and then ate Cheerios out of it the next morning (de-spite rumors that it had been recently used to potty train another player's child).

While New Jersey teams dominated the early and late years of the '70s, a shift started in the middle part of the decade, a shift that saw the rise of an alternative vision and venue for Ultimate. At some point around 1976 East Coast players began to hear muffled rumors of a distant land. It was a mythic place where the game was played differently. This land went by the name of Santa Barbara.

It was there on a spring day in 1975 on the sloping Santa Barbara Mission lawn framed by peeling eucalyptus trees that the sport finally broke free of the eastern seaboard and a form of something very close to Ultimate burst out. It was not brought west on a stagecoach by the game's brave Jersey pioneers but rather sprung up spontaneously, coevolving and then coexisting with East Coast Ultimate for a while, a slightly different version of essentially the same thing, like bands of Homo sapiens living over the hill from tribes of Neanderthals. Ultimate Frisbee was invented in Jersey, no doubt about it, but it was on those mythic fields of California, that shining hill far above the beach, that Ultimate *should* have been born.

The man most responsible for the invention of this new West Coast game and the gathering of the players who threw themselves into it was Tom Kennedy, who would soon become universally known in the Ultimate community as "TK." If Santa Barbara looked like the place Ultimate should have been invented, TK looked the way a real Ultimate player should. Not some Jersey geek, but tall, handsome, and thin with a beard and long hair of brown-gold. He was also a gifted athlete who could throw a backhand far and true, and would at one point simultaneously hold the world records for both Frisbee accuracy and distance. Boston's Heather Morris, who was one of the pioneers of the women's game and has a strong claim to being the best women's player of all time, remembers first meeting TK in California: "He was like a god to me as a young player. He was *it*. I went gaga. Pure puppy love."

But back in '74, in those pre-Internet days, TK and his friends in Santa Barbara hadn't yet heard of Ultimate's existence, and in fact their initial interest was in simply throwing and catching. In

TK's own written recollection of the roots of West Coast, there is a distinctly California vibe:

> My path toward becoming deeply involved began innocently enough in a park on a Sunday afternoon late 1973 when I asked a stranger holding a Frisbee if he wanted to toss it around. That stranger turned out to be my lifelong friend and Frisbee partner Tom Shepherd. This event took place at Palm Park in Santa Barbara, California. Palm Park is a flat, lawned area directly adjacent to the beach near the Santa Barbara pier. The park is an especially beautiful place to play both because of its picturesque setting and a steady flow of unimpeded wind. For those reasons alone it is still a very popular spot among freestylists. However, when we first began meeting there to play, an added attraction for us was the music which was played as an accompaniment to a group of folk dancers who also gathered at the park every Sunday. Tom and I soon formed a relationship revolving around weekly Sunday meetings at Palm Park. We soon began to increase how often we played and included the Mission Lawn as one of our regular playing venues. With the beautiful ocean vistas, large rolling lawn and location adjacent to the historic Santa Barbara Mission it is a natural place to play Frisbee.

Perfect. While East Coast Ultimate starts on a parking lot in Jersey, West Coast Ultimate begins with palm trees and music and folk dancers and views of the ocean. Soon the two Toms were heading down to the Rose Bowl in Pasadena, California, to watch the first World Frisbee Championships. There were all sorts of Frisbees being thrown and Frisbee golf being played but no Ultimate, not yet. Still, the boys returned to Santa Barbara excited and before long had other locals coming out to join in their throwing sessions.

And then: "It was at one of these group throwing sessions in the spring of 1975 that about ten of our friends were gathered on the Mission Lawn. We were basically just throwing, running, and catching when we came up with the idea to figure out a team game we could all play." The group was filled with real athletes who had backgrounds in traditional sports, and at first they just used shoes and shorts as markers for the corner of a field and played something close to touch football with a disc. But then the huddles disappeared and the disc began to flow more freely and they played until dark. "As we were leaving, I remember how excited we were by what we had created," TK remembered, "and we decided to try and recruit more people to join us."

This would prove to be the beginning of what would become the Santa Barbara Condors. Not much later, TK came across the article about Ultimate in *Time*, and the Condors began incorporating the rules that had developed on the East Coast. At that moment in December of 1975, fifty-three Ultimate teams were known to exist, with only one existing west of the Mississippi, a possibly fictional team from Bakersfield College. But before long the Condors would join that list, as would other California teams as Columbia High School graduate Irv Kalb and his fellow Rutgers superstar Stork Roddick moved west. By 1976, Ultimate tournaments were springing up all over the West Coast and those tournaments were all being won by the Condors, who went undefeated. A year later, in July, the Condors won the first Western Regionals, which gave them the right to play the winner of the Eastern Regionals, Penn State, in what was the first actually *national* National Championships. The Penn State team was made up of college kids who hadn't played since school had let out while TK's team had real athletes with an average age of twenty-seven. It wasn't even close, the Condors winning 32–14. The next year the Condors again advanced to the finals and beat Cornell 23–17 for their second consecutive title. California Ultimate had arrived.

By the time I headed to college, in 1979, Harvard was one of more than a hundred schools that listed Ultimate as a club sport. Joel Silver's Johnny Appleseeds had done their job well. I never thought much about the game's history, didn't know yet about Columbia High School or what was going on in California or any of that. I just started playing.

These days a year passes with the snap of my fingers, but back then, during the first year of college, a month seemed an eon. The same week that I went to my first Ultimate practice, I walked into a classroom in Emerson Hall and discovered Walter Jackson Bate, a Harvard English professor with wispy white hair and a rubbery face that could go from gentle to stern in zero flat, and whose right hand would rise above the lectern like a fluttering leaf as he lectured. He spoke of the struggles of his hero, Samuel Johnson, and of the poet John Keats, and I would quickly learn that he had written biographies of both writers (and that both books had won Pulitzers). I also heard the story of how, near the end of his life of Keats, Bate grew sick in sympathy with the poet, developing a cough that sounded almost tubercular. "Great" was one of Bate's favorite words—and soon was one of mine—and he was fond of quoting Longinus: "The hunger of youth is for greatness." When I first heard him say those words, sitting in my hard wooden seat in Emerson 101, it was all I could do not to jump up and yell "Amen!" By the end of the term, having listened as Bate seemed to personally usher English literature from the eighteenth century to the nineteenth, I began to harbor secret dreams of becoming a great writer myself. I told no one of course, not back then.

One of the proudest moments of my freshman year came when I was walking back from practice up what was then still Boylston (soon to be Kennedy) Street, cleats over my shoulder, with a bunch of Ultimate teammates. I was keeping quiet, as I usually did back then, when Stuart, our captain (the same guy who had talked me into coming back to play that first day), asked me what I planned to major in. The most common answer to that question, in my brief experience at Harvard, was Economics. But I told Stuart about how much I loved Walter Jackson Bate's course and how I had decided to major in English.

"You're a real renaissance man, aren't you?" he said.

Maybe he was teasing but the question made me happy. Made me proud.

I *wanted* to be a renaissance man, you see, I really did. But there were some obstacles in my effort to achieve this ideal.

Chief among those obstacles was alcohol, with marijuana running a close second. My decision to frequently indulge in both together was unfortunate, since in those days the latter made me paranoid and the former aggressive and occasionally violent. I had five suitemates my freshman year, including George Parker, the son of the famous Harvard crew coach Harry Parker (who knew a thing or two about amateur sports). We were all trying to start to find our way in the world, all in different styles. George was neat, a little persnickety, on his way to med school, and spent a lot of time on homework, which made us natural enemies. I played Ultimate, drank and smoked too much, and my corner of our suite stank like a wolf's den, with my muddy sweats and cleats draped wherever I had taken them off, and empty beer bottles stacked like soldiers. I was mean to George, once peeking through the keyhole while he was unlocking the door and slamming the door hard outward into his body, and I regret it.

"Blow it off" became the rallying cry of my freshman year. I'd begun to read Hunter S. Thompson, who I saw not as a crazed '60s caricature of wild drug use, but as a role model. The renaissance man never really stood a chance. After a fall in which I got three A's and a B, I began to test how little work I could do, and how many classes I could blow off while still getting passing grades. As an alternative to attending classes, I did midday bong hits and played an inordinate amount of Frisbee golf. Fairly early on during our freshman year, Simon Long had laid out an 18-hole Frisbee golf course that meandered through the buildings and grounds of the Harvard Law School and then back toward the Museum of Natural History. The first hole required a strong drive over the Cambridge Street underpass—often enough we ended up scrambling down onto the busy road to reclaim our discs from traffic amid honking cars—with the "hole" itself being the space between the second and third neo-classic columns of the School of Public Administration's Littauer Center. Other holes provided a course in art history. The second, for instance, required hitting the Discus Thrower, a bronze life-sized replica of the original sculpture in the Vatican by Jonderia Chiurozzi that stood in front of the Hemenway Gymnasium, and the fourteenth had as its target Bessie, the three-ton bronze sculpture of an African rhino that was created by the American artist Katharine Lane Weems and that, along with its twin rhino, Vicky, guarded the door to the bio labs. We must have played that course a thousand times, though it took me a while to figure out that since Simon was left-handed the whole course was laid out for his lefty thumber.

There was something darker going on, too. One night I went out drinking with my roommate Will, who played for the varsity baseball team, and my friend Griff, who had come to Harvard to play hockey but had badly injured his knee. We staggered home late and drunk and I found myself in our floor's communal

bathroom, leaning against a sink while staring at my own reflection in the mirror. The character I saw there was brutish. Hair
long and disheveled, body well muscled but thick, eyes unfocused,
goatish and vague, a slob really. I didn't like him. Not at all.

It wasn't just that the character I was looking at wasn't *great*
that bothered me. It was that he wasn't *good*. Somewhere inside
that brute was not just a more refined man but a better one.
Although I stared hard, however, all I saw was a long-haired beast.
At that moment I hated that beast.

I was still leaning on the sink, arms straight, palms on the porcelain, when these thoughts occurred to me. And then, just as my spasm
of self-loathing peaked, I felt the sink give a little below my weight.

When the sink gave I, instead of taking my hands off, pushed
it down a little farther and then pulled it back up. Then, before I
knew it, I was yanking the sink up and down, pushing down hard
and pulling up with violence. Soon I was determined to liberate
the porcelain base from its long confinement against the wall, to
break it free of its moorings. And I did. When the last pipe broke
and the sink fell to the ground, a great geyser of water spurted into
the air, water that before long was flooding the bathroom and
cascading down the dorm stairs to the lower floors.

It was an act that might have gotten me thrown out of college
were it not for what I did next. Overwhelmed by what I'd done, I
ran to the T.A.'s door and knocked on it. I told my story. That, I
found out later, had been what saved me. They had gone easy on
me because I had confessed my sins.

In Tom Kennedy West Coast Ultimate players had a model for
how the game should be played: with athleticism and fire of
course, but also with grace and fairness. David Barkan, who would

later rise to prominence in Boston with a team called the Hostages, has never forgotten how Tom Kennedy came up to him and praised him after he had played well for the Jam, a team from San Jose, in 1978: "I felt anointed. Recognized by the king."

Like many others at that time, Barkan looked on the Santa Barbara Condors with awe: "They were real athletes, a bleach-blond army of studly So-Cal dudes. And TK was the biggest and the studliest of them all. He walked in and it lit up around him. 'That's the guy I want to be like,' I thought. That's how I want to hold myself. And this is how the game can be played.'"

Later, during my junior year at Harvard, I would come across this line in one of Walter Jackson Bate's books: "The boldness desired involves directly facing up to what we admire and then trying to be like it (the old Greek ideal of education, of paideia, of trying to be like the excellence, or arête, that we have come to admire . . .)." My pen bore a deep furrow under those words, one I can still run my fingers over all these years later. *The arête, the excellence.* The idea excited me, thrilled me. *Arête* was the quality the ancient Greeks most admired in athletes, and as I learned more about it I found that any definition of the quality included "virtue, skill, prowess, pride, excellence, valor and nobility."

I'm not claiming that the Santa Barbara Condors were running around the field in togas or were waxing philosophic during time-outs. But there was something going on there. Led by their enlightened leader, they played with the conviction that it was possible to be both great and good. It wasn't just that the Condors won but how they won. They had begun in the spirit of play, of fun, of tossing a disc around in the sun in a park by the beach while folk music played. Somehow they held on to this spirit, though of course it could get eroded during hard-fought games, and by the fact was that the Condors, like everyone else, had jerks on their team. But they also had Tom Kennedy. TK would evolve into a sort of philosopher-king of the sport, a great talent but also a great guy, who seemed equally interested in winning and in helping spread the game. Before long he would become the national director of the fledging Ultimate Players Association, running tournaments, printing the Ultimate newsletter in his spare bedroom, and even writing the first book about how to play Ultimate with Irv Kalb. If he didn't build up the sport singlehandedly—there were plenty of others, most importantly Stork, who, ensconced in his Wham-O job, helped create the game's infrastructure—it is hard to imagine the game growing like it did without him. A machinist by trade, his real work during that time was Ultimate.

"It was a moment in my life," he said. "And that moment lasted a few years. It *was* my life. That's all I did. Ultimate. It was all-consuming."

It was also around this time that the phrase "Spirit of the Game" was written into the rules, and it was officially decided that Ultimate would move forward without referees. It's unlikely that the actual phrase was bandied about as those original throwing sessions in Palm Park and the Mission lawn evolved into a running sport, but the idea of *espirit* had always been there, as much in the air as the chords of folk music. In those days Tom Kennedy simply called it "fair play." Winning was great, but they were there for fun.

The origins of Spirit are murky, even to the protagonists. There is not a whisper of the notion of Spirit of the Game in the revered first edition of the rules. Of course the earliest games at Columbia High School had been unofficiated not due to any lofty ideals but because there were no refs handy. But what had been a practical reality was gradually elevated into the lofty position of a code of honor by the writers of the rules. Pragmatism begat idealism, an idealism that some would later find rather sticky and unctuous.

What is clear through the murk is that in the late '70s discussions between TK, Irv Kalb, and Stork Roddick yielded up some language that found its way into the rules, first in the form of relatively vague talk about sportsmanship and then more explicitly in a section of the 1982 version of the rules that states: "In Ultimate, an intentional foul would be considered cheating and a gross offense against the spirit of sportsmanship. Often a player is in a position where it is clearly to his/her advantage to foul or commit some violation, but that player is morally bound to abide by the rules. The integrity of Ultimate depends on each player's responsibility to uphold the Spirit of the Game, and this responsibility should not be taken lightly."

And so Ultimate made its grand stab at idealism, a decision that would have consequences that were sometimes less than ideal.

In my classics course at Harvard, I read about Marcus Aurelius, the great and fair-minded Roman emperor, who led the Roman army as they fought back the invading barbarian hordes, and then, after a day of battle, retired to his tent to write the immortal philosophical work known as the *Meditations*. The scholar Brand Blanshard wrote of Aurelius: "If his place is unique in history, it is because he set himself a transcendent aim and came heroically close to reaching it."

I am not suggesting that some blond machinist dude from Santa Barbara who got really into Ultimate Frisbee merits comparison with one of the greatest minds and military leaders of the ancient world. Just that at that point in the young, unformed sport there were certain possibilities in the air, certain ways to be, that were as yet unexplored.

As for me, I tried to play fair but I rolled my eyes at the more pious notion of Spirit. As my reaction to Walter Jackson Bate attests, I was not unidealistic. But the Spirit of the Game seemed too much. It reeked of the perfectibility of man and I thought it silly the way that it was writ large in the rules as if its origins were biblical. It was a nice idea, like communes and free love, but it neglected one small factor: human nature. I had played enough pickup basketball to know what really happened when people made their own calls.

Despite TK's influence and efforts, Ultimate back then was still in an adolescent stage of its development. Throughout the '70s there had always been a kind of pulse between the players' desire to excel at the game and the original spirit of Joel Silver's "anti-sport." This was typified by the early Tufts team's response to the numbered jerseys that Irv Kalb and the Rutgers team wore. The Tufts captains, Jim Pistrang and Ed Summers, wanting to puncture what they saw as the pomposity and over-seriousness of the three-time champions, decided that they would wear numbers, too. So the next time they played Rutgers the whole Tufts team sported shirts with the number 3 on their backs.

This was the perfect embodiment of a different kind of spirit. A screw-the-man, nothing-is-above-mockery spirit that was there from the sport's beginning and that continued for all the years that I played, and that even continues, to some extent, today. If it is a cliché to say that Ultimate was born as a "hippie sport," it was also in many ways wrong. Ultimate was invented not at a California Be-In but by the ironic geeks of Columbia H.S., and came into the world not as some love fest but in the same cauldron of 1960s and '70s rebellion and irreverence that, fueled by everything from Hunter S. Thompson to *Mad* magazine to the first tongue-tasting acid, formed the *National Lampoon* and *Saturday Night Live*. By the time I was playing the sport, people were as likely to give the finger as a peace sign, and if peace signs were given, they were usually given ironically.

It was one of the things I loved about Ultimate from the first, and in some ways made up for the fact that we as players weren't taken seriously. Or perhaps, more accurately, it was the upside of not being taken seriously. We could smoke joints or drink a beer on the sidelines, wear clownish uniforms without numbers or with ironic numbers, and have teams with names like the Hostages, the Seven Boozy Idiots, Chicks and Salsa, Chicks with Dicks (a team composed of men in skirts), Lady Godiva with its go-dive pun, and the all-Jewish team, Let My People Throw.

Like Joel Silver, we were not above mocking the game we spent so much time playing. This continues today: at a recent college National Championship, some members of the crowd, made up mostly, as always, of players themselves, turned to the ESPN cameras and started chanting "Not a real sport."

Like those around me, I was quick to deprecate the game I played, but with each passing month it seemed to have a deeper hold on me. I began to bring a Frisbee along wherever I went, throwing it ahead of me when I walked to class, tossing it up in the air and running it down as I jogged along the Charles River. It became part of my identity, my security blanket. And it was my weapon, too, since discs, unlike balls, have always had a warrior aspect. If Captain America carried his shield and Thor his hammer, I now had my 165-gram Wham-O always at the ready.

Moreover, that piece of molded plastic was becoming the object of my affection. During the majority of weekdays over the next four years I would reenact the walk I had made on the first day of school, over the Charles River on the John F. Kennedy Bridge, down past the hoary stadium that looked like it still might stage gladiator fights, to the little uneven slice of grass, off to the side of the soccer field, which we had talked the Harvard administrators into letting us use for practice.

In that era of long hair and short shorts, I found a home on the Ultimate field. If I was a sometimes indifferent and lazy practice player, games brought with them a special adrenalized excitement. There was a carnival feel to those weekends in the fall or spring when we would often either host tournaments behind Harvard Stadium or head out on the road, to UMass Amherst or SUNY Purchase, or, once a year, as far away as Washington, D.C. There would be as many as a couple dozen teams at a tournament, and on Saturday mornings, before the first game, anything was possible. Soon enough the good teams would beat the bad and the pecking order would be reestablished, but for the moment you could imagine yourself winning it all. If your team did make it to the quarterfinals, that would mean you would play on Sunday, and if you made it to the semis, you would play again, and if you reached the promised land of the finals, yet again. Back then games were timed and lasted an hour and a half, with a typical score of a close game being, say, 15–13. That meant that on a successful weekend a player could conceivably play ten to twelve hours of Ultimate and well over a hundred points. Which is why Sunday evenings meant cramped legs and Mondays brought general enervation after an entire weekend of running.

During the spring of my freshman year a player named Chris Heye took a term off from Wesleyan and came to Harvard for the term. Chris, a slim man who did yoga stretches during warmups, was a great thrower who opened my eyes to possibilities in the game I had not yet glimpsed. Soon enough I learned that if I made eye contact with him, then faked as if I were coming back to the disc, I could take off long as he unleashed arcing bombs for me to run down. He also introduced us to "overheads," direct nonfloating passes thrown in the style of a football. We had seen these throws before but had mostly laughed at them and considered them a novelty. Now I saw not only how these spearlike throws could be used to advance the disc, but how much fun they were to throw.

I had started to think about winning Nationals, too, or rather to fantasize about it since there was no way Harvard was going to win it all. But I liked to turn the idea of it around in my mind, and imagine being on, or putting together, a great team capable of doing just that.

Even with the temporary addition of Chris Heye, Harvard was just a good team, not great. We beat most of the other Ivy League teams though we sometimes struggled with Columbia, a geeky team that played zone defense against us. That spring we lost at sectionals to a Dartmouth team that featured the future New York great Pat King. We were up by two with a minute left, but then they scored and one of our players threw it away after catching the ensuing pull. That tied it and Dartmouth went on to win in overtime.

We sometimes even had a hard time beating the one prominent high school team of the time, Bronx Science of New York City. The star of that team was a skinny seventeen-year-old who didn't look like he had yet shaved, but who possessed preternatural skills as an Ultimate player. At 6'3", he ran like a gazelle and timed his jumps perfectly so that the Bronx Science strategy was often just to huck the Frisbee long to him. His name was Jeremy Seeger and by the time he was done he would have a place of prominence in Ultimate Frisbee lore comparable to that of his famous uncle, Pete Seeger's, place in the world of music. We rarely called him by his real name, however, but by the nickname Simon had invented for him: God.

I was always assigned to cover Jeremy and since it was my only hope I often got pretty physical with him. I *had* shaved at that point and made it a point to act like a stevedore around this upstart high school kid, pushing and shoving a little and grunting and saying "fuck" a lot and snorting and blowing my nose on the ground in that gross one-fingered way, hoping to scare him a little with my relative manliness. It didn't work. He often left me plodding far behind as he outraced me to the disc. His trademark was a kind of gliding grace while all I could offer in return was grunting effort. No one was ever going to nickname me after a deity.

But I had my moments. Like the one time I blocked a pass to Jeremy and raced to the other end of the field to catch a pass in the end zone. Those moments, more and more, were what the sport was about for me. Moments when I, a person who spent too much time thinking, escaped from my brain and became fully immersed in the game. Moments when I was absorbed, a part of something, and not just spinning around on the narcissistic hamster wheel of my own mind.

The Santa Barbara Condors' reign didn't last, of course. It couldn't. The Condors won National Championships in 1977 and 1978, but by the time I entered college in '79, Jersey was back on top. Glassboro State, and Timba, beat the Condors that year by a single point.

TK, exhausted from the obsessive work of trying to turn Ultimate into a real sport, was ousted from his position as head of the Ultimate Players Association (UPA) by East Coasters who thought he had claimed too much power. He had been older than many of his peers when he started to play, and after a knee injury, his level of play fell, and he was past his prime by '82. Very soon the East Coast's metaphoric Belushi would smash the West Coast's folk guitar. Punk, not Crosby, Stills, Nash and Young, would provide the soundtrack for Ultimate's next period.

Before the enlightened era of TK ended, however, the Condors had one last hurrah. Some new younger players had joined the team, and they would make a difference, especially on defense, giving the team what TK would call "that young juice." In 1981 more than half of the players on the team were rookies, players who made up in athleticism and effort what they lacked in experience and skills. One such player was David Ellsworth, who everyone called Buzz or Buzzy. Buzz had something relatively uncommon in Ultimate at the time—real muscles—and he looked like a slimmed-down and miniaturized version of Hulk Hogan, the pro wrestler. Everything about Buzz screamed California, from his blond good looks to his Cali twang to his muscular arms to his love of surfing, but his dark secret was that he hailed from Worcester, Massachusetts. I had known him there as a kid, and even gotten in a fight or two with him, something I would never try with this new, improved, sinewy version.

There is something archetypal about Buzz's movement from Worcester to the West. He was following the sun and following discs. He described this to me once in typical Buzzy fashion, heartfelt, a little over-the-top, but earnest.

"In the winter of 'eighty-one, I left school," he said. "It was a mutual decision. I dropped out of UMass before they kicked me out. I hitchhiked out to Santa Barbara. I was destined to go out to California. Destined to play Ultimate."

Buzzy was just a beginning player back then who barely made the team, but he was part of one of the best man-to-man defenses to play the sport at that point. It was another player, however, Keay (pronounced "K") Nakae, an athletic twenty-year-old from Southern California of half-Japanese descent, who would prove to be the star of that Condors defense (D). The next year I, and the

Keay Nakae flying

rest of the Ultimate world, would become familiar with Keay when TK and Irv Kalb's book, *Ultimate: Fundamentals of the Sport*, came out. Page thirty-eight of that book (still dog-eared today, almost forty years later) featured a photo that I greatly admired: a picture of a thin, strong, muscular Keay with a wild, slightly simian look on his face, laying out and extending fully, "getting totally horizontal" as Ultimate players called it, and all of this three feet off the ground. To me Keay seemed like a superhero, and for an obvious reason. In the picture it looked almost exactly like he was *flying* after the disc. All that was missing was a cape.

Keay's beginnings as a player point to both the randomness of our life choices and the powerful hold Ultimate can start to have on some people. He had been riding his bike home from work through the Southern California town of Woodland Hills when he found himself approaching a traffic light. If the light turned green, he would go straight and cut through Pierce College but if it stayed red, he would turn right, a decision he made every day. It was green so he cut through the college, where, next to the gymnasium, he saw a guy spinning a Frisbee on his finger in what Keay would later find out was called a nail delay. Keay almost rode right by but thought, *Wow, that looks cool*, and so walked over and introduced himself to the guy, Bruce Allison. They talked and threw a little and Keay made a first attempt at a delay himself, and then Bruce told Keay about a sport that they played on those fields on Sundays. The next Sunday Keay came out.

"I just watched them play from a distance for a while," Keay remembered. "I didn't know what it was. Finally I walked up to Bruce on the sidelines, and he said, 'Go ahead, jump in.' So I did."

The usual happened. The disc hovered and Keay dove for it or he skyed in the air and caught it or he dove and blocked it. Whatever it was something clicked. He came out again the next Sunday. And the next.

As he put it later, the whole "vector" of his life shifted on that day. It turned out the team he had scrimmaged with was called the Woodland Hills Hot Socks, and he soon joined the team. He got better quickly, particularly on defense, for which he had a rare talent. He loved to run and stay right with the offensive player he was covering, and he had an unusual ability to completely shut down opposing players, limiting them to very few catches—sometimes none at all. The team was good, but they didn't stand a chance against the best team in California, the Condors, led by Tom Kennedy. Keay was beginning to sense that he could be one of the game's best players, but he needed to play with a better team. Then something pushed him over the edge. The newly formed Ultimate Players Association, with none other than Tom Kennedy as its national director, had begun to put out a newsletter. It was really not much more than a pamphlet, stapled together, but I remember always being thrilled to get my hands on it, to see pictures of players from other parts of the country, and hoping that maybe one day, with luck and hard work, I'd see a picture of myself in those pages. Keay, like many other Ultimate players, read the newsletter religiously, and he was particularly excited by the 1981 special championship edition. On its cover was a picture of an ecstatic Timba D'Urso, the Glassboro State star, being held aloft on the shoulders of his teammates with his hands raised over his head in victory. He wore a black T-shirt with white lettering that read WORLD CHAMPS. As soon as Keay saw that picture he knew that that was what he wanted. To be the best. To be a world champion.

The next year he quit his job, ended his lease, and headed north to Santa Barbara. He made the Condors squad and focused hard in practice, listening to TK, his new mentor, and trying to improve his game in every way he could think of. One way he did this was by attacking private track workouts, workouts designed by his brother, a high school track coach, and tailor-made for Ultimate, focusing on the kind of long sprints needed to cover the best players of the other teams. Keay started by doing a series of 220s, but then, to more closely simulate the game, began running sets of five 50-yard sprints. He dedicated each individual sprint to the best offensive players on rival teams. The first was always reserved for Danny Weiss, a great thrower from Santa Barbara's in-state rival, the Berkeley Flying Circus. The next were dedicated to other great players. People said you could never entirely shut down a great offensive player. Keay Nakae wanted to show otherwise.

The Condors won Nationals that year, 1981, beating the Knights of Nee, another New Jersey team, 15–13. Keay was a star, the fierce defensive warrior we all dreamed of being. He could now proudly wear a WORLD CHAMP shirt if he wanted.

He felt great after the win, which he kind of expected. But he also fairly quickly felt something he hadn't expected. Over the next days he learned that winning it all was not going to alter his life, not really.

"I mean there were great intangible benefits: a real sense of accom-

Timba D'Urso celebrating

plishment, a bond with my teammates, and a bolstering of my status in the fantasy world of Ultimate Frisbee. But right away I saw my life was not going to change."

It was great fun and he was happy to drink beers and toast the victory with his teammates. But there were no offers to turn pro, no money, no covers of magazines. In fact, he wouldn't earn a penny from winning it all, and he had to be back at work on Monday.

The buzz of winning stayed with him. But over the next weeks he began to see Ultimate for what it was, not his life but a hobby. It was a hobby that he wanted to excel at, and he took pride in trying to be great at it, but he started to put Ultimate in the proper place in his life.

"I wanted to be the best," he told me. "But winning in the right way became very important to me."

I asked him what this meant in practice.

"It means 'Don't be a dick.'"

More loftily, his feelings toward the sport echoed the Greek concept of arête, the idea Walter Jackson Bate celebrated, the excellence, and, like the Greeks, he saw athletics as a part of his life, not all of it. He was an amateur, an impassioned amateur but an amateur, and in this Keay was the perfect embodiment of TK's philosophy, a philosophy he would adapt and make his own. To be a good man and great player. A player who knew that winning was glorious and that losing could be intensely painful. But also a player who disagreed with the Lombardi adage. Winning *wasn't* everything. You didn't let the game *become* your whole life. You stayed balanced and kept perspective.

As it turned out, Keay Nakae's time at the top of the game would be brief. He would continue to train and play defense like a warrior, but five years later, at the still young age of twenty-seven, he would tear his ACL, and was more or less done. Like a lot of Ultimate players, he did not have health insurance, and could not afford the necessary operation. That would take another year of scrambling to get a job that had insurance, during which he tried to play on his bum knee. Even after the operation, he was never the same.

While I dreamed of arête of my own, specifically of becoming a great writer, I barely wrote a sentence outside of my school papers and the essays that helped me bullshit my way through exams. I'd put such a burden on myself, heaped such expectations on the idea of being a *great* writer, that I'd paralyzed myself. But during my sophomore year I found another outlet for my creativity. I'd always had a gift for caricature and spent hours as a kid copying the cartoons in *Mad* magazine and then trying my own hand at caricatures of TV characters like Arnold Horshak, Vinny

Barbarino, and the rest of the cast of *Welcome Back, Kotter*. Fairly early I started drawing political caricatures and I cut my teeth on Nixon with his famous ski jump nose, hanging jowls, shifty eyes, and five o'clock shadow. When Nixon resigned, my cartoon Ford practically leapt off my pen, looking like a friendly orangutan with gently eroded features. My Carter started as a smiling hayseed, but then shrank smaller and smaller along with his prestige. And then came Reagan—the bobbing head, hanging wattle, upward-swirling pompadour, and happily vacant smile. I spent hours perfecting my Reagan and then more hours readying my first batch of political cartoons for inspection by the editors of the Harvard *Crimson*.

Those first cartoons were stiff and it took me a while to realize that mine was the art of bluntness, that I was best when I was most direct. Every week or so I would bring my batch of cartoons in to Paul Engelmayer, the editorial chairman, and he would look them over with the *Crimson*'s president, who at the time was Bill McKibben. McKibben would later become famous for his books and activism against global warming but back then I mainly knew him as a tall and distant figure, somewhat Lincoln-esque, a news junkie who practically lived in the *Crimson* and whom I only occasionally caught a glance of. Gradually my cartoons began to appear in the newspaper, mostly on the editorial pages but also as a special full-page ad that featured Reagan in his bathrobe. Seeing my last name below the cartoons gave me my first twinges of artistic pride.

There were other positive signs that I might emerge from my brutehood. Though I'd almost died when I drunkenly jumped out of a dorm window and fractured my skull during my sophomore year, and though it would be hard to say that I'd gotten my drinking under control, several factors dovetailed to lend more stability to my life. For one thing, because I wanted to be great at Ultimate, I started to train, which meant longer runs along the Charles River (often sweating out the booze from the night before). For another, I suddenly found myself in a relationship with a very smart, funny, and outgoing young woman named Rachel from Newton, Massachusetts. Rachel had asked me to go see the movie *Fame* with her at the old Church Street Theater in Harvard Square and one thing led to another. Over the next couple of months we set about losing our virginities together. This did not occur in a great fit of ardor, but more in the spirit of a science experiment. Neither of us knew what we were doing. But even with our overworking and undermining Harvardian brains slowing us down, we finally figured out that tab A went into slot B.

For me that moment was as great a triumph as any I'd had on the Ultimate field. A monumental breakthrough. I'd convinced myself that I would remain a virgin forever. I was already almost twenty and I carried my virginity like a dark secret. I'd had girlfriends in high school but had always wilted when the moment arrived. Not my penis so much as my will. I would get to a point and simply stop. But now, suddenly, I was no longer wilting, and the effect of this on my mood was extraordinary. My shyness decreased; my confidence rose. Our relationship would carry on for another year and a half or so and then, as if it had served its purpose, would die out, though not in any mean way. We still joked around when we saw each other at parties after that and we still keep in touch today. There was love between us but it was also a utilitarian relationship and it had achieved its necessary result.

My relationship with Rachel calmed me. In my better, more sober, moments I could envision a more balanced life, a life of the mind, a life of the body, and the elevated life of an artist. I still *wanted* to be a renaissance man, I really did. Not some vulgar, sink-ripping, skull-breaking drunkard, but a man of intellect and culture like Walter Jackson Bate. A pursuer of arête. A writer no less!

But as much as I may have wanted this refined life I couldn't have wanted it very much, or at least not as much as I wanted another kind of life: a life that was wilder and funnier, that was more animal and physical, and more fun. While I might have had some ideas about elevating my life, I seemed more committed than ever to undermining those lofty notions. Ultimate played a large part in the undermining. It wasn't solitary and noble like writing or drawing, but communal and wild, a sort of constant athletic party. While my roommates had begun to go to their Harvard Finals Club (the Owl) for their socializing, I went to the fields. There I was creating a new self out of the shy raw material with which I started college. This self was not timid; he was raucous, bold, full of laughter. And, it goes without saying, this self was still often found consuming large amounts of alcohol.

While publication and sex were good for my ego, Ultimate still remained the most exciting thing in my life. By sophomore year the older generation of Harvard Ultimate players had graduated, and Simon, Jon Epstein, and I inherited the team. The team was bolstered by the return of two players who had been taking terms abroad during our freshman year, Bennett Goldberg and Tom Baker, and by our own efforts at improvement. My throws were getting better, but my favorite part of the game remained catching, more specifically "skying." Skying meant going up and getting the disc at its highest point, leaping over other players and timing that leap, then coming down with the disc. I loved nothing better than ripping down a disc in the end zone, and I was pretty good at it. As generally deluded as I was in those days, I wasn't deluded enough to think my jumping was something special among the more general athletic population. During those winters I was playing in pickup basketball games at Harvard's Indoor Athletic Building, and while I had managed to dunk a couple of times by running up without dribbling and using a rubbery ball I could palm, I was playing against guys who were regularly dunking over me, with my hand reaching their elbows if I was lucky. But my timing was good, and against the limited athletic pool that constituted Ultimate players back then I rarely had anybody sky me. In fact, I started to take a good deal of pride in coming down with the disc. At that point, those moments were the highlights of my life.

The Condors victory in 1981 was a kind of final coronation and confirmation for Tom Kennedy, who was once again and for the last time a world champion. It was, as he said, a *moment*. Brief and almost miragelike. The spirit of the game lowercase, without the unctuous pretension. Fairness. The arête, the excellence. The shining city on the hill.

Kennedy's team of philosopher-kings from the fields above the beach had shown that you could win without squabbling (too much) and that goodness and greatness were not incompatible. From that point on the Spirit of the Game would be embedded in the rules and over the next forty years no article or TV piece on Ultimate would fail to mention it.

But Spirit was about to come in for a beating. One of the fascinating things about Ultimate in those days was that it was not just a game without referees but one without coaches and media coverage as well, which meant no objective commentary on each player's subjective experience. Or, to put it more bluntly, players, including me, often thought we were much better than we were. In theory this was a kind of ideal from the game's 1960s roots, the sense that everyone was valuable no matter what some coach said. But in practice it often led to an overgrowth of unchecked egos, something that would profligate over the next decade as the game grew.

A certain brutish ugliness was about to descend on the Ultimate world; an overly competitive and overtly ambitious period was dawning. Jimmy Carter had been whisked out of office and the age of Reagan was beginning, and as the country went, so would the sport. The Spirit of the Game would remain in name but more and more it would seem that the most competitive teams would use the fact that players made their own calls to their own advantage. A reasonable person might question whether Spirit had ever existed at all, or whether it was a myth on the order of the hippogriff or unicorn.

It would not have been crazy for someone standing there on the sidelines at Nationals in Austin, Texas, in 1981, watching the Condors win, to imagine that they might do so for the next decade. At the very least it would have been reasonable to assume that the National title would be traded back fairly regularly between East and West, with some South and Midwest champions thrown in for good measure. But *reasonable* would not be the tune of the coming era.

In fact, the next time the Condors would win Nationals would be twenty years later, when a team made up of players who were young enough to be TK's children finally brought the title back to Santa Barbara. During the gap that constituted these two decades a different type of team and a different type of player would ascend the sport's highest rungs. And during those years, nice guys would almost always finish last.

"Our team was kind of going in all different directions," Keay would say later. "We didn't have that one obsessive leader who forced us to practice and made all the hard decisions. TK was a great leader but not that kind of leader."

The coming era of Ultimate would match the times and have more to do with ambition than fair play. A new version of Ultimate would emerge in places like Chicago and Boston and New York City. And this new version would not be heavy in either Spirit or spirit. Or perhaps it was just a different kind of spirit. Something sharper, angrier, darker, and more complicated but still vital and striving toward a kind of excellence.

In fact, from the twenty-one years between when I started to play and the end of the millennium, the tally of National Champions would read like this: West Coast 3, Midwest 3, East Coast 15.

The game's move to California had been a brief one and now it would turn toward somewhere else. If you listened hard enough, you might have been able to hear distant drumbeats. Something was changing; the barbarians were rising up. And they were not coming from the West.

In that age of Reagan I lived in what was perhaps the citadel of the new era, not just Harvard, but at the very top of the Harvard pyramid, in the snootiest of all the Harvard Houses, Eliot House. Walter Jackson Bate might still talk of arête, but for many students that was just a word to study so you could ace a test. Most of my classmates saw Eliot as a jumping-off point, and if that is where they were jumping from, there was little question where they were jumping to. It seemed that half the university was frothing to get to Wall Street and make buckets of money.

Harvard freshmen spend their first year in Harvard Yard but then head off to various residential "houses," which are basically fancy dormitories for upperclassmen. My freshman roommates, understandably appalled by my general behavior and by the rank hole of books, cleats, and cartoons that was my corner of our suite, had initially decided not to invite me along when they moved to Eliot House. My roommate Dan, who had been picked by the others to tell me and chose to do so when I was in the shower of our communal bathroom (the sink-ripping bathroom), must have been surprised by my reaction. I started bawling, stung by the rejection from those I thought among my only non-Frisbee friends at college. I guess I really didn't understand that to them I must have seemed a kind of erratic brute. Anyway, I created enough of a scene to make Dan reconsider and, after reporting back to the others, change his mind and invite me along to Eliot.

It was odd that I still wanted to stay with roommates who had rejected me, but a part of me, a part that I had glimpsed below the brute when I looked in the mirror before I tore the sink from wall, knew that it was the smart and responsible thing to do. If I had instead gone off to Kirkland House, the jock house, with my other roommate Will and my friend Griff, the rest of my days at Harvard would have been one long keg party. The quieter part of me understood that the Eliot House roommates were more serious and that there I might become more serious, too.

And so for the next three years I dragged my muddy self back from Ultimate practice or from weekend tournaments to what might have been the country's truest bastion of all things preppy, the bright-colored sea of Lacoste shirts that was the Eliot House dining hall. Of course, Frisbee was preppy enough in its own way but this was a whole different level of preppiness at a time when preppy was at its peak, when *The Official Preppy Handbook* was a bestseller and Reagan had ushered in his new unashamed age of privilege.

I had few friends in Eliot and so sometimes I opted to eat dinner elsewhere, following Simon Long back to Adams House, the artsy house where he lived. After dinner, Simon and I would either head out to throw or up to his room to party. (I think we probably listened to Springsteen's *Nebraska* five hundred times.) I was becoming less shy but was still relatively quiet. Meanwhile, Simon's favorite form of speech was the loud monologue that he, brooking no interruptions, could keep going for surprising stretches of time. Even if it was sometimes hard to get in a word edgewise, he was a good and generous friend. Already, he was beating many of our classmates to the punch by playing the stock market, and, after a particularly lucrative surge, he bought me a gift.

By then I'd stopped playing barefoot and was wearing a pair of narrow Adidas cleats barely held together with athletic tape. One day while Simon and I were walking up Mass. Ave., throwing a Frisbee as always, we saw a new pair of expensive cleats in the window of a sports store. I wanted them but couldn't afford them. Simon told me that if the stock market did a certain thing, he would buy them for me, and the next week the market obeyed, so he did. I was ecstatic. They were big black Johnny Unitas–style high-tops with long plastic spikes that were painted silver so that almost everyone I covered over the next couple of years asked the same frightened question: "Are those *metal* cleats?"

The cleats would signal the official end of my barefoot days, and in a way nicely mirrored what was happening with the sport at large. Ultimate was becoming more athletic, ambitious, physical, competitive, intense. If it had ever been hippie-dippy and groovy, that was going away, at least at the top level.

Not only were the cleats physically impressive, but they had a name that I liked.

They were called Barbarians.

3.

The Hunger of Youth

Though Ultimate players still sometimes wore beads and funny hats and grew their hair long, it slowly was becoming clear that there was something else, something decidedly less groovy, going on out on those fields. It may sound oxymoronic, but there was such a thing as "Frisbee ambition." The people who played the sport wanted not only to win but also to be considered great at what they did, not just in their own eyes but in the eyes of other players. It was the pursuit of fame, really, though a fame closer to the ancient Greeks than *People* magazine, existing only among the bands of players from around the country who, retelling stories of great players and great plays, created the oral tradition through which, in those dark days before iPhones, the sport was remembered.

Ultimate had begun to change my life, but during my last two years of college the sport itself was also changing. I wasn't the only convert to cleats; soon no one was playing barefoot. The time of the hippies was over if it had ever really existed at all. Sure, people still had long hair and beards, but they also had these new things called muscles. Moreover, teams were getting *serious*. This was happening in Boston and also in New York and Chicago and Santa Barbara and St. Louis and San Francisco. Harvard was a decent college team but the real action was with the club teams that were made up of college graduates and, increasingly, of people who dropped out of college to play full time. All over the country these teams were taking the sport to a new level. Down in Jersey, the sport's birthplace, the players from Glassboro had formed a club team called the Gang while out in Chicago a team called Windy City played with a kind of angry edge, a willingness to fight for their self-made calls and an open desire to win, if not at all costs then at quite a few. The Windy City players never went anywhere without their discs, and they excelled at other Frisbee disciplines like the game of Guts, which involved throwing hard, bladelike passes at each other with points scored if the disc was not caught. The Windy players then carried these throws over to Ultimate, becoming some of the best throwers ever to play the game. They were pushed by their rival, the St. Louis Tunas, a squad made up of ex–high school jocks who had emerged from that city's massive summer league and who seemed to have taken the athleticism level of the sport to a new high. Meanwhile, on the West Coast the Santa Barbara Condors were still going strong, restocking their team with hordes of young athletes, enough to fill two practice squads as well as the traveling team, while in the north the Berkeley Flying Circus was ascending.

Also, there was this: people had started to *train*. In the old days practices had consisted of pickup games; now teams began instituting running drills and holding track workouts. Maybe it had once been about flow and friendship and camaraderie, but suddenly it was all about *winning Nationals*. If you were going to train all year, if you were going to give up normal things that normal people got in life, then you had better get something, some smidgen of recognition or glory, in return.

It was true that in those days fewer than a hundred people might watch your Nationals win, but that wasn't the point. Among the ever-growing Ultimate community, among *the tribes*, you would be *known*, your name would be made and then remembered. That was at least part of what drove individuals, and teams, as they pushed the boundaries of what one could do with a Frisbee on the field.

Part of the appeal of playing serious Ultimate, I was just beginning to understand, was that life took on the simplicity of quest, a little like stepping inside of a good science fiction or fantasy novel. There were archenemies (who else gets to have archenemies these days?) and beautiful exotic lands to travel to, with the year culminating in Nationals, the great annual quest for the Grail. My father said that I didn't live in the "real world," and he was right. Instead it was like a game of Dungeons and Dragons and you were in it—right inside it—complete with your weapon and your own special magic powers. A secret world where you were part of a secret tribe.

At around the same time that I was catching my very first goal at that tournament in Maine, a seventeen-year-old named Kenny Dobyns was discovering Ultimate on a rock-hard field in New York City. No one watching him at the time would have ever guessed he would one day be considered the greatest player in the sport, or that his influence on the game, during my era at least, would exceed even that of TK or Irv Kalb. Back then Kenny grew his hair long, wearing it in a ponytail that hung almost down to his butt. Just 5'6", he was solid and strong but didn't yet have the large muscles that would later sprout from his arms, and he'd spent the better part of his high school years getting kicked out of one school after another, once being expelled after hitchhiking to procure a quarter pound of pot and being picked up on the way back to campus by the school's headmaster.

Not only that; Kenny barely knew how to throw a Frisbee. Though, as anyone watching could see, he did know how to throw his body around. His brother Brian, three years older, had started playing Ultimate up at Hampshire College, and when Brian began attending pickup games in New York City, Kenny, the worshipful little brother, followed him like a puppy. And, like a puppy, he chased down whatever Brian threw.

"I figured if I caught everything, they couldn't kick me off the team," he later said.

From the beginning Kenny Dobyns had a unique way of launching himself up and out, Superman-style, flying after discs before landing with a thud on those hard fields. He would later rupture a kidney in this manner, only to return the next year wearing a flak jacket, but what was amazing is that he didn't do even more damage to himself. He had begun flying through the air as a kid, even before he discovered Ultimate. Back during the 1976 Olympics, Kenny had become fascinated with high jumping. He spent that summer at his grandparents' house in Newport News, Virginia, where his grandfather built him his own high-jumping setup, complete with a bamboo crossbar. But what the grandfather neglected to build, and what Kenny never thought to ask for or add himself, was any sort of landing area. By the end of the summer Kenny was regularly clearing four to four and a half feet, not Fosbury-flop style but straddling sideways, and was landing not in a pit of foam but on the ground. He would go to sleep with bruises all over his chest, and then get up and do it again the next day.

This was an early hint of what would make Kenny Dobyns great. On the Ultimate fields in New York, he was the shortest and youngest player, but also the most determined. In his very first real game he was so excited that he smashed into another player and bit through his own lip. His brother looked at him and decreed, "You're fine. Go home." So Ken rode the bus home bleeding into his shirt. This didn't stop him for long. At one of his earliest tournaments he had one of those moments of anointment that always seemed to be happening in Ultimate: Jimmy Herrick, who was one of the country's best Ultimate players as well as the winner of an all-around individual Frisbee skills world championship, came up to Kenny after a game and said, "You learn to throw and you're going to be something." After that Kenny dedicated countless hours to his throwing.

He somehow managed to get his high school degree but then only made it through one term at Reed College in Oregon before being expelled for not going to class. When he came back east he had no confusion or doubt about what he wanted to do with his life. He wanted to become a great Ultimate player and he wanted to play for a team that would win it all. That was all he cared about.

What Kenny Dobyns would come to represent in the sport of Ultimate, over the next decade or so, was a kind of living embodiment of drive and ambition. He *wanted* things. And he was willing to sacrifice to get them. Running down a Frisbee and throwing his body after it was not just what he did best on earth, it was also the perfect metaphor for *wanting* itself. He would see something, go after it with all his might, and get it. He would reduce life to its simplicities, its fundamentals. *I want. I run. I get.* To say he would eventually come to play the Visigoth to TK's renaissance man would be too simple. Kenny was smart, funny, and, it would turn out, a helluva writer. But he also represented what happened to a person who desperately wanted a thing he didn't have. He would turn himself into a kind of living missile, a projectile of desire and effort.

"The hunger of youth is for greatness." That line from Longinus, the one Walter Jackson Bate often quoted during his lectures, was still taped to my wall. In the world of Ultimate Kenny Dobyns would become the most obvious embodiment of this hunger, though he clearly was not alone. If other people were not as blatant about their desires, if they tried to cover up the ugly rawness of their need with something more decorous, they still felt the pull of the essentials of the thing. It was in the air. This desire, this need, this whatever you wanted to call it, was spreading through the country like a contagion. The age of Reagan had arrived and, for some, part of Reagan's appeal was that he pulled the curtain back and showed us that it wasn't so bad to want. Maybe greed *was* good. Certainly ambition, which had become a dirty word in the '60s, was. Even if you despised Reagan's politics, you had to admit he had driven down deep into the zeitgeist, and that the well he'd found there was gushing upward. It was now okay to *want* again. It was okay to *strive*. And, it went without saying, it was okay to *get*.

My writing ambitions continued to slumber, but other ambitions were waking up. If you were to distill these ambitions down to their essence, you would be left with two words: *Frisbee* and *Reagan*.

While sentences still weren't coming to me, political cartoons were. By then I was drawing every day, and I drew dozens of cartoons of the president: Reagan as a blind man stumbling over a cliff, Reagan starring in the then-hit movie *Seems Like Old Times*, Reagan as the Statue of Liberty with the caption "Give me your rich, your white, your upper classes, earning to be free."

These cartoons were all being published in the *Crimson*, with one of them even gaining some national attention when it was attacked by Harvard's newly formed conservative newspaper, the *Salient*. That cartoon was a picture of Reagan, recognizable mostly by his pompadour, seen from the back. He was urinating on a black homeless man who was sleeping, covered with newspapers, in a gutter. It was called "The Trickle Down Theory."

This was around the time that I made another discovery that would greatly impact my burgeoning creative life: I began to drink coffee. Properly fueled, I would stay up late, hunched over my drawing board, drawing Reagan after Reagan. The next morning I would sleep in, blowing off classes, waking up in time to head down over the bridge to the practice fields to pursue my other chief obsession.

Walter Jackson Bate's classes were the only ones I deigned to drag myself to. Though I hadn't yet written a sentence of my great novel, I remained under the spell of Bate. The thrill of his lectures had come first—his malleable face, trembling voice, and hand floating above the lectern—but soon his ideas began to infect me. I took long walks by the Charles muttering to myself, mulling over the notion that literature must retreat from modern games and return to essentialism, whatever that was. Back in my room I hunched over his biographies of Samuel Johnson and Keats and his little book *The Burden of the Past and the English Poet*, underlining everything, feverishly scrawling notes and quotations.

A t one of the several high schools that Kenny Dobyns had gotten kicked out of, a private school named Riverdale in New York, he had briefly been a schoolmate of an extremely tall boy two years his senior named Steve Mooney. Dobyns would always

*Walter Jackson Bate
in his office*

remember that in Steve's
yearbook picture he was
holding a pair of skis. This
seemed somehow perfect
since Steve Mooney was
just the all-American sort
of guy whom Kenny natu-
rally loathed. Later during
an interview with George
Plimpton about Ultimate,
Steve Mooney would ap-
pear wearing a nice blue
sweater with a collared
shirt underneath, and for Dobyns that pretty much
said it all. This guy wore *sweaters* for Christ's sake.

The sweater-wearing boy would graduate from high school
(without getting kicked out once) and go on to Wesleyan University, where he grew to be 6'7" tall and became a varsity soccer
player. If Steve Mooney did not outwardly appear to be as intense
and competitive as Kenny Dobyns, it was only because he hid it
better. He had grown up as the middle boy in a household ruled by
a distant and accomplished man named Richard Mooney. Steve's
younger brother, John, once said that Steve could "talk his way
out of anything" as a child, and was ridiculously competitive at
everything, but added, "there was always an element of sportsmanship to everything he did." For Steve himself there was "no
separation between consciousness and the desire to win." He had
started at age five to play baseball, basketball, and soccer and to

run races in his household of brothers, a household not so unlike the Dobyns' household, it turned out, with the mother, outgoing and athletic herself, as the central figure and the distant intellectual father off writing (or doing crosswords) in the other room. Ken and Moons would say the exact same thing about their mothers: both grew up before Title Nine and, had they lived in a time when women were encouraged to play sports, they would have been athletes.

As for Richard Mooney, he was a Yale graduate who worked for the *New York Times*, first as the Paris correspondent and then, after moving back to New York, as a writer of features and editorials. He had once held up Steve's report card in front of the boy's face and asked, "So do you *want* to go to college?" Steve was a good student but not a great one, and though few people knew it, he was insecure about what he saw as his academic failings. Where he really excelled was playing sports: baseball, tennis, basketball, soccer, you name it. "It was all about winning in my family," he would say. His height, which was often an advantage athletically, could also be a hindrance. By his junior year he had earned a position as a starting forward on the Wesleyan soccer team but by then he'd honestly grown too tall for the sport. In the meantime his classmate and friend Nick Donahue had convinced him to try another sport, this one played with a Frisbee, where his height would help, not hurt. Moons, like Kenny Dobyns, could barely throw at first, but he could run forever and was exceptionally coordinated for such a tall man.

After his junior year, Steve spent a summer in Berkeley that changed his life. He took a photography course at the university, where the professor asked him what his major was; when he said "History," the professor urged Moons to switch and dedicate himself fully to being a photographer. That summer he also began practicing Ultimate with Berkeley's Flying Circus, and one day the team's captain gave him a similar talk. When Moons told him he had to head back east early for soccer camp, the captain shook his head.

"You're playing the wrong sport," he said. When the fall soccer season ended, Steve reached the same conclusion and from then on it was all Ultimate. Moons brought something new to the game, not just a real athlete's skills but a love of training that before him was almost unknown in Ultimate.

Steve was also a great organizer. He had been good at running the games back in his Pelham, New York, neighborhood and Ultimate was just a bigger neighborhood to run games in.

After graduating in 1981, he moved to Boston and formed a team made up of some of the best players on his Wesleyan team along with the best players from rival colleges. The team was called the Rude Boys.

The Rude Boys would become the game's first überteam, capable of sporting a starting seven with an average height of 6'4" and overwhelming other squads with size, talent, speed, and depth. When Harvard played them we never stood a chance. The Rude Boys blasted teams like ours into oblivion like some sort of Frisbee version of Vader's death star.

From the start Moons was fully committed to the sport, and his new team trained as no Ultimate team had trained before. Pushed by Moons, the team attacked their infamous early-morning track workouts at MIT and ran double sessions in summer. To some more groovy-minded Ultimate players this was unheard of, almost against the rules. The Rude Boys didn't care for grooviness: they wanted to win.

At first it looked like they would, and for a very long time. They had taken the sport to a whole new level and their reign seemed inevitable. But there would prove to be one small obstacle on the way to their coronation. That obstacle wouldn't yet be Kenny Dobyns and the New York team he would form or the well-oiled machine that was the Condors of Santa Barbara. Instead it would be a small, scrappy team called the Hostages that came from, of all places, Boston. There was a year or two when Moons and the Rude Boys could travel all over the country, and the world, and thrash any team that lined up against them. But they just couldn't beat their crosstown rival when it mattered most.

It was my good fortune to be able to witness many of the early games between the Hostages and Rude Boys. While I loved playing Ultimate, from the very beginning I relished the stories about the sport almost as much as the sport itself. Up in Simon's room after practice, we would ride the buzz of endorphins, beer, and pot, giddily talking about Ultimate, barely able to contain our excitement. Simon and I would analyze the Hostages and Rude Boys, blatantly hero-worshipping great players and their best plays. We'd also try to decide such weighty issues as who was the game's greatest player—Kenny Dobyns had not yet entered the picture but we considered Steve Mooney, along with David Barkan and Steve Gustafson of the Hostages, with the young Jeremy Seeger coming on strong—and who would win at Regionals and Nationals.

You couldn't have invented more perfectly contrasting rivals than the Hostages and Rude Boys. If the Rude Boys were the death star, with Moons at the fore, then the Hostages were a scraggly band of rebels, fighting against all odds. They'd taken their name during the Iran crisis and, since there were fifty-two hostages, everyone painted that number on their shirts. While the Rude Boys wore more standard black uniforms with the team name emblazoned across their left breasts, someone on the Hostages had gotten the idea to put T-shirts up against a chain-link fence and spray-paint them, leaving the shirts stained with a pattern of chain link. To complete the uniform, some players tied yellow ribbons around their wrists. The Rude Boys looked tall and handsome, like premed or prelaw students out for one more fling before getting this "Frisbee" thing out of their blood, but the Hostages had a decidedly grubby look, with a minor punk rock theme running through the team's general anti-establishment motif.

But it wasn't merely sartorial differences that separated the two rivals. There was a distinct Dudley Do-Right element to the Rude Boys, and they seemed oddly organized in a sport that until then had favored disorder. They were not only a large team physically, but their numbers were huge so that they kept fresh and their opponents had the sense of a swarm of players coming at them in waves. By contrast the Hostages were a smaller team that intentionally kept their numbers low to ensure camaraderie and tightness, with everybody getting a lot of playing time. During warmups, while the Rude Boys stretched as a team, the Hostages were in disarray, some players smoking joints or sipping beers. One Hostage, Jimmy Levine, wore baggy sweats and unlaced work boots right until the game started, and indulged in his own particular psych-up ritual, the pregame cigarette. When the Rude Boys circled up before the pull there was the we-mean-business air of a football huddle with Moons outlining the team's strategy. Meanwhile, the Hostages told dirty jokes and razzed each other, completely disorganized except for their one concession to ritual. That was when, right before they took the field, they would stand in a circle and hook arms and repeat, in unison, "May our passes be linked as our arms are now." Many of the Hostages worked together as stock boys at the Ski Market Warehouse in downtown Boston, and lived together in warrenlike apartments, and they seemed to have an almost telepathic communication. Despite the fact that the Hostages didn't stretch or prepare, their passes often *were* linked. The Hostages were led by David Barkan, a manic whirlwind of a man who popped around the field on pogo stick legs and who, at only 5'6", provided every possible contrast to the more staid leadership of Moons. Barkan would sprint wildly across the field, eyes full of fire, always ready to huck his backhand long or pump his fist or argue a call. He was also a great thrower, and in this he was not alone. The Hostages' Tommy Conlon, who played the game with the shambling nonchalance of a scarecrow, could, in his own casual inimitable style, do things with a Frisbee that no one before had ever tried. Jimmy Levine, meanwhile, in cleats not work boots but still looking grubby and irritated, was developing into a virtual artiste with the disc, throwing overheads that would tail off backward into the hands of cutting receivers, so that one often wondered if he wasn't growing concerned less with the throw's effectiveness and more with its marks for creative difficulty. The Hostages weren't only great throwers; they were daring ones. They took more risks with their throws, in part because they were a sure-handed team, and the onus was on the receiver to make great catches. The other reason they took more risks was because, against a team as powerful and consistent as the Rude Boys, they simply had no choice.

As might be expected, the Rude Boys and Hostages played entirely different defenses. The Rude Boys relied on their long legs and numbers to wear down teams with an aggressive man-to-man D. While the Hostages might be just as fast, their small numbers made them tire sooner, and if they tried to cover the Rude Boys man to man, they would open themselves to severe height mismatches. Instead they played a zone defense that they tightened like a vise around increasingly nervous throwers. At the center of this network, playing deep in the zone, was Steve Gustafson.

While Barkan was the team's catalyst and Conlon, if the spirit moved him, could take a game over, Gustafson was the Hostages' best player. Just six feet tall, he would, as a deep, be required to cover huge distances and engage in sky battles with the much taller Rude Boys. But he had an uncanny field sense and always seemed to be in the right place. He played the game with a cat's quickness and his throws were absurdly creative and ballsy. Later, at a reunion tournament, one of his teammates would nickname him "Elvis," because he'd gained weight and had the has-been look of the King during his suede-suit Vegas years. But during those early years he was Elvis in his prime, handsome sleek with a cocky curl to his lip, possessing a predatory charisma.

Barkan and Gus were the headliners, but what really made the Hostages special was that they were a tight team where everyone knew their roles and played them well. "We weren't about stars," said Bill McAvoy, a gritty and smart handler who joined the Hostages after playing for a team called Dark Star in Oregon. "We were about flow and movement. That was the fun of it. Playing as a unit and trusting each other." This was embodied by players like Roger Gallagher, not flashy but always dependable, and Jeff Sandler, nicknamed Wheels, who never developed into much of a thrower but caught half of the team's goals, and Neal Lischner, who anchored the zone in the middle and was the team's best defender. On the other end of the spectrum was "Rasta" Bill Newman, known more for his dry wit than his athleticism, and Craig McNaughton, who could throw almost as well as Levine, but focused just as much of his energy on heckling other teams, getting under their skins like no one else.

Nineteen eighty-one was the first year of both the Rude Boys' and Hostages' existence, and Simon and I watched each battle between the two with a connoisseur's delight. It was, we told each other, like having free front-row seats at Celtics-Lakers games. Though our natural instinct to root for the underdog made us favor the Hostages, the Rude Boys were dazzling in their skills, throwing the disc upside down and at sharp angles with great accuracy, and as a whole were better sportsmen than the prickly Hostages. They traded games through the season but at the sectional finals the Rude Boys won handily and, going into Regionals, they seemed so strong and well prepared that they were almost prohibitive favorites. Only one team would emerge from Regionals to go on to Nationals that year, and Simon and I were pretty certain that would be the Rude Boys, a feeling the Rude Boys themselves obviously shared as they had already bought their plane tickets to Austin, Texas, where Nationals would be held. Harvard had been eliminated before Regionals, and so, for the first time that year, we wouldn't get to see the two teams clash. We considered driving out to Amherst to watch the game, but figured, with the Rude Boys peaking, it might be lopsided and not worth it. Later we'd wish we'd made the trip.

Watching the Hostages and Rude Boys play, I imagined being not a mere fan but one of the players, maybe, even, one of the stars. Why not? It seemed no less improbable than my other lofty goals.

"The hunger of youth is for greatness." Over the next decade my own hunger would be a gnawing one and it would manifest itself in two primary ways. Cartooning was fun but it wasn't a big enough container for what had started to pour out. My emerging goals were simple. I wanted to become a great Ultimate player and win Nationals. But in my secret heart I harbored another goal, one that was both intertwined with and greater than the first.

Living in Eliot House, the air was thick with ambition, though I couldn't help but feel that my own ambitions were so much stranger than those of my schoolmates. While I didn't like Eliot, feeling like an interloper there in that preppy epicenter, there was one advantage of living there. Walter Jackson Bate—the great man himself—lived only a few doors down from me and I often saw him eating in the dining hall, not twenty feet away. There he was, taking his breakfast or lunch, wearing mismatched plaids or what looked like pajamas, often eating alone, absorbed in his Salisbury steak and profound thoughts. At least a hundred times I picked up my tray and started across the room to sit with him, but I always chickened out. Though I was taking another of his lecture courses, I'd never encountered him in person outside of class. I could have gone to see him during office hours, but by then he meant—he symbolized—too much to me, and I didn't have the courage to approach him.

That was left to Jon, my bolder and less self-conscious roommate. Jon and I had become good friends and it was in Jon that I confided my growing hope that I might one day become a writer. I also confided how much Bate meant to me. "Why don't you just go over and talk?" Jon asked, logically enough. Finally one day, fed up with my equivocations, Jon, with my halting blessing, marched over to Bate.

Jon introduced himself and soon the two were friends. Three months later, when Bate invited him up to his New Hampshire farmhouse, it was a crushing blow. I hated hearing the stories from that weekend, but of course I asked Jon to tell them again and again until I knew them by heart. I heard about Bate and Jon spending the day pitching horseshoes and walking through the woods, then drinking hot cider and rum that evening in front of the fire with Bate reading out loud the poetry of his "old friend Archie MacLeish."

I was devastated.

But if Jon knew the actual man, I still believed that I alone understood his ideas: "The boldness desired involves directly facing up to what we admire and then trying to be like it," I read. "It is like the habit of Keats of beginning each new effort by rereading Lear and keeping close at hand the engraving of Shakespeare." And so I tacked pictures of Keats and Johnson, and yes, of Bate, too, above my desk. In his biographies—his stories, as I saw them—great writers always struggled and eventually persevered.

Near the end of that year I finally got up the nerve to visit Walter Jackson Bate during office hours. There he was in person, white hair disheveled, sitting behind a large desk and slamming his empty pipe on a glass ashtray. I stared into his watery blue eyes and wondered what to say. I knew I needed to make an impression, to become his friend the way Jon had. We had just begun to talk when he managed to shatter the ashtray with a particularly sharp whack from his pipe. He called in his secretary and the three of us got down on our knees, sweeping up ash and gathering broken shards.

When we resumed talking I tried to explain how much his courses and books had meant to me. I admitted that I wasn't a very good student overall but that I'd spent the better part of the last four years prowling Widener Library and reading, as Samuel Johnson had put it, "by inclination."

He studied me closely, brushing ash off his pants.

"It sounds like you've given yourself quite a self-education," he said.

That was as close as I would come to a blessing that day. We had a nice chat, but there were no invitations up to the old New Hampshire farmhouse, no special advice conferred. I left his office happy to have finally spoken to him but disappointed that I hadn't performed better or garnered more pearls of wisdom. "There are a series of answers available in man's long and groping quest," he had said in class, "answers that can shed some light on our problems now, can teach us what might work, and what not to do." That was what I really wanted, some of those answers.

It didn't matter, though, not really. Unbeknownst to him, Bate had already given me his blessing. It had been during a survey class called From Classic to Romantic in the spring of my sophomore year. In a lecture during that course I heard him speak about the possibility of a "new romanticism," a return to the essential tenets of romanticism that might rise out of the compost heap of postmodernism. He described how the romantic movement itself grew out of neoclassicism, in part born of a rebellion against neoclassicism's "worst excesses": the eighteenth century's increasingly rigid emphasis on unity of form, order, decorum—that is, "the rules." Then he suggested the parallels to our current situation, comparing the worst excesses of postmodernism and deconstruction to those of neoclassicism: a dry emphasis on reason, on mind; a focus on games, a literature that had moved away from essentialism, from a direct connection to life. "What is literature if it isn't relevant to how we live?" he asked the class. Though a scholar and not a prophet, Bate speculated that the next logical movement in the arts would be toward a kind of "new romanticism."

It was just a theory, of course, maybe even an offhand remark, but in my fervid young brain it quickly became much more than that. In my mind's eye I saw Walter Jackson Bate floating above the stage, clad in a tunic, reaching over with a blazing sword that he placed on my shoulders. In my head his new romanticism became *The New Romanticism*. Was there any doubt who the first great New Romantic writer would be?

I f you've ever played balls out, do it now!"
   That is what Gus, his arms linked to his Hostage brothers, told his team before the fateful Regional finals against the Rude Boys.

The Hostages had lost to the Rude Boys the week before and due to the odd math of the tournament they came into Regionals ranked fifth despite being the winningest team in the region that fall, a fact that infuriated the team in general and David Barkan in particular. They wore that low ranking like a chip on their collective shoulder, feeling disrespected, hating everyone but their bros. *Us against them.* Barkan spray-painted the words *No Mercy* on his shirt and that was how they played, destroying other teams in the run-up to the finals.

When it comes to the game against the Rude Boys, different players remember it in different ways. Mark Honerkamp of the Hostages saw it as a bit of a fluke. The year 1981 was the last one that games were timed instead of played to points, and in timed games funny things could happen. The Rude Boys came out a little tight, made some turnovers in the wind, and suddenly found themselves down a few points. The truth was it hadn't even been that windy, just enough maybe to stop the Rude Boys from throwing long or over the top on every play. Or maybe it wasn't the wind at all but their minds that slowed them down. Remember they had already bought their plane tickets to Nationals in Texas—they felt they were *destined* to win. So they became cautious, swinging the disc back and forth instead of trying anything more daring. With each swing of the disc there was a chance it would be dropped and turned over to the Hostages.

Another factor might have been that the Hostages felt they had even less to lose than usual. In the game before, the semifinals, they had lost one of their best and tallest players, Matt Williamson, to injury, and in at least one Hostage's mind, Mark Honerkamp's, they didn't really stand a chance. So they played loose to the Rude Boys' tight, still not quite believing they were going to win. That belief didn't settle in until near the end of the game when the Rude Boys, down by 2, called time-out. The Hostages gathered together in a circle and linked their arms the way they always did, then all of a sudden here came the injured Matty Williamson (everyone seemed to have a y on the end of their name with the Hostages: Jimmy, Billy, Jeffy) hobbling out to the huddle with a big smile on his face.

"Guys, there's only a minute left," he told them.

They couldn't believe it. But when they went back out the Rude Boys turned the disc over again and all that was left was for the Hostages to run out the clock. Mark Honerkamp, the fatalist who was sure they would lose, ended up with the disc as time expired and he threw it as high as he could in the air.

David Barkan remembers it differently: "For the first time all year I was sure we would beat them. We were still angry about being seeded fifth and our energy was up. *I just didn't think we could lose.* No one was going to fuck with me and I was going to do everything I could to make us win. They scored first, shredding our defense, but then we scored and they choked it away to our zone. Then we scored and they choked it away again."

Barkan would play for many years and would later be elected into the fledgling Ultimate Hall of Fame (yes, it really exists), but as good as he was over the long haul, his game never came close to reaching the white heat of those early supernova years in Boston. Barkan had the great gift of energy. Of sprinting across the field in one direction, making a little hop—a kind of bunny hop—and then suddenly sprinting in the other direction, wide open. When he played he was transparently emotional, yelling and pumping his fist in joy when something good happened and throwing his head back and howling when it went bad.

Later, Kenny Dobyns would perfect the role of the sport's undersized bad boy, but back then Barkan was a kind of early-model Dobyns. He had a McEnroe component, too, and sometimes Hostages looked the other way when he made a particularly questionable call. Steve Gustafson, trying to cool him off, would call time-out and say, "Let's value the disc," and then Barkan would go out and immediately huck a wild throw long and walk back to the sidelines, head down, sayings, "I know, I know." But if he was volatile, he was also one of my favorite players to watch, always engaging, always exciting, zipping around the field and popping into the air. And his throws, the smooth backhand and chopping forehand, were impeccable.

The first half almost ended with a long throw that Barkan dove for, touched yet couldn't quite pull in. But the Hostages got the disc back and once again Barkan ran deep and this time Gus uncurled a long backhand. Running at full sprint Barkan launched himself after the disc. He was four feet in the air and any spectator who'd showed up at that minute and saw him would have thought he was flying. This time he was able to get his hands on the disc and he somehow pulled it in and landed hard, in-bounds, a foot shy of the back of the end zone. Still lying face down he started screaming, and kept screaming after he got up. The other Hostages carried Barkan off the field. It was now halftime and they were up 6–2.

After they grabbed some water they gathered as a team, not on the sidelines as usual but right in the middle of the field. The message was clear: This is *our* field. Our turf. We own it.

And they did.

"We started to feel a collective flow," Barkan remembered. "You don't get to feel it that often but when you do, it's awesome. When everyone's on the same wavelength. It feels like you can't possibly be vanquished."

As great a game as Barkan had played, Gus was every bit as good. He had always had terrific court awareness, a sense, as Bill Bradley put it in John McPhee's book, of where he was. He was one of those blessed few who could say, without exaggeration, that the game slowed down for him. Though their players were taller, the Rudies were reluctant to huck deep against Gus, and for good reason. His timing was great and he was cunning: sometimes if he didn't think he could get the disc high in the air, he went up early as if he could, luring the player he was defending into a mistimed jump. He would also pretend to be farther away from a defender or not looking and so bait throwers into making throws and then pouncing.

"I remember one play from that game when a Rude Boy had beaten Gus deep," Ken Dobyns said later, "but he got there and just managed to tip the trailing edge of the disc and push it out of reach."

Gus and Barkan did things on the Ultimate field that no one had done before, like throwing to space. If Barkan was covered so Gus couldn't get it to him, he would instead throw it to an area where it would hover and Barkan could run it down. In what became known as "the Hostage Cut," a player would cut in toward the thrower and then suddenly cut away as the thrower perfectly looped a leading pass. The Rude Boys would eventually counter this by allowing their downfield defenders to poach; "checking in at the home office," they called it. But that came later. On this day in 1981 the Hostages were unstoppable.

David Barkan throwing to Steve "Gus" Gustafson
at the 1981 Regional finals against the Rude Boys

That game proved one of the most influential games in my Frisbee life, though I didn't see a minute of it. Simon and I had stayed home and missed the finals, figuring a Rude Boys victory was a foregone conclusion. When the reports came back, we could barely believe it. The Hostages had somehow pulled it off! I had always bought into the romance of the underdog, and here it was. The game's most talked about moment, the one that made it back to us, was when David Barkan, at 5'6" more than a full foot shorter than Moons, had supposedly sprung into the air and blocked a pass, skying over the taller man. It was a dramatic victory that we, back in Cambridge, hooted over, listening to friends who had seen the game and then recreating it with our own words. Later, we pored over the UPA newsletter with its pictures of Gus and its descriptions of Barkan (spelled alternately "Barkham" and "Barkum") as "a fire hydrant who couldn't stop running" and who "couldn't be stopped no matter who the Rude Boys put on him."

I wasn't the only one who would be influenced by that game.

It was a game Kenny Dobyns wouldn't forget either. As he put it later in his career, "When I saw the Hostages at Regionals in 1981 I said, 'That's the team I want to be like.' The Rude Boys were more athletic but I never looked at the Rude Boys and said that."

If losing to the Hostages did not sit well with the Rude Boys, it was particularly irksome to Steve Mooney. How the hell had *that* happened? Losing to the shorter, undermanned Hostages didn't make sense, it didn't have any logic in the Ultimate universe, and furthermore it just wasn't *right*. It offended Steve's sense of how things should work. In the Rude Boys, Moons had attempted to create a kind of East Coast version of the Santa Barbara Condors, a shining city, an Athens on the Atlantic. Boston, as Moons saw it, was the Mecca, and all of these great players had traveled there, postponing their lives, to play together. The ideal of the Rude Boys was to both win and to play with spirit, and in one part of his brain Moons held firm to those noble ideals, the idea of arête. Moons clearly wanted to be both good and great. The idea was to win but also to win in a classy way. The problem was that when that winning was threatened, as it had been by the Hostages and soon would be by Kenny Dobyns's New York teams, another part of his brain became engaged. Then the moral landscape became murkier, shiftier. Then he was suddenly back in his childhood, that middle sibling who knew just one way to prove himself. Because, you see, Steve Mooney *really* wanted to win. Not just as much as you and me but more. He had to win. And to some degree, given his team's personnel and their preparation, he felt he *should* win.

Which made it particularly frustrating to lose to the Hostages, a team that acted and sometimes even played like they didn't give a shit. A team that spent the weeks after beating the Rude Boys not thinking about winning Nationals but drinking and blowing off practice and wondering how the fuck they were going to get to Austin, Texas. A team whose leader, Gus, drooled on the National Championship trophy after failing to make the finals in Austin (the place Moons had plane tickets to, remember). A team that clearly thumbed its nose at the idea of Spirit of the Game and sometimes argued long and loud. And a team that, at root, didn't seem to take the sport seriously. How could the Rude Boys possibly lose to these drooling idiots?

Myths would grow up around the Hostages' defeat of the Rude Boys at Regionals, and over what happened during the next year in Boston. The two teams took away different narratives from the game. The Hostages came to believe, at some level, that the Rude Boys could train all they wanted. What mattered more than some boring work ethic was a kind of magic ability to raise one's play in the clutch. And clearly the Hostages had magic on their side. It was true that this belief led to a subpar performance at Nationals, where injury reduced them to eleven players and where they ended up going 2–2 and not making the finals. But the next spring, still barely training but filled with the bravado and confidence of their big win the fall before, they managed to win every major tournament, including April Fools in Washington, D.C., and Easterns, while losing only *one* game the entire season. Clearly the team had a bag of magic dust that they could sprinkle on themselves whenever they needed it.

The Rude Boys, on the other hand, responded to their failure by training even harder. They trained as a team and individually and were soon inspired by a new teammate, Finlay Waugh, who arrived from Stanford and began to engage in a kind of private hell called interval training. He would take to the track and put

AC/DC on his Walkman and run 400s as fast as he could, with only short breaks in between. Waugh had founded the team at Stanford and played against Keay Nakae and he had it in his mind that he would not be outworked by anyone, Keay included. On the West Coast he had been a very good player, but he was no longer interested in being "very good." He wanted instead to be great and he thought he knew how to attain this. It wouldn't be through his throws, which never rose above the level of proficient, but through the three things he had going for him: he was tall, he could run like hell, and he had desire. His signature move would be diving on D and then not just blocking the disc but catching it—a play the Rude Boys dubbed the "Craw"—which would send a jolt of energy through his team while thoroughly demoralizing the astonished victims. When he moved from the Bay Area to Boston he was ready to shed his "very good" self, and while his movement was West to East, not the other way around, he set about reinventing himself in quintessentially American fashion. This refashioning happened at the track and it happened mostly alone. Of course since he played for the Rude Boys he was already training more than 99 percent of the Ultimate world. The early-morning MIT practices and Rude Boy scrimmages gave him a good base but it was not enough. Those were the *team* practices. Which meant you would only be doing what everyone else on the team was doing and, therefore, logically, you wouldn't be putting any separation between yourself and the rest.

Which was what led Finlay to devise his own workouts. Decades later track workouts would be common in Ultimate, and teams would come to understand that theirs was a unique sport with regard to running, close to soccer perhaps, but with a lot more sprinting. Finlay's times in those 400s were extraordinary; on one day when he let it all out he ran one in forty-eight seconds, only a couple seconds above the then NCAA record, though he naturally ran his sets at a slower speed. As he ran he imagined shutting down players like Pat King, and uttered his name again and again like an incantation. "Pat King, Pat King, Pat King . . ." He attacked the workouts with a fury, readying himself for Regionals.

In contrast the Hostages still barely trained. They sometimes ran something called Indian sprints, where the team would jog around the field in a line, one player after another, and then the last person in line would have to sprint to the front, at which point, as soon as he got there, the person who was now last would take off for the front. This is not to say they were fat or out of shape. They were all in their early twenties and some individuals like Barkan and Neal Lischner were obviously in top shape, but most of them stayed in shape by playing and training to play, not by *working* out.

It might be oversimplifying but if you wanted to, you could see the split between these two cultures as one between the '70s that were being left behind and the '80s that were emerging. The classic '70s athlete was a Kenny Stabler who stayed out partying late the night before a game and then rose to the occasion, or a Pete Maravich wearing schlumpy socks, or a Dr. J—the ABA Dr. J, mind you—with a huge Hendrix 'fro, or a Bill Lee throwing Moonballs or Luis Tiant chomping cigars or even a baseball-hat-wearing Dave Wottle coming out of nowhere to win the Olympics 800. It was a wilder, less-polished athlete with less of a focus on control. Because what is training about if not control? The benefits of training are very real, of course. "Fatigue makes cowards of us all," as Lombardi said. And training also gives the players something to do as they wait for big events, sometimes for months or, in the case of the Olympics, years. Nationals came only once a year and it made sense to train all year for it. But winning Nationals, or even just getting there didn't only hinge on ability, talent, or desire. It also hinged on performance in the moment.

What the Hostages excelled at, at least during their first year or so, was exactly that: performance in the moment. Call it being clutch, call it magic dust—whatever it was, it wasn't just about training or fitness or muscles. Churchill called it "the field of chance." If one is to excel in the moment, there needs to be a sense of play, a sense of uncertainty. A sense of humor doesn't hurt either.

Steve Mooney was a steely competitor, a great leader, and he would become one of the greatest Ultimate players of all time. But he would also turn out to be a wee bit of a control freak. This, too, in its way was a positive in the athletic world. Keay Nakae believed that the Condors would have benefited from more of a take-charge leader, and Tom Kennedy for all his talents was not that. Over the next two decades Moons would gradually take complete charge of Boston Ultimate. That included running practices and being the coach, trainer, road manager, and captain all rolled into one. In a game without coaches you needed someone who took control.

But you can only control so much. Over the next year, during which the Hostages beat the Rude Boys fairly often, they played a zone defense that took away the Rude Boys' greatest strength, their long legs, and forced them to stand still and make precise throws over and around the zone. It became more of a static game, more of a mind game. And the necessary precision became more of a challenge when the wind was up. Had the Hostages been a more superstitious tribe, they might have gathered early on the Sunday of each tournament and prayed to the wind gods. Playing in the windy Northeast in the fall and early spring, wind was a huge component, and generally speaking, the Hostages played their best when the weather was worst. A calm, sunny day was nothing to celebrate. Their success against a bigger, more fit team required aid from that invisible element, and the randomness somehow perfectly matched the Hostage spirit. Steve Mooney could do a lot to beat the Hostages; he could control a lot. He could make the team practice regularly; he could prod them to work out; he could urge them to be spirited but competitive. But even Steve Mooney couldn't control the wind.

Looking on, I never knew quite who to root for. I found myself caught between competing mythos. "Blow it off" had been my early college motto and I loved the idea of taking it easy and partying until the big moment and then sprinkling on the magic dust and finding something inside that allowed me to become more than myself. It fit nicely with my academic philosophy at Harvard of doing little work and then trying to ace the essay exams. But more and more another part of me, a Rude Boy part, was rising up. My father might not have believed it, but by nature I was a goal setter, a worker. The idea of training began to catch hold of my imagination. I, like Keay Nakae and Finlay Waugh, wanted to be able to wear a shirt with the words WORLD CHAMPS written on it. To control that outcome I was beginning to suspect that I would need to outwork those who shared a similar dream. To control that outcome I would need to start to train.

I f I could go back in time, I would counsel myself to try and combine the effort and preparation of the Rude Boys with the edginess and sense of the moment of the Hostages. To work my ass off before tournaments but to always bring along my magic dust to the big games. Of course I can't go back in time and while there would soon be a player who brilliantly combined these two philosophies, it would not be me.

At that moment Kenny Dobyns was still a mere spectator at

the biggest games and that could not have sat well with him. He had never even made it to Nationals. He must have watched the Boston duels between the Hostages and Rude Boys like a boy locked out of the house, staring in through a window.

I once heard a story about something that Kenny's mother said to him. Mrs. Dobyns, as she was known to the whole Frisbee world, would always come to her sons' tournaments, and would bring along a fold-out table on which she spread cold cuts and bread and desserts for her New York boys, providing a homey contrast to the usual intense warlike New York vibe. Mrs. Dobyns herself, in my memory, was always sweet, even to Bostonians, white haired and wearing granny glasses and looking like someone you could picture on a bag of Pepperidge Farm cookies. But apparently it wasn't just his famous father, Lloyd Dobyns, a driven NBC reporter, who Kenny got his competitiveness from. On the ride home from a tournament in which New York had been beaten by Moons and the Rude Boys, Kenny said something like, "We're getting close. Just a couple of points here and there."

"No you're not," Mrs. Dobyns replied. "That's not it."

Kenny asked what she meant.

"You're simply not good enough," she said. "They're better than you."

After he thought about it a while, Kenny knew in his heart that his mother was right. If you were going to get there, it required guts, and it required a strong will to win, but it also required a certain amount of talent. So he took action. He recruited new players and dreamed of a new, better team. Meanwhile, he worked out harder than ever, running through the New York streets, doing intervals at the track, and beginning to lift weights. He pushed and pushed and pushed.

Later, during an interview in *Quest to Be Best,* a 1985 film narrated by George Plimpton, Kenny would say, "What drives me is an insane hatred of losing. Especially to Boston."

He really did hate losing, and in his case this was not just a sports cliché. To onlookers, *hate* clearly seemed part of the fuel that drove him so wildly around the field. It certainly wasn't some lofty notion of arête. New York at the time was the perpetual little brother, never quite able to beat its older siblings. There was a kind of rage to the way Ken worked out, lifting weights and sprinting by himself after practice had ended. I will go as far as to say that there was a hole inside of him, something unfillable that he needed to fill. Strangely he had decided to fill that hole by excelling at a sport played with a Frisbee, a sport few outside of it took seriously.

Fair play was an occasional casualty of his savage drive. When I first competed against him he still wore the ponytail down to his ass, but if I thought I'd come across another Ultimate hippie, I was disabused of that notion fairly quickly. On game point, with Harvard about to score, Dobyns made a traveling call on a Harvard player named Peter Sanborn. Sanborn then took the disc back and threw the game winner but Dobyns again called it back. When Dobyns made the same call again, a third time, the usually calm Sanborn, a thoughtful and quiet Midwesterner who majored in social studies at Harvard, went ballistic, screaming and yelling at the shorter man. But more to the point he proceeded to throw the disc away on his fourth attempt (after the third call) and Dobyns and his team marched the disc down to the other end of the field and scored.

"I think it's fair to say I was developing an extreme personality," Dobyns would later admit. "I can say that in the moment of competition I could be a complete asshole. I was insanely competitive. I had a total commitment to greatness and winning. And when I saw people who didn't have that it infuriated me. When people dropped the disc I would berate them. I wasn't a good teammate back then."

It would turn out that prep schools and colleges were not the only thing that Kenny was good at getting kicked out of. The Heifers were the best team in New York and by the time he was nineteen Kenny was clearly one of their best players. Despite this, his incendiary manner and sheer aggressiveness, even toward teammates, made him hard to play with, and the team held a meeting, deciding to cut him. Some of the players simply couldn't stand Kenny. Others were frankly scared of him.

"When they cut me they were right," he reflected later. "I was an embarrassment. I was hard to be around."

It must not have always been a pleasant thing to be inside Kenny's skin. If there was such a thing as Ultimate ambition, then here was that ambition fully distilled. He had no interest in joining the ranks of TK's philosopher-kings, no interest in creating an Athens. In fact, later on, when his New York teams were at their full power, they would gather in a huddle and loudly quote several lines first spoken by Arnold Schwarzenegger in the movie *Conan the Barbarian*: "What is best in life? To crush your enemies. To see them driven before you. To hear the lamentations of their women."

Yes, their tongues were in cheek, but not entirely.

Dobyns would become one of the game's great performers, a man who rode moments like an expert surfer. And he would combine this with an almost absurd sense of commitment to the sport.

"I don't know if you can achieve total success at anything without devoting yourself to it totally," he would say.

Over the next dozen years he would rarely waver from total devotion.

4.

Commencement

If you have only casually tossed a Frisbee in your life, you have likely thrown only backhands. It's the natural way to throw discs, to curl and uncurl, not so dissimilar from a tennis backhand really. This is the throw most of us use naturally, the one you see at picnics and the beach.

The forehand, again like its tennis counterpoint, originates on the opposite side from the backhand. But it isn't a swing, as in tennis, or really a throw at all. Rather it is an intense downward flick, a cranking of elbow and wrist that sends the disc spinning downfield. By the time I began playing, having a good forehand was de rigueur, and I spent my first year both embarrassed not to have one and determined to learn to throw a good one. Unaware of the sport's history, I would have been astounded to learn that only seven years before almost no one threw a forehand. Practically all of those early New Jersey games had been played using backhands and a geeky-looking thing called the overhand wrist flip, a throw that was regarded mainly with squirming embarrassment by the time I started playing but that was commonly used as late as the mid-'70s. In other words in the early days almost no one used the throw that would soon become the sport's most important, and often—overheads and blades aside—most dramatic.

The founding father of the forehand, the George Washington and Louis Pasteur combined, was a brash Brooklynite named Victor Malafronte. Back when all the Frisbee world was uncurling backhands he came barging in with the throw he called "the two-fingered macho sidewinder," which was essentially a modern forehand that he could snap off to the tune of 100 yards or so. Malafronte would use it to win the overall men's title at the first World Frisbee Championships Rose Bowl in Pasadena, California, in August of 1974, the same event that Tom Kennedy drove from Santa Barbara to watch. He would also use it while barnstorming with the Harlem Globetrotters and performing their halftime show.

Before Malafronte no one saw much promise in this strange nonthrow. In the early '70s the International Frisbee Association put out a newsletter, edited by Dan "Stork" Roderick, that included a series of tests where you could, by passing each one, advance from Frisbee beginner to expert. This appealed to the Boy Scout in Irv "Dr. I" Kalb, and he went about passing those tests as earnestly as he had once set about getting his Webelos badge. Most of the hurdles were fairly easy, especially for the man whom almost everyone considered the game's most accomplished player at that time, but "the sidearm" stumped him for a while. The sidearm, which was the modern forehand, didn't really fly very well, at least the way he threw it, and while he earned his badge, neither he nor any of his buddies imagined it would be very effective in Ultimate.

That changed during Kalb's trip to Michigan and the International Frisbee Tournament in 1972. It was a twenty-four-hour drive to the Upper Peninsula and a twenty-four-hour drive back, but what pushed Irv and a group of his Columbia High School and New Jersey league alums to make the trip was the usual missionary zeal, the desire to spread the seeds of the sport they loved. *We are the apostles of Ultimate and we want you to try it!* In those days Guts, not Ultimate, was the top Frisbee sport. Irv watched it for a while and simply couldn't understand the appeal of a game that involved standing on a line and throwing the disc as hard as you could at each other with the intention of it *not* being caught. It was as if the promise of Frisbee flight was being intentionally squandered.

"Here we have this beautiful flying object and they are doing exactly the wrong thing with it," Kalb said.

The intention was to put on a demonstration of Ultimate that would reveal to the Guts players the one true sport. The apostles had come to convert the unholy, and thanks to their demonstration they did their share of that, but then, during the distance competition, came a twist: the converters became the converted. The scales fell from their eyes as they witnessed Malafronte throwing a disc the length of a football field *with a forehand.*

He didn't throw it so much as *crank* it, whipping his arm down and letting it rip. And the disc jetted off with rocket speed, traveling even farther than their best backhands. That moment signaled the death knell of the overhead wrist flip and the thumber. Right away the boys from Jersey started to practice the new throw, though it would take a while to infiltrate the sport. At that point its rise was inevitable, though. All you had to do was watch Malafronte to see that this was the future. He *cranked* it! Soon Jim Pistrang of Tufts, who had been on the trip, was using the forehand in games, and then Irv himself, and then great early players

like Jon Cohn were abandoning their thumbers or wrist flicks, and
then it spread like wildfire.

My own forehand had begun life modestly, as a kind of soft
noodle-armed thing. For my first year I rarely used it at all,
mostly acting as a receiver and then throwing short backhands to
more skilled players. But it became clear pretty early on that if I
was going to be great, I would need a great forehand. So I spent
the summer after my junior year completely retooling the throw,
breaking it down and building it up again. I began to consciously
imitate the chopping downward motion of David Barkan's forehand, which was Malafronte-like in its emphasis on the downward crank. My reading of Walter Jackson Bate had always
stressed that we can't become great without models, and I had
one in Barkan. Over the summer I engrained this new motion by
forcing my younger brother, Scott, to play catch with me for
hours. I threw thousands and thousands of forehands.

I returned to school early for my senior year so that I could live
at Simon Long's family home in Brookline for a week while com-
muting over to MIT for the 6:00 a.m. track workouts run by Steve
Mooney of the Rude Boys. It was a little like going to football
camp, but for me football, by the end of high school, had been
obligatory, dull, and exhausting. This was different: a sport I really
cared about and wanted to be great at. Even better, I was training
with and playing against my heroes from the club teams, the gods
of the sport, which filled me with adrenaline.

Many of the players on the Rude Boys had jobs, so the MIT
practices started before work. I am a habitual early riser now, but
back then six was an ungodly time. It felt like real discipline to get
up that early to train. Like everyone else in the world, I had seen

Rocky five years earlier and I attributed virtue to early rising, though I skipped the raw eggs. It felt like we were doing something important and consequential, though it was still only Frisbee.

My memories of that week in Simon's house are imprecise, impressionistic. I know we ate at least two breakfasts, one before practice, one after. I know we were ravenous and always thirsty. The foods I remember devouring were bagels, lots of bagels, with cream cheese and capers and caviar, the last something we stole from Simon's parents' secret stash. Orange juice, not Gatorade, was our sports drink of preference, and we drank prodigious amounts of it, so much so that Simon's mother commented, wondering where the gallons had gone. We even had a punish name for the liquid, calling it "O. J. Anderson" after the then St. Louis Cardinals running back.

The MIT workouts were eye-opening. We began with a big lap around the field, with Moons out front, and then went into a series of throwing and catching drills, followed by Monsters. Monsters were essentially basketball suicides, except on a football field, a sprint to the 20-yard line, back to the goal, to the 50-yard line, back to the goal, to the 70-yard line, back to the goal, full field, back to the goal. I don't remember puking but I remember coming close, and it was now becoming clear to me how inadequate my own training—which consisted mostly of playing Ultimate, jogging, doing sit-ups and push-ups—had been to that point. We also did something called Dive Factor, which Moons had adapted from a drill the goalies did on his soccer team back at Wesleyan, which consisted of one player throwing the other a bad but catchable pass and the other player diving for the disc in one direction and then, as soon as he got up, being thrown another pass to dive for in the opposite direction, leaving everyone with bloody knees and raspberries.

Laying out may be what truly separates Ultimate from other sports, and almost every Ultimate player capable of rudimentary thought has pondered its meaning. Rude Boy Phil Adams, known to all the Ultimate world as "Guido," once wrote this:

> Running as hard as you can, laying out fully and snaring the disc. Never available in basketball and hockey, rarely in football, seldom in baseball, but abundant in Ultimate. And of course the defensive corollary, the diving block. . . .
>
> Ultimate's diving catch is where physics meets metaphysics, in a sort of deterministic morality play. With a baseball or a football, there's a ballistics-underpinned arc with the ball ending up at a certain spot based on the laws of gravity. Making on the fly projectile calculations, you pretty much know if you're going to get there or you're not.
>
> But with the disc, not so much. Time and time again, I've seen discs hover at the last second, rewarding a run that seemed quixotic based on the laws of physics, but perhaps not based on the laws of karma. You try, the disc waits to reward the effort with a chance for a catch. You give up, and it falls to the ground on its prescribed arc.

Diving was about risk and full commitment, and it was about something that your body, wary of being broken, might not do naturally. The idea of the Dive Factor drill was to habituate us to leaving our feet, making it automatic, instinctive.

Once all the diving was done, we, exhausted and bloody, the morning's sweat having left a layer of drying salt on our skin, would begin the intellectual segment of the practice. We sat on the sidelines and had deep philosophical discussions on such issues as how to beat the zone, with Moons in the role of Socrates. To Simon and me this might have been merely theoretical, but to the Rude Boys it was urgently practical. They needed to be able to beat the zone, and there was little question whose zone they were trying to beat. *Everything* depended on it.

When we finally got around to scrimmaging I focused mostly on defense. I was out of my league to some extent, and the way I compensated for this was playing furious D, the usual chip firmly planted on my shoulder. I always tried to cover Nick Donahue, a fiery redhead who was one of the Rude Boys' best players, and who was known for a strong forehand that he liked to zip into tight places, as well as for diving around the field. One thing that always helped me play defense was to develop a dislike for whomever I was covering, and with Nick I focused on the fact that to me some of his dives seemed unnecessary. "Hollywood" was how I described him to Simon. It often seemed that he could have made the catch or the block without diving, or at least without diving in such a flamboyant way. I'm not sure if this was true or not, but I know it helped me build up the necessary hate, which in turn helped me run faster. I also created a narrative in my head: in this story Nick didn't know who I was, which could well have been true, and I told myself that if he did know who I was, he certainly didn't respect me, treating me as insignificant. This was fiction but it worked. I needed anything that could help me run faster. Anything that I could use as fuel.

Our workouts helped Simon and me that fall, and our team was stronger. We added some players who did not play for Harvard, like the Miller brothers and Bobby "Speedo" Carvalho, and we had Charlie Bliss, a strong runner and great defender who went to Harvard Law School, and a few others, including a great pure thrower named Emmett Thomas. We named ourselves the Hecklers. The name derived from the heckling of other players that we did, usually during the semifinals and finals of tournaments, by which point we, invariably, had been knocked out. We gave both the Hostages and Rude Boys good games, but of course could never beat them. In one game against the Rude Boys I remember going deep on Moons and having the disconcerting experience of him running me down. Then, as I tried to go up for the disc, I looked up to see his 6'7" frame blocking out the sun.

At some point that fall I broke my wrist in practice after going up high, colliding with a teammate, then trying to break my fall with my left hand. I kept playing for the rest of the season with a cast on my wrist. Injuries and even the occasional concussion were part of my regular life. The year before, for instance, I had skyed over a player from another team, after which we both began writhing on the ground. It would turn out that I had lost part of my tooth and that that part had lodged itself in the top of the other player's skull.

But we, the Hecklers, were just a small side story during that fall of 1982. The Rude Boys were the headliners, and it was during that season that all of their training would pay off. They romped through the fall, beating everyone in their path. They shut down the Hostages with tough man-to-man D. Finlay Waugh, reveling in the effects of his interval training, decided one weekend to shut down Neal Lischner, one of the Hostages' best players, and was then dubbed the "Neal-stopper" by his teammates. The Rudies even managed to control the speedy David Barkan. A year before he had seemed impossible to cover with his zigzag cuts but now the Rude Boys found a man for the job. The man was Alan Cave, a quiet, tall, nonflamboyant, athletic runner who, miraculously, seemed to keep up with Barkan stride for stride no matter how he zigged, zagged, faked, hopped, or spun. Simon and I, watching from the sidelines, could barely believe it, and this, too, soon became part of the lore. Alan Cave became the Man Who Could Guard Barkan.

The balance of power in Boston seemed to have clearly shifted, but then, at sectionals, the Hostages did it again. Just like that they sprinkled on the magic dust and beat the Rude Boys soundly. Despite some cross-team friendships, bad blood was common between the two teams in those years and in the course of the sectionals game the Hostages made a couple of calls that the Rude Boys objected to. These calls, as usual, centered around David Barkan. Barkan was still and always the lightning rod. The very things that made him great—his fire and passion and intensity—made it hard for him to see events calmly and objectively in the heat of battle. He might call himself in-bounds when he was out or call a travel on the other team when no one else had seen the travel. And he wasn't the sort to back down or change his call.

If the players on the two teams were enemies, some of them were also friends. The Stooges and the Rudies, as they were known locally, would eventually have many parties together and more than one girlfriend in common. They all lived in the same city, after all. Bill McAvoy of the Hostages and Peter Farricker of the Rude Boys were roommates and close friends (and would remain so until Farricker's tragic early death from ALS), and other friendships developed, too.

And yet . . . they were *different*. It might be going too far to call it a culture clash since they were all white kids who had spent at least some time in college, but the teams just *felt* different. There was something misanthropic and edgy about the Hostages. It was true that the Rude Boys also prided themselves on their nonconformity, singing Clash songs and wearing their ska-style shirts, but they looked good in those shirts, good and successful, and would later appear in slick magazines and get more media attention than any team before them. The Hostages were the opposite of slick. Once, when Moons was being interviewed for TV, Gus stood immediately behind him, chanting, "You're a whore, Moons, you're a whore. . . ."

Moons was the focus of most of the Hostages' ire.

"There was sometimes a dissonance between what he said and what he did," Barkan recalled.

Because of the ugliness in the earlier sectionals game, Moons and Barkan met in Boston the week before the climactic Regional finals, like two chieftains determining the rules of battle. Though the Rude Boys had been beaten badly in the game in question, they were most upset about one traveling call the Hostages had made. As Barkan remembers it, during their meeting Moons suggested that they embrace the Spirit of the Game and not make any traveling calls at Regionals. In Ultimate traveling is called if someone moves their established pivot foot when throwing. Yelling "traveling" as someone is making their throw is a way to negate the completion and send the disc back to the thrower. There would be none of that, they agreed. This game would be as clean as possible. They shook on it.

At Regionals there was no repeat of the Hostage upset. The supply of magic dust had dwindled. At a crucial point in the game, when it looked like the Hostages had scored to go up at the half, a Rude Boys player called traveling and Barkan ran up to Moons and objected, reminding him of their summit meeting. Moons said, "Dave, I'm receptive to what you're saying, but I really can't tell my player what to call." This enraged Barkan and in his mind seemed to perfectly point out the hypocrisy of Moons. He wouldn't be able to trust the taller man for many years afterward.

But the truth is that one call did not determine the outcome.

After the half, the Rude Boys started running away with the game and that one play was just a blip. The Rudies were in their glory now, living out their favorite Clash song, "Rudie Can't Fail," and the long legs of Finlay, Stick Dissoway, Pete Farricker, Alan Cave, and Moons were churning up and down the field. They won going away and there was a sense of liberation and not a little exaltation among the Rude Boys at having finally vanquished, and exorcised, their crosstown rival in a big game.

Luckily for the Hostages, that year the National Championships had been expanded and two teams would go from the region, so that they, placing second, would join the Rude Boys back in Austin, Texas, which again hosted the event. The tourney was supposed to be at the University of Texas but biblical rains made the fields unplayable and so the games were moved to some local fields that most agreed were the worst they had ever played on. The rains continued through the weekend, as the Hostages beat the Berkeley Flying Circus in a four-and-a-half-hour marathon, winning 19–17. Most of the teams at Nationals had sensibly upped their rosters to twenty men or so, but the Hostages stubbornly stuck to their insistence on a small, tight band of brothers, and brought only fourteen players, a number that was then reduced further by injury. Still, they only lost one game in pool play, a 20–18 overtime loss to the Gang, a team of former Knights of Nee and Glassboro players. The night before the semifinals they won their last game with Chicago's Windy City, which was delayed by rain until seven thirty, and didn't end until ten. An hour later they were eating pizza and wondering how they were supposed to play the next morning at eight.

While they staggered into the semifinals, the Rude Boys romped. Undefeated in their pool, understandably feeling on top of the Frisbee world, might some of them have greeted the sight of the Hostages in the semis with a little queasiness? They had traveled two thousand miles only to meet their next-door neighbors. No matter how good they were feeling they must have known that between these two teams it could always go either way. The last thing they wanted was to have an element of chance, of randomness, intruding on their perfect and perfectly choreographed season. All their planning, all their training, and now . . . what? More than one Rude Boy went to sleep the night before wondering how hard the wind would be blowing the next day.

My old teammate Chris Heye, a Rude Boy now, said he felt pretty good about their odds when he saw Gus limping in the parking lot before the game. Gus was really the only Hostage who had a chance in the air against the taller Rudies. But you never really knew with the Hostages. Would they be sprinkling on the goddamn magic dust again?

If there was a sense of queasiness, it could not have been helped when the Hostages scored the first point. Then the next. And the next. David Barkan wondered if another miracle upset was in the offing. *Oh no*, thought Steve Mooney, *this can't be fucking happening. Not again. Not after all our work and dedication.* He wasn't the only one on his team thinking those types of thoughts. Oh shit. They tried to exorcise memories of the previous year's Regionals and that goddamn magic dust.

One player who wasn't worried was Finlay Waugh, who had not been there for the previous year's failure. He could see just how tired the Hostages were and how few of them were healthy, and he was licking his chops, ready to run them into the ground. And as it turned out Finlay, Moons, and the rest of the Rudies quickly steadied the ship. In the notebook he kept of the season Moons would write, "Stooges were tired. We choked up three quick ones but that was all. We rolled to the finals . . . Many agree that winning this one outweighed our loss to the Hostages in '81." The Frisbee universe was no longer out of whack. All was right in the world. The Rudies won 21–14.

In the finals the St. Louis Tunas were their surprise opponents, a distinctly unhippieish and athletic group of tireless runners who would win the National Championships two years later. They were a strong team just coming into their own with two great handlers in Doug Parrish and Tom Heimann, and deep players like Rick Linck and Randy Ricks, who were tall enough to battle the Rudies in the air, but on that day there was no stopping the Rude Boys. Finlay Waugh, having built his base by running all those 400s, was particularly brilliant and felt like he could have run for hours. There is one photo of him in the UPA newsletter's story about the game that I studied when Simon showed it to me in Cambridge two months later. In it you can see that the stadium where the finals are being played is mostly empty, a testament to the fact that Ultimate still wasn't a "real sport." But the picture also tells another, opposite story. Finlay is well off the ground, catching the disc at the peak of his jump, and there is little question that this is a real athlete doing the catching. It was another level of Ultimate being played.

The Rude Boys won the finals 21–12 and now, at long last, they were National Champs. When it was over they carried Steve Mooney, the conquering hero, off the field on their shoulders. They had destroyed the competition, the Hostages being the only team they played that even broke into the teens. Furthermore it was agreed that they had won with good spirit (unlike the nasty Chicago team who the next year would spike and break the trophy). They had fulfilled the arête ideal, had been both good and great, and this was the almost universal appraisal. *Almost* universal. The few remaining

The Rude Boys celebrating

skeptics pointed out that the closest game they had had been against the Hostages, and they had beaten them by seven points. Wasn't it easier to be "spirited" when you were crushing people? Didn't things get a little messier when games were close? These were questions for the future, however. For now it was time for the Rudies to celebrate. They returned to Boston triumphant.

We always simplify when we remember, imagining that in some past time we were feeling *one way*. But I was feeling a hundred ways during that year, my senior year, and half of those were some form of scared. Scared of graduating and scared of my father's "real world" and scared that I was making all the wrong choices. Scared that I didn't have what it took to make it out there. Powerless, too, and no doubt one function of my Ultimate ambitions was to help create a world where I had some power, not to mention a disc-shaped weapon.

It may seem evident that I didn't need to introduce another unstable element into the already murky stew of delusion and ambition that was my young personality. But I did anyway. It was during the spring of my senior year that I began to experiment with psychotropic mushrooms.

The first time I ate them was in the company of Nathan, the man who had knocked my father to the ground with his backhand. We drove down to Washington, D.C., in his van to what was always the year's first Ultimate tournament, April Fools, or Fools' Fest. Parked in the van near the fields, after the Hecklers were eliminated, we listened to Peter Tosh and I nibbled on dry stems as a light rain pattered on the van roof. Nate told me that I should be with someone I trusted during my first trip. Right then, at that moment, I trusted Nate, which turned out to be a good idea. However wild he could sometimes be on the field, he proved a fine and consistent friend and guide during my first excursion into psychedelia. I remember laughing after we climbed out of the van and started throwing a Frisbee, banking it around trees that were waving their leafy arms as if playing defense. I swear that as the disc arced through the sky it was trailed by its own psychedelic tail like fireworks. Gradually, we wandered over to the fields. I remember hearing the noise of the games first, the cheers and yells from the players, and then wandering up to the sideline and feeling so close that it was as if I were in the game.

It was the first time I saw the Flying Circus play. The Berkeley Flying Circus, as they were known then, were a San Francisco–area team that wore face paint and Mardi Gras beads—as if you'd given the Merry Pranksters cleats. But it wasn't the costumes that stirred me. It was the style of play. The word "huck" is Ultimate for throwing deep, and that day I watched the Circus huck the disc almost every time they got hold of it. I didn't know their names back then but I was likely watching Danny Weiss throw his deep backhand to receivers like Ronar, who would sky for it in the end zone. Who it was, what their actual names were, didn't really matter, not to me. What mattered was that it was an aggressive, risky, swashbuckling, and fun way to *play*. It was the way, I knew right then, that *I* wanted to play. The way I dreamed of playing.

What I didn't know at the time was that the Circus had come into the game determined to make up for a poor performance at Nationals the year before and that, playing with a small team of thirteen players that included a couple East Coast ringers, they were having the day of their lives. "It was like Hoosiers," said Paul "Sack" Sackley, who'd picked up with them. "Actually it was crazier than any movie upset." To even get to the finals against the Rude Boys they had had to beat Windy City and the Hostages, and they had done so by becoming bolder and bolder. Often this style is a recipe for disaster but on that day it all went right. "I've never hucked so much during a game before or since," said Danny Weiss.

And I don't think I've ever enjoyed watching a game as much as I did watching the Circus beat the Rude Boys. The drugs were part of it, but only part. It was like watching a team full of Errol Flynns, and in my receptive state, it seemed not just a style of play but a way of being.

I liked tripping, it turned out, and I did it again when I got back to Harvard. The first time was when I wandered down to the Charles River with Will, my good friend and former roommate who played for the Harvard baseball team. When we got to the field by the government school we threw a Frisbee around for a while, and when Will drifted off I kept throwing and catching by myself, hucking backhands up high and into the wind and then catching the disc when it boomeranged back. My main memory of that day is of throwing one of those big backhands and then forgetting about the disc as it flew up into the sky. I started to think about something else, something profound in a mushroomy kind of way, no doubt, and was lost in thought when the disc angled back down out of the sky and hit me dead center in the forehead, knocking me backward.

Will and I crossed the bridge over the river and snuck into the football stadium. There we howled like wolves, listening to our howls echo off the cavernous walls. Not two months later we would back up my AMC Spirit, pop open the hatchback to reveal the keg inside, and play a game of pickup Ultimate, my last at Harvard, not with the Harvard team, but with about twenty friends.

The world of mushrooms was not unlike the worlds of Frisbee and literature. Once you were inside everything took on the power of symbol. The mushroom world was an Emersonian one where every item in your physical world related to a corresponding item in your psychic one. I remember once tripping on the beach on Cape Cod and saying to myself, "I'm going to run to that warm rock," which made no sense, but then after I ran there, at speeds I could never attain while straight (or so it seemed), I was warm from the exertion and sweat, and suddenly "get to the warm rock" became my personal shorthand for focusing on short-term goals. While tripping you could feel the rightness of the universe. It was as if you had returned to an earlier time in history, before God was dead, or at least before gods were, and everything, but particularly the weather and the natural world, held portents.

At the same time, as the individual trips wore on, the symbolic faded and you began to focus on your more purely animal self. You could see that you were just this sweating physical thing. It was like the movement of human thought from the early vision of a cosmological human-centered universe to a more scientific and materialistic view—the thing itself.

After Will and I left the stadium, we prowled the athletic fields. It was a late-winter day and there was no one else around; Will wandered over to the baseball field and just stood there on the pitcher's mound, taking in his home field, considering his turf from a new psychotropic perspective. I did the same on the Frisbee field where we practiced, and both of us spent almost an hour pacing the perimeters of our territories. It struck me as profound that the Frisbee field was my *place* at Harvard. I considered making a small fire to keep warm, or maybe digging a hole where I could camp, or, possibly, live.

I felt safe there, on my turf, but the truth was I was scared. Graduation was only a couple of months away and I still had no idea what I was going to do for a living. I didn't even know for sure if I would keep playing Ultimate. I was frightened that if I did finally start my great novel and put sentences on the page, they would not live up to the perfectionist ideal I had in my head, frightened that I would fail so much in this thing I cared so much about, and frightened that I wouldn't get a job doing the one thing other than Ultimate I could already do well: cartooning.

Over the next two months I made a desperate scramble to land a political cartooning job. I sent out hundreds of letters and portfolios of my work, starring "The Trickle Down Theory," to every newspaper in the country, vowing that I would move wherever I got a job. I also flew out to a political cartooning conference in San Francisco to show my work to other cartoonists and editors. The keynote speaker at the conference was Charles Schulz, and I remember that he stressed the importance of dailiness—that is, of sitting down in your chair and cartooning every day. I wrote that on my drawing pad and vowed to start when I got home. Soon after I returned to Cambridge, however, the form letters started pouring in, rejections from all the newspapers where I had applied.

As it turned out a friend of my family knew the editorial editor of the *Boston Globe* and he agreed to meet with me. The *Globe's* cartoonist, Paul Szep, had once been a hero of mine, but by then I'd outgrown him, or at least his style, preferring the dancing lines of the *Washington Post's* Patrick Oliphant to what I saw as Szep's more ponderous style.

The editor sat behind a large oak desk and was polite and formal, while I, the supplicant, laid out my work for him. He said what a lot of people said about my cartoons: the ideas were strong, the drawings somewhat less so. It was pretty clear after five minutes that there would be no magical offering of a job, nor would there be an internship with Paul Szep.

In fact, the highlight of my meeting with the editor had nothing to do with cartooning. When he stood up to announce the meeting's end, he lifted a stack of papers from his desk. In the shuffling, a single piece of paper dropped from the stack, and in the strange way that paper has of falling it slowly started cartwheeling toward me. I stood up and quickly shot my hand out, catching the paper in midair between my thumb and forefinger. The editor seemed excited by my catch, as if I had accomplished something important.

"That was amazing," he said, shaking his head. "How did you do that?"

It was perfect really. He was more impressed by my hands than by my work.

My senior year in college coincided with the peak of Boston Ultimate. In the years since, Boston men and women have won many titles but never was the city as deep with players. Within the city limits of Boston in the fall of 1982, we had, arguably, the two best men's Ultimate Frisbee teams in the world, and a strong third team, which had placed fifth in the Northeast

Regionals. On top of that we had Suzanne Fields, who was as close as Ultimate would get to its own Billy Jean King. Fields and her team, BLU, or Boston Ladies Ultimate, had won the very first Women's National Championship the year before, down in Austin, Texas, where the Hostages had fallen short. The pool of women's teams was admittedly small at the time, and the pool of talent smaller, but that a league existed at all was due to Fields and her fellow pioneers.

There were women Ultimate players from the very beginning, of course. Back at Columbia High School a few women had always played alongside men, and that continued more or less through the '70s. The Harvard team had actually been started by a Columbia High School graduate named Sara Schechner, one of the Johnny Appleseeds, and during my freshman year I played alongside a young woman named Beth Heckscher. The early etiquette in these matters was never entirely clear: sometimes the other team would put in one of their women to guard our woman, or sometimes a man would cover Beth. If a woman was covering a man, it was bad form for the man to run deep and take advantage of height and strength, but there were no written rules to this effect.

Suzanne Fields and a few other pioneers would change all this. Suzanne had started playing in 1977 while a public policy grad student at UMass. From the start she had good throws, better than most of the men, and when she graduated she brought her love of Ultimate back to her hometown of Boston. When the blizzard of 1978 shut down the city, she partied with her neighbors in the apartment across the hall and learned that they shared her love of throwing discs. After the blizzard stopped and the sun came out they took to the snowy streets, happily free of cars, and threw for hours. Her next step was starting to play with men at the Boston

Frisbee Club, and then the next was to be the only female member of Boston Aerodisc, one of the best teams in the country. Suzanne, it turned out, was a natural marketer, and she managed to convince Nike, which was not yet the giant it would become, to sponsor Aerodisc, providing them with uniforms—green striped '70s-era short shorts, green shirts, and turf cleats. Suzanne was not on the official roster of the Aerodisc team that went to Nationals in 1980, but she did manage to play a couple of points for them in a rout of the Santa Barbara Condors.

In fact, Suzanne Fields had landed herself in a very nice situation, surrounded by twenty men on one of the best teams in the country, and at that moment was in no great rush to advocate for an all-women's division. It was actually another Boston woman, Louie Mahoney, who was most determined to start a team, recruiting both women who were playing on men's teams and some who had never played Ultimate, or even played any organized sports, before. In those days, when it was often tough to get enough players, men or women, out to practice against each other, the idea of getting the few women who played together to form a league at first seemed impractical. But Mahoney and women like Kelly Green of Michigan State, who would found one of the first great women's club teams, the Fishheads, kept pushing. Meanwhile, Lisa Dally was starting a team at Cornell called the Wild Roses, and, on the other side of the continent, Michele Pezzoli had already formed the Lady Condors in Santa Barbara.

The year 1981 saw six women's teams at Easterns, and at that same tournament a reporter from Ms. magazine interviewed Suzanne, who had by then fully embraced the idea of a women's division. The next step was confronting Tom Kennedy and the Ultimate Players Association, insisting that women's teams compete at Nationals, an offer that TK couldn't refuse.

Suzanne Fields

Suzanne's article, "Do Women Have Fair Representation?" appeared in the UPA newsletter and began, "I am not so sure I want to support an organization that doesn't want to support me as a player." It continued: "Women players have been neither active nor vocal in letting their concerns be known about the game, nor their part in its development." Of course with the letter's publication that was changing. "Competitive sports have long been dominated by men," Suzanne wrote. "We in Ultimate have the opportunity to change that trend. The main actors in the UPA have been silent in support of women players. If they truly believe in Ultimate as 'the sport of the future,' a sport that will grow through the UPA's efforts, then the UPA's future must include the promotion of women as competitive players in the overall development in the sport."

The women's division officially began at the next sectionals. In the first women's Nationals, the team that Fields and Mahoney had formed, BLU, Boston Ladies Ultimate, beat Synergy, an all-star team of women from the Pacific Northwest, in the finals 8–7. On a strange foggy morning in a nearly empty stadium, BLU took an early lead and then, after Synergy tied it up late, scored one final goal to win. Even in an era that saw few fans, the lack of spectators at that first championship game was disappointing. But still, the first women's National Championship had been played and the first National Champion had been crowned.

Though the history of the game is my current subject, I can't pretend that my interest in women's Ultimate at the time was entirely academic. It manifested itself more in terms of crushes. The formation of BLU and later of the Spinsters and Lady Godiva, amped up what was already a powerful Frisbee social scene in Boston. Suddenly it wasn't players and a few girlfriends who were partying together, but whole teams, and tournament after-parties were taken over by BLU, Rude Boys, and Hostages. Both the men and the women were obsessed with Ultimate but they were also a little obsessed with each other. It was the early '80s: coed naked hot-tubbing was not uncommon and coke was the drug of choice. Out of this nearly incestuous mix came hundreds of couplings, dozens of relationships, and, in the end, more than a few marriages.

The members of Suzanne's team and Moons's team were insepa-rable. Later Suzanne would often remember one tournament on Martha's Vineyard during which the members of BLU and the Rude Boys rented a house together. The house had only one outdoor shower and Suzanne remembers a line of naked men and women, with towels over their arms but not covering their waists, waiting patiently and casually for the shower, chatting with each other.

As a college player I was on the outside looking in. This was the club scene, after all, and by "club" I don't mean Studio 54. Club Ultimate players were those who had left their college teams behind and were out in the real world, playing for the closest thing Ultimate had to professional teams. As a mere college player, I could watch the women play but could only dream about the naked-hot-tubbing part. One of my main crushes was on Heather Morris, a lithe, long-legged woman who was quite simply the best female athlete to play the sport in those early days. Heather was the BLU player who broke the tie in the National finals by throwing a goal and giving the Boston women their first title. In a player like Morris you could glimpse the future of the game, but again, my interest at the time was less grand and more direct. I was more concerned with her legs than her place in Ultimate history.

Then there was Stephanie Kirsch, who I had been fixated on for the better part of a year. At the time Steph was in the process of dropping out of UMass and moving to Boston to play with BLU. She lacked the athleticism of Heather, but her throws were strong—though, again, it would be dishonest to claim that it was her Frisbee ability that most concerned me. She had been born in Israel and had a radiant smile; she tended to wear loose clothing that almost, but not quite, hid her curves. Once, the previous fall, she walked up to me while I was patting a puppy, and I had been too tongue-tied to say anything more than a stammering hello. In my mind I was not in her league—she was just too far above me. Even after our meeting at the puppy, I doubt she knew I existed. I was smitten, though that might be too delicate a word. I was particularly fond of the way she arced her back when she threw her backhand.

As it turned out, Stephanie, along with Suzanne Fields, would play for a team that would win the first World Championship. The dominance of Boston Ultimate spilled over from the fall into the spring of 1983. Following their win at Nationals, the Rude Boys traveled to Sweden to play in the World Championships, and several Boston women went along. The women who went didn't have enough players to form a team but by picking up a Belgian woman and a tall non-Ultimate-playing girlfriend of one of the Rude Boys, they managed to create an eight-player team they dubbed Melting Pot.

By then it wasn't just American men and women who were dreaming of glory on the Ultimate fields. Frisbee missionaries had begun to spread the gospel around the world. Tom Kennedy had traveled to Japan and toured shopping malls and schools, creating some early converts to the game in 1980. Even earlier, in 1976, Dan Roddick had put on freestyle demonstrations in small towns in Sweden, and for one sixteen-year-old, Paul Eriksson, this was enough to prompt him to put together his first Ultimate team. From the UPA newsletters he would learn the names of great Ultimate players in the United States.

The Rude Boys and Melting Pot traveled through Belgium, France, and London, throwing Frisbees in the narrow streets and putting on Ultimate exhibitions as they went while also drinking all the alcohol and smoking all the pot they could get their hands on. Sweden, Holland, Finland, Italy, and Japan all had teams at the World Championships in Rothenberg. The Rude Boys romped through the field. Steve Mooney had conquered Boston, then conquered the country. And now he conquered the world. Moreover, he did it in just the way he had always dreamed of, as a representative of Athens and arête, an embodiment of TK's vision of good and great. Moons had an ability that Ken Dobyns would never master: he could switch into a fun, playful, almost silly mode when the situation was right, making fun the priority. The Rude

Boys didn't just win the tournament; after the victory they danced with the other teams to Prince singing of a far-off 1999, and won the award for good spirit, an award usually reserved for lesser teams with good guys, not the tourney winners.

Left unsaid again was the fact that it was easy to be spirited when you were winning by double digits. But for the moment it didn't matter. It looked like the Rude Boys might be on the verge of a dynasty. As it turned out there were a couple of teams in the Midwest that would have something to say about that, one a kind of grittier and more talented version of the Hostages.

But that was all to come. For the moment Steve Mooney was king of the world. And a nice king, a dancing king.

Suzanne Fields's Melting Pot also won, though they had a harder time of it with their tiny numbers, and relied heavily on their BLU players Kelly Waugh, Stephanie, and Suzanne. The finals were played in a huge stadium in Rothenberg and were televised nationally in Sweden. Women's Ultimate had officially arrived.

Both Steve Mooney and Suzanne Fields would return to Boston as World Champions, members of the first Ultimate teams to be able to truly say that.

My father liked to talk a lot about the "real world," a world he clearly believed I did not inhabit. Who could blame him? As graduation approached my Harvard roommates worried about which companies to go to work for. Meanwhile, I'd secretly begun to wonder which of the great Boston Ultimate teams, the Hostages or the Rude Boys, to try out for after college. By then I'd become completely wrapped up in the lore and the lure of the game, and while I pretended not to be sure, it wasn't so much a decision as an inevitability that I would continue to play after school. Why? It was simple really. I was addicted to that feeling I experienced when I dove through the air and a disc stuck to my hand or when I jumped high and ripped one out of the air above someone. Nothing else made me feel so alive; nothing else gave me that sensation that Tom Wolfe, writing of Chuck Yeager and the other young fliers at Edwards Air Force Base, called "rude animal health." Playing Ultimate was one of the few times in my young life when I felt potent, and I was quickly becoming an addict of that feeling. Trying to describe the feeling now, I keep coming up with words like *primal* or *tribal* and I'm afraid this might reek of the once-fashionable neoprimitivism of the men's movement, but there was nothing contrived or literary about the feeling I was after, and I knew it to be real: I had been inside of it, and if anything in my world was true and to be trusted, it was that feeling. I was ready to follow it anywhere.

Sometimes I think we choose the things we spend our time doing just because of the difficulty and pain they cause us. A positive way of looking at this might be to say we like to "test ourselves," while a more cynical view might hold that we are all, to some extent, magnificent self-torturers.

I'm pretty sure that I chose to become a writer at least in part because I hated to be criticized and rejected. This hatred was partly due to living with my father, who, for all his good qualities, was a ferocious critic, both in the form of teasing and outright reproach. It was from living with him that I learned to be self-deprecating, a habit that I used as a kind of preemptive strike, beating him to the punch by mocking myself before he could mock me. Given this, you might think I wouldn't choose a profession that would lead to years—decades really—of outright rejection. You would, of course, be wrong. In this light, my choice to try to become a writer seems equal parts inspiration and masochism.

If possible, Ultimate Frisbee might have been an even more perfect instrument of self-torture. What better way to inspire loathing in my father (and self) than to choose as my other passionate pursuit a game that was considered by most, if they considered it at all, to be on par with Hula-Hoops. That it was a running sport that required real athleticism didn't fly. To go to my father after leaving school to tell him that I was committed to Ultimate was akin to telling him that, having graduated from Harvard, I'd decided to forgo traditional careers like law and medicine and, instead, planned to focus all my time, passion, and energy on competing in hopscotch tournaments.

In fact, my choice to stay in Boston after graduation to play Ultimate must have seemed almost completely insane to my family. It did to me. But I did it anyway. My priorities set, I left school in June of 1983 for the world my father liked to call "real." In that world one of my college roommates, Dan, a good Harvard boy, immediately made $300,000 a year working for some rich Texans named the Bass Brothers. Meanwhile, I, instead of heading off for Texas or L.A. or New York, moved into a cramped apartment in Somerville. I played Ultimate fanatically while also making elaborate vows about, and a few outlines of, the novel I would soon start.

There was, of course, the immediate problem of money. I found a job as a bike messenger, but that job lasted less than a day, when, on the way to report to work, I was buffeted by the wind blast of a passing truck and slammed into a curb. The next week I took a job as a security guard in a telephone store in Kenmore Square, which, despite the position's name, was decidedly less dangerous. With my Harvard degree in hand, I sat by the door for eight hours in my guard uniform and watched people shop for phones.

But if my working hours were dull and my writing hours still nonexistent, my Frisbee hours were vital enough to lift my life. I was getting better and stronger, my throws sharper. Two nights a week I would drive out to Wellesley High School and play in their famous pickup games. Closer to home I joined a coed summer league team that played in the shadow of Harvard Stadium. If I was excited that there was a Rude Boy and Hostage or two on that team, I was more excited by the fact that I was, through luck of the draw, teammates with Heather Morris and the newly minted world champion Stephanie Kirsch. Though I still barely had the nerve to really talk to them, I could manage a "nice catch" or "good throw."

Then, in August, something miraculous happened. I was asked to play on a pickup team made of players from both the Hostages and Rude Boys in a tournament in Santa Cruz, California. Usually the two teams treated each other with the type of distrust and suspicion reserved for feuding hillbilly clans, but for some reason they had decided to get together for this tourney. When they asked me to come along I was thrilled.

I needed to find a way to get to California. My Harvard friend Griff, and Ken Fay, a high school friend who had been an All-ACC knuckle curve ball pitcher at Duke, had also just graduated. We decided to make the trip a grand tour of America, though our budget was less than grand. This was my very first thrilled glimpse of the interior West, and the tournament itself was equally exhilarating, allowing me, for a while, to leave behind the confusion I felt about my life and my future. Of course I considered it a great honor to play next to the men whom I'd long rooted for. Our makeshift squad was named FRAC-29, after the license plate on a team member's van. I played well the first day, and, the next morning, had an even greater honor conferred on me. David Barkan of the Hostages asked if I would join his team. I didn't say yes right away, and, after our meeting, as I walked around the fields to mull my decision, Steve Mooney approached me. He asked me to play with the Rude Boys in the coming fall.

I circled the field again, bursting with pride. My roommate Dan might have turned down Goldman Sachs to go to work for the Bass Brothers, but had any young man ever gotten two such prestigious offers in one day? And, even as pride came over me in waves, I knew that my decision was no decision at all. If I had previously been unclear about my feelings regarding the two different teams, in that moment everything crystalized. My walk became a jog. It was obvious. I would turn my back on the sure thing, the defending National and World Champion superteam, the Frisbee equivalent of corporate success, and I would play with the scrubby underdogs. Of course, a small ambitious voice nagged. If my father had cared enough about Frisbee to give counsel, he might have reminded me that the Rude Boys represented a better chance for *achievement*, for fulfillment of my goals. But a louder voice drowned out any nagging, and I didn't hesitate for a second. I would thumb my nose at Moons. I would be part of a gritty band of rebels taking on the powers-that-be. I would become a Hostage.

II

Glory Days

And I hope when I get old I don't sit
around thinking about it, but I
probably will.

—Bruce Springsteen, "Glory Days"

5.

The Glorious Fall

In some ways, in many ways, I suppose, that fall of 1983 was the greatest of my life. It can't compare to the birth of my daughter, true, or to the steady confidence I would gain as an artist in later years. But in its rawness, in its wildness, in its highs and lows, it was like no other year I have ever lived through.

Fall was—and is—the most important season for Ultimate club teams. That fall, my first as a Hostage, I would suddenly have fifteen new friends, friends who I would band together with through some great victories and bitter defeats, friends who I remain close to today after all these years. I would live in a beautiful place during a beautiful season and as a consequence would make living in such places a priority for the rest of my life. Also, for the first time I would glimpse certain possibilities and, however tentatively, I would finally start to write. And finally, not to be underestimated in its overall effect on my state of mind, I would have my first and only fling.

It would also be my first taste of my father's "real world," though how real it was is open to interpretation. While Boston would be the center of much of my life over the next decade, my first move was out of my dingy Somerville apartment, and down to Cape Cod. My father and mother had bought a cottage on Cape Cod in 1962, the year after I was born. Or rather they had bought a plot of land for one of those ridiculously small amounts that make later generations so envious, and then my resourceful mother had discovered an old Cape Cod–style house that was being torn down due to the new highway being built through the town of Middleborough, and had paid fifty dollars for the post and beams, and moved them to the land they had bought on Cape Cod. The result was a beautiful little Cape with cedar shingles, sitting on a hill above a harbor named Sesuit, and it was there, not Worcester, that my lucky family (minus my father left working back in Worcester) spent our summers. The house had never been winterized, and no one had ever spent an off-season in it. But here I was, a recently graduated, more or less unemployed Ultimate Frisbee player and there was that house that I loved, sitting empty by early September when my family, and all the rest of the summer people, left Cape Cod. I had read my Thoreau and knew that his paradise was based on squatting on someone else's land and after some squabbling with my father, and earnest promises to pay for upkeep, be prompt with the bills, and winterize the house, determined that I would do the same. "My father's house" was how I often referred to it during that fall, though I'm not sure why since it was as much my mother's and was fully her inspiration. Maybe it was simply because my father had lodged himself so deeply in my head space as I left college behind, and I felt as if he was watching my every move. It was perhaps best that he did not know my real plan that fall: I would live on Cape Cod but commute to Boston, not for work but for Frisbee.

Our first practice was in early September and I played well. At the end of practice the team jogged a big lap and I found myself running next to Mark Honerkamp. He was a tall, skinny kid with a shaved head in the punk rock style, and everyone called him "Hones." After practice he invited me out to a bar called the Bustop with his Hostage roommates, David Barkan and Jimmy Levine, and soon there I was drinking beer with my old hero, Barkan, who was now my teammate. We drank beer after beer, at least Hones and I did, and then we headed back to the apartment in Allston where they all lived. We kept drinking, and I soon doubted I was going to be driving the hour and a half back to Cape Cod. In fact, I would spend a decent part of the fall season sleeping on the couch in that living room on Abby Road in Allston.

Like I said, I had played well at practice and was now intent on showing just how normal, funny, and essentially un-Harvardy I really was. If anything I overcompensated in this direction and became pretty drunk, a not uncommon occurrence during those days. After Jimmy and Barkan went to bed, Hones and I kept going and at one point Barkan came out of his room and asked us to keep it down. Later that night I would wake from a drunken sleep on the couch and wander into the kitchen and grab a handful of Barkan's leftover lasagna in the fridge. He would find my handprint in his casserole the next morning and perhaps begin to question the wisdom of asking me to play for his team.

Of course I didn't know then that Honerkamp would become a lifelong friend. He was two years older than me, which meant something back then in a way it doesn't now. He had played with Barkan for The Jam on the West Coast, a team that was made up of some friends of his from San Jose State, where he went to school. He had dropped out of college to move to Boston to play Ultimate. Let me repeat that: *he had dropped out of college to move to Boston to play Ultimate.* This made my own rebelliousness seem relatively tame.

Hones was into punk and back then looked down disdainfully on anything that smelled of "selling out." There would be a long list of such things, from REM to the Rude Boys. He had sported a buzz cut for the last year (and was, I learned later, one of the inspirations for Stephanie Kirsch soon doing the same). With Jimmy and Barkan gone, Hones and I headed into his bedroom, where I admired the decor. His room was already taking on the hoarder's flavor it would more fully realize later on, with boxes full of photos and records, and a wall plastered with Frisbees from the various tournaments he had played in. This still seemed very cool to me back then. As did his bamboo bong that had no base and rested in a gray ceramic mug, though in truth it rarely rested, not in that house. He sat at a small schoolboy's desk and I took a seat next to him in his crowded bedroom. He used an upside-down Frisbee as a dish to separate the seeds from the pot. He packed a little hit for himself.

While he pulled in the smoke and the bong gurgled, I told him how I had quit smoking pot.

"This is the year I'm going to keep my body in perfect shape," I said drunkenly. "This is the year I'm going to put everything into Ultimate."

He nodded, holding the smoke in his lungs, as I continued on in this vein, describing the rigors of my workouts and the deep level of my commitment, and of course the discipline it would take to not smoke pot for the entire fall. I went on and on about my training, and, God help me, I may have even mentioned arête. When I finished my lecture, and after he'd finally exhaled in a great cloud, Hones refilled the bowl with a finger pinch and tilted the bong toward me.

"Want a hit?" he asked.

"Sure," I said.

Soon the water was burbling and I was sucking the smoke into my lungs.

It was the beginning of a beautiful friendship.

While the Rude Boys were the defending champions, and the Hostages had restocked with four new players including me, more radical changes were occurring a couple hundred miles to the south. The best New York team, the Heifers, had endured a fall 1982 season that in almost every way was the opposite of the Rude Boys' glory. The decision to kick Kenny Dobyns off due to his hotheadedness had been a disaster. Without him the team had no fire, no heart. They lost badly at Regionals and once again did not make Nationals.

One Heifer who had never understood the decision to cut Kenny was their best young player, Pat King. Pat's objection was not due to a lack of understanding about just how thorny and difficult Kenny could be. In fact, Pat had encountered the unsolvable problem that was Ken Dobyns quite directly the very first time they clashed on the field.

"When I first played against him he spit in my face," said King, who would be Dobyns's co-captain and slightly more rational counterbalance on the New York teams to come. "Really. He *spit* right in my face. My teammates couldn't believe it but I knew Kenny well enough to know that that was just part of his gamesmanship. I wiped off the spit and went back to beating him."

King was tall and lanky and played the game with a more controlled and goal-oriented version of the shambling grace that Tommy Conlon had brought to the Hostages. As a youngster King had moved from Utah to New York City, where he was a jock who played varsity football, basketball, and lacrosse at Trinity High

School while also falling in love with playing jazz saxophone. He was good at pretty much anything he did but then one day a friend told him about a game played with a Frisbee, and, thinking it would be a good way to stay in shape for lacrosse, King gave it a try. The games took place at the fields below the Fifty-ninth Street Bridge and would start at 11:00 p.m., after the softball players were done, and go until two in the morning. Like so many others, King loved Ultimate right away, but unlike many who played, he had no problem putting a finger on what it was he loved.

"It was a combination of three things," he decided. "First was the running. I loved all the running. Second was the flight of the Frisbee. I had played a lot of ball sports and the way a Frisbee floated changed everything. It slowed things down and made things more creative."

And the third?

"The third was the sense, right away, that I could be really good at it. One of the best players, maybe even the very best."

Soon King was heading out to the Fifty-ninth Street fields three nights a week. He was full of adrenaline as he approached the fields and was still excited when he headed home in the early-morning hours. The next year at Dartmouth, King got hurt playing freshman football in the fall, and that winter saw a poster announcing the formation of the Dartmouth Club Ultimate Team. "I'm good but I doubt I'm good enough to play *college* Ultimate," he thought. But at that first meeting, held in the field house, he was clearly not just the best player but the best thrower and by the end of that meeting he was anointed captain. Not bad, he thought, for a freshman.

King would get better and better, but his Dartmouth team would never be much, even losing to my Harvard team a couple of times. During his sophomore year he left school for a while and headed back to New York to try and make it as a jazz saxophonist, and there he started playing Ultimate with some very strong players from Columbia (the university, not the famous high school) while dreaming of putting together a team that would be better than any that had yet played. After finally graduating from Dartmouth, he returned to New York to pursue his twin goals of music and Ultimate.

If you were a top Ultimate player in New York, at the time you played for the Heifers, but the Heifers were a cut below both the Rude Boys and Hostages. The Hostages fascinated King, and their win over the Rude Boys in '81 was revelatory for him. He felt that it was that particular game that opened his eyes to a new way to play Ultimate. It also sparked the beginning of a kind of chemical change in him, a movement from desiring just individual greatness to team greatness. Watching the Hostages beat the clearly more talented Rude Boys he began to see that it was the *team* that mattered, the chemistry and flow and togetherness, and not mere individual achievement. That game, he later wrote in a letter supporting David Barkan's Hall of Fame candidacy, was "one of the most powerful experiences in my life as an Ultimate player." He continued:

> Sure the Hostages managed to play the Rudies close a few times that fall, but everybody knew how this one was going to end. . . . Ok. So everybody was wrong. But how they won changed the way I thought about Ultimate. These guys were tight as a team—a cohesive unit that played with a confidence and looseness that comes from trust . . . For me it was like waking up from a dream. All I'd ever known was plodding cutbacks and hitting receivers across the field like an NFL quarterback hits a receiver on a crossing pattern. But the Hostages were

using the natural float of the Frisbee to run a type of offense that was new to me. Soft tosses to space. Making passes before the receiver started to cut.

The "beautiful lesson" that King took away from that game was this: "flow and chemistry beat talent every time."

But as much as he loved the Hostage style, there were noticeable design flaws in the model, like their choice to keep their numbers small to assure that everyone could play. That inevitably led to a tired team playing in a tournament's last, and most important, game. What if you could have a team with a large number of great players while, at the same time, keeping the cohesion of a smaller team? Yes, what was needed was a large team that played like a small one.

This was one reason that it made no sense to him for the Heifers to cut Kenny Dobyns. There simply weren't enough great players in New York to do without one, whatever his flaws.

"I knew from the beginning I wanted to dominate the sport," King would say. "And I knew I couldn't do it in New York without Ken Dobyns."

After the Heifers' loss at Regionals that fall, Pat King decided to break away and form a new team, Kaboom!, taking some of the Heifers' best players with him. He also recruited some of his old jock friends from Trinity High School and of course Ken Dobyns. From that point on all New York teams would decide it was worth it to make a deal with a devil named Kenny. It might mean yelling and screaming at practice and in games, it might mean being pushed to extremes of fitness and patience, and it might mean being perceived by other teams as assholes and sometimes cheaters. But it would also, they would soon discover, mean a whole lot of winning.

Pat King throwing around John "Johnny Sky" Alcott

While Pat was the classic Ultimate player, a long-limbed, grace-ful athlete who could run all day, Kenny was an unlikely star, a short, squat fireplug of a man who wore a sneering expression that led the Chicago players, among others, to call him "the Troll." Pat was hardly above arguing, but there was a sense of cool about the way he played. Kenny, in contrast, was all heat. If Pat moved around the field to the soundtrack of his beloved Jazz saxophone, Kenny was driven by the beating of a tribal drum. He played angry with a chip on his shoulder and moved in bursts of fierce energy, hurling himself around. This hurling would lead to many injuries (mostly incurred, some inflicted), but that would barely slow him down. He was short but built like a tank, and he was smart, poaching by prowling in passing lanes on defense and anticipating throws. He had a lot of bounce in his legs, though his stature meant he would never reach as high as some of the game's very best skyers. Instead of sheer height it was his sense of timing that made him a great deep receiver. He also excelled at diving. It was a given that if you played Ultimate you dove for the disc, but for some of us diving was a kind of crumpling, a direct route to the ground. Not for Dobyns: there was height to his dives; he sprung up and out, and usually hit the ground hard when he landed. All that high-jumping had paid off.

Most of all, Dobyns had a sense of the moment. Early on this came out in his goal catching and blocks but later he would turn himself into a strong deep thrower, carving forehands and hurling overheads far down the field. He did all this with a kind of angry scowl on his face, eyebrows lowered in troglodyte fashion, but there were also moments of sheer joy when the pass was complete, the game won.

Together over the next decade Dobyns and Pat King would lead New York squads that practiced on rock-hard fields in the middle of the city, teams that would effectively wring the last drop of grooviness from Ultimate.

While there would be many great players for Kaboom! and later for the team known only as New York, New York, these two would be the most recognizable, and the most vocal, leaders. In terms of ego they were fairly competitive. While Kenny was unbridled ego, Pat's ego, though every bit as big, was hidden, barely, under a sardonic wit. Pat's scratchy voice, which had a timbre similar to Ed Burns, the actor from Queens, could be heard both exhorting his teammates and dropping one-liners. He had once replied to a TV interviewer who asked him why he liked Ultimate by saying, "Because *I* play it." Pat seemed relatively restrained but only in the context of Kenny. Kenny was raw, angry, direct, willful.

Sometimes Kenny would rub Pat the wrong way.

"A lot of it was an act with Kenny," he said. "Theater."

Pat could see through this and wondered why others couldn't and when what little media attention that Ultimate got in the

Ken Dobyns with Kaboom!

coming years focused on mighty Ken Dobyns, the proud and willful warrior, he could not help but be a little envious. But he was also Ken's friend and understood him as few others did. And he never forgot how valuable Ken Dobyns was to his concept of a great team.

Summer stretched into fall in 1983, and then, just when it seemed as if the cold had come, Indian summer broke out, bringing one of the warmest falls on record. I had always known Cape Cod in summer but that was the year I truly fell in love with the place. While living on the Cape meant I would have to commute for Ultimate practices and tournaments, it also meant I could train on the beach. The beach would later become my classroom, observatory, and muse, and I would write my first book about my love for it. But that fall it most plainly served as my gymnasium. I vowed that I would get in the best shape of my life. Before the trip to California with FRAC-29, I'd read an article about Herschel Walker, the Georgia running back, that focused on the sprint and hill workouts he did. Walker figured if he worked harder than any of the other players, he would be better, and that made sense to me. I copied his workout, which included not just sprinting but hundreds of push-ups and sit-ups, and jumping rope. Better yet I ran the beach, sprinting repeatedly up a high dune near Corporation Beach, sometimes with a large piece of driftwood strapped on my back for added weight, and then running intervals on the hard, flat sand of low tide. Out of an old Dunlop tennis racket cover and some rope I fashioned a quiver, which I wore over my back and in which I kept my trusty Frisbee. On the way home I'd toss the disc into the wind and run it down, or float it out in front of me and dive after it. "First, be a good animal," said Emerson, and those words became my motto. I fancied myself a noble savage. When my workouts were done I'd cool down by plunging into the icy fall water.

If it sounds like I'm romanticizing that time, the truth is I romanticized it even as it was happening. I was twenty-two and my moods fluctuated between supreme confidence and deep insecurity, the insecurity perhaps due to the fact that I didn't know what the hell I was doing with my life. To purge my insecurity I'd work out even harder. "Exorcise through exercise," read a note I'd scribbled on a scrap and tacked to my wall. When I felt afraid, I simply turned around and did hundreds of push-ups and then flexed alone in the shower, admiring myself, cranking the Talking Heads on the boom box while the water burned my scalp. I showered at least twice a day, listening to "Burning Down the House" or "Girlfriend Is Better." My hands had never felt more sure and I would toss the soap up in the shower and try to catch it between my thumb and forefinger, like pincers. I wrote myself a note that I never could, and still can't, decipher. "Bodily fluids are crucial," it said.

During that fall I also had the only "fling" of my life with a young woman who came up to me after my first tournament as a Hostage. The tournament was the Tufts Invitational and it was one of the few we didn't win that fall. After our last game I stood around the keg, proudly wearing my new but already torn and muddied Hostage shirt. As I sipped my beer, a girl named Lizzy walked right up to me and started talking. She touched my arm at one point, I remember that. She was cute, with pretty brown hair and a dimply smile, and she drank a couple beers with me and told me she was at school at Tufts and I told her that I lived on Cape Cod and she seemed to think this romantic. I told her she should come visit me on the Cape, never for once thinking she would take me up on it.

After Lizzy's visit to Cape Cod there was no stopping me. "The world doesn't revolve around you," my father had always said, but now I wasn't so sure. It certainly seemed to: the wind, the salt, the sand, the sex, the leaves, all of it rustling and churning and gyrating and pressing in. *Maybe I brag too much*, I wrote in my journal, *but why shouldn't I brag?* I felt strong and alive. I even began to hear messages in the crow's cawing at the beach. "The crows of hope," I called them. Perfect that I could understand the animals now. I was the Tarzan of East Dennis.

There was, of course, the small problem of money. It was a problem that fall and would remain one for the next twenty years, during which time my annual income would remain under the poverty line.

But while it was a personal, and very acute, problem for me, it is also a more general problem for any woman or man who throws her- or himself fully into a passion that doesn't pay. Starving artist, starving writer, starving Ultimate player, whatever. The choice not to make money one's priority sounds noble, but by making that choice, money, and its lack, loom large and have the power to cause nearly constant and stabbing anxiety. If I flew back in time and told my young self that I would not make over $12,000 a year until I was forty-two, would I have said "No, thanks" and sensibly given up my dreams? I'm not sure. But I do understand why so few people choose unconventional courses or at least fail to stick to unconventional courses. To choose these things means to give up traditional rewards, something I would discover very soon.

Ultimate players, until very recently, were all amateurs. Flying to tournaments was not cheap, and training like a pro without a pro's time or cash was always a problem.

"Ultimate is addictive," Steve Mooney would say near the end of his career. "You might look at my expenses over the last fifteen years and say that work is what I do between tournaments. My job was always secondary to athletics. It goes back to when I was five. What was most important? Sports."

Moons, though, was one of the lucky ones. He had a stimulating and relatively lucrative profession putting his photographic and management talents to use as the creative director of a Boston company specializing in interactive media. Most of the Hostages, meanwhile, went to work every day packing boxes in the warehouse at the Ski Market, biding their time and collecting their paychecks until the next practice or tournament. Working at menial labor to support their addiction.

Many Ultimate players took whatever job came their way, just as young writers work as baristas and bartenders. Kenny Dobyns provides a fine portrait of the artist as a young Frisbee player, putting off his non-Frisbee priorities until well into his thirties. He worked a variety of odd jobs during the Kaboom! years, running photocopy services at the Columbia Law Library, working as an assistant manager at the Delacorte Theater in Central Park and as a fire marshal at the Big Apple Circus. Making money, other than making enough to survive and get to tournaments, was simply not a priority.

What drives someone to do this? What drives someone like Kenny to throw virtually all of his passion and energy into something that will not pay him a penny? And something that, in the case of Ultimate, will, if you dare tell someone what you spend all your time doing, likely be greeted with laughter?

Amateurism, of course, was not something that was valued much in the rising age of Reagan. Many of my classmates and most of my roommates, the best and brightest, had headed off to Wall Street to cash in. And why not? This is what smart and ambitious people did after all. This is what they got excited about. They certainly didn't spend all their hours dreaming about chasing a piece of plastic. That would be crazy.

Oddly, my own hopes for making money were even more directly tied to Ronald Reagan. I did not live alone on Cape Cod, but with my oldest friend from Worcester, Dave Rotman. Dave and I had become friends in second grade and had remained close over the years, talking so often on the phone that at one point my sister told me she suspected we might be lovers. Dave had always been an entrepreneur, selling hot dogs on the lawn in front of the Worcester Galleria while in high school, and rugs to returning students at Brown while he was in college there, and together we had struck on a way we thought we might be able to make money.

At the time the best-selling poster in the country was something called "Poverty Sucks," which portrayed a scene of glorious wealthy excess. In that poster rich folks thumbed their nose at the poor, which apparently seemed amusing to enough people to make it popular. Inspired by that poster's success, Dave and I decided that we would make a poster out of "The Trickle Down Theory," my cartoon of Reagan pissing on the poor guy in the gutter. We were hoping to equal the success of "Poverty Sucks," but not really thinking through the fact that ours had almost the exact opposite message. Ours was not lighthearted: poverty really *did* suck.

At first we considered simply making a poster of my original drawing, but then decided to hire actors and photograph them acting out the cartoon. We hired a limousine and two actors to play a chauffeur and the homeless man, while getting Dave's grandfather to play a generic rich guy in place of Reagan. As the director, it was part of my job to coach Dave's poor grandpa in simulating urination, which he did by spraying the water from a mustard bottle onto the man playing the bum in the gutter. Dave and I filmed the thing in the backstreets of our hometown, Worcester, Massachusetts. We had a professional photographer shoot the scene but apparently he wasn't feeling all that professional that day; when we got back the ten thousand copies we had ordered, wrapped in brown paper bundles of five hundred, we discovered that the lighting in the poster was too dark and muddied.

It may say all you need to know about our business acumen that we thought we could turn a profit by selling a poster of one man urinating on another. Somehow it never occurred to us that this concept—a guy pissing on another guy—was not going to make us rich. Amazingly, Dave convinced my father of the efficacy of our plan, and he co-signed a loan from the Cape Cod Bank and Trust that provided the funds for ordering the first batch of posters. We also drove down to Providence to sell carpets to incoming students at Brown, as Dave had while in college, which put a little cash in our pockets and helped further fund our poster business.

We would learn a lot over the next few months. We would learn how to roll posters, between our thumbs and forefingers, so that they fit in the small plastic wrappers we shipped them in. We would learn that being an entrepreneur is a risky thing, and that you have to ride the ups and downs of an uncertain profession, and that the time to pay back loans always comes a lot faster than you think it will. Mostly we would learn that the country was not too excited about buying copies of "The Trickle Down Theory."

I was making it a habit to pursue ridiculous things, and now I would begin my postgraduate life in debt, a debt I would spend the next few years paying off. After it became clear that "The Trickle Down Theory" was not going to make us rich, I set to work on our second poster, which, this time, I would draw. It would be called "Ronald Reagan: A Physical Examination," and it featured a large drawing of Reagan, naked except for boxer shorts patterned with the presidential seal. Arrows from the outside of the poster would point in and identify different parts of the president's anatomy: itchy trigger finger, gender gap, nuclear warhead. The jokes would be slightly dumbed down in hopes of increasing sales, but I determined that the drawing of Reagan would be the best thing I had ever done. I spent hours up in the attic room of the house, hunched over the drawing board, drawing draft after draft of Reagan, breaking his face into components, working for days on the swirling pompadour and lopsided grin. I knew that time was running out before we had to get real jobs. But maybe, if I drew Reagan well enough, I could rescue us from financial doom.

Meanwhile, the Hostages were rising up and having a spectacular fall, suddenly casting ourselves in the favorite's role. Along with me, we had added Bobby Harding, a great runner from Michigan who would become a close friend, and two brothers, Chris and Adam Phillips, from New York. Many thought this

*The author throwing to fellow Hostages David Barkan
and Adam Phillips*

the strongest Hostage team yet. After a slow start, we began click-ing and soundly thrashed the Rude Boys in the two tournaments building up to the all-important Regionals, winning one of those games by the absurd score of 18–6.

And it wasn't just the winning that jazzed me up. I loved hav-ing fifteen new friends, loved being part of a tribe and pouring my entire self into becoming a great player. The Hostages prided themselves on the number of college dropouts on the squad and they teased me about Harvard, which, in this looking-glass world, was a badge of shame. But the teasing itself was just part of the fun of my new life, part of belonging to my new instant family.

I quickly became close with Hones, and with Jimmy Levine and Bobby Harding, and that closeness translated to the field. "May our passes be linked as our arms are now," we said in the huddle before the games—and more often than not they were. It wouldn't be long before I could see Bobby fake a forehand and know it was time to sucker my defender toward that sideline before sprinting to the opposite end zone for his backhand. As in love, no words were required.

But if it was great to be playing beside my college hero David Barkan, another of those heroes had gone missing. Steve Gustafson had suddenly quit before the season began. This was no small thing for the Hostages. Gus, perhaps more than any other Hostage, was a believer in and a seeming beneficiary of the magic dust theory. He rose up in big games and he made ballsy and outrageous throws, sometimes to the point of seeming not to care.

While he was a great player on the field and often made honorable calls, off the field he treated the sport with a kind of casual disregard that sometimes bordered on disgust, ridiculing its lack of athleticism. It was an argument that people had made since the sport began and that people make still. And there was no denying it: the prospect of getting just one division 1 basketball player on a team made people salivate.

Moreover, if TK was a philosopher-king, then Gus had refined the role of clown-prince. Exhibit A was his famously drooling on the trophy at Nationals. He also liked to sometimes kiss other Hostages on the mouth to shock other teams. He professed not to give a shit and sometimes it seemed like he didn't.

Back then Gus also, if possible, drank more than I did—and not just beer. If TK was the enlightened face I hoped to see when I stared in the mirror, Gus was sometimes the dark, goat-eyed creature who had torn the sink from the wall.

It was always a mystery why Gus quit when he did, after two straight trips to Nationals for the Hostages. David Barkan thought he just wanted attention. Or perhaps he simply knew his moment. He was a perfect fit for a wilder, less-restrained time, for that era of Pete Maravich and Kenny Stabler and Dr. J, but not so much for the coming era of workouts, of striving, of wanting more than anything to win. He was Belushi, left behind with the outgoing era. And there might have been a more practical reason for quitting. At the last Regionals he played in, the Hostages, after losing to the Rude Boys, played UMass to see who the second team to go would be. UMass had been way down until they struck on the strategy of hucking deep to Jeremy Seeger. Gus, as deep in the zone, was forced to cover the taller Seeger, who had two or three inches on him, not to mention speed and jumping ability. Again and again Jeremy went up over Gus, eating him alive. Gus had complained about lack of athleticism but now he got to see the results when one of the new breed, a real athlete, went up against him. It was a dilemma all of us would face in one way or another as Ultimate began to change. We wanted better athletes in our sport and we wanted our sport to grow. But we also wanted there to be room for *us*.

As it turned out, it would be my job to replace Steve Gustafson as deep in the Hostage zone, a position that would require air battles with the taller Rude Boys. Realistically, I had no right doing this, but realism was not the theme of that fall. I began to have flying dreams and then one day, jumping on the beach with a strong tailwind, I thought I might have gotten some lift. It didn't seem entirely out of whack with the way things were going that I might actually learn to fly.

During the last few weeks before Regionals my world sped up. Then, at a party one night, one of the Rude Boys' best offensive players, who I'd been assigned to cover, approached me. After joking around for a while, he turned serious. "I shouldn't tell you this," he said. "But the other night I had a nightmare about you guarding me." That pretty much sent me over the edge. I was invulnerable! My already substantial ego stretched even larger. I glimmered with a near megalomaniacal confidence.

These delusions were no doubt aided by the mushrooms I ingested a couple times that fall. The residue of those trips—during which I felt I got down to the essence of my animal self, sweating, running, drinking, pissing—spilled over into my so-called normal life. I lived inside a fever. Now, the fever so long past, I see myself for what I was: a scared little boy playing at life. Humans can be narcissists at any age, but there is no narcissism like that possible in one's twenties, particularly one's early twenties. With time, even the dullest of us gets at least some wisdom pounded into our brains, but there is pleasure as well as pain in the time before wisdom. What I really had going for me that fall was the advantage of inexperience. With writing, for instance, I hadn't yet begun and so could still live fully in the fantasy that what I wrote would be brilliant. Unlimited possibility still seems possible before we begin a thing, and before we realize that our bonds define us, that without constraints we have no shape, without limits there is nothing. But the illusion of limitlessness is a drug beside which mushrooms pale.

In the end, all this moralizing won't do. It's the feeling I remember from that glorious fall, a feeling I have never felt since and am quite sure I'll never feel again. I was full of sap and muscular and strong, and, of course, quite deluded. A young Icarus with enough literary training to be pretty sure where all this was heading. It was hubris plain and simple, but one thing they don't tell you about hubris is how good it feels. In fact, in some ways, though I now know what it will lead to, I still think of that fall as the high tide of my twenties. In some ways I still think of it as the high tide of my life. Though a happier and better man now, I still miss that time, and if there were a way, if granted a wish, I can't pretend I wouldn't run right back and crawl inside that lunatic's skin.

After dominating the late-fall season we were seeded first going into Regionals in Purchase, New York.

We played well on the opening day, a Saturday, going undefeated.

According to the schedule, we were to play the number two seed in the game to go to Nationals late that afternoon. We were ready, maybe slightly tired, but exhilarated and full of ourselves with a kind of wild anticipation of victory. But in those early days the roles of players and administrators were blurred, and suddenly there were mutterings that the Rude Boys, Moons's team and the number two seed, were arguing that the game should be postponed until the morning. Their games had gone longer, and been closer, and it was, they argued, getting too late in the day to start.

"They" meant Moons, who was about the closest thing the sport had to an authority figure back then. When we caught up with him in the parking lot of the SUNY gym, he was talking steadily and intently to the tournament director, pushing home the point that there might not be enough light to finish a game if we started now. Barkan joined the fray, and then other Hostages, including even my outraged rookie self, joined in, too. Our point was simple: we want to play *now*, just as the schedule said we should. The longer we argued, of course, the more Moons's case was made. Moons's voice, in argument, was reedy and insistent and it was pretty clear that he was not going to accept any other decision but postponement. We moaned in complaint as he filibustered away.

This is what drove us so crazy. The Hostages, just like the later New York teams, would come to regard Moons's supposed calm as an affectation. Nationally he had a reputation as a kind of statesman of the game, but not regionally. It was his very reasonableness that got most under the skin of the teams he played against. We didn't see it as actual reasonableness, of course, but a feigning of that attitude as a disguise while, behind the mask, he tried to achieve his own ends. He was just like us, wanting what he wanted but pretending he only wanted "what was right." The superiority of it, the affectation of judicial calm, was the most infuriating part.

In the end it was decided that it was too late to play, and by the time the argument died it probably was. Soon I was under a hot shower in the Purchase gym, letting the scalding water steam my bruised and muddy legs. A small bad feeling began to spread in the back of my mind, not just about the argument we had lost but about the next day. The truth was that the reason we had wanted to play immediately was that we knew that *right then* we could beat the Rude Boys on the field. We didn't want to have a night to think about it. We wanted to play them *now*. We weren't sure we could postpone our inner feeling of invincibility.

Meanwhile, as the light faded, the New Yorkers were fighting for their lives. They'd come into the tournament with some high expectations, having had big wins over the Rude Boys and a couple of other top teams. The team had gelled, and seemed to be fulfilling Pat King's vision of a large but tight squad. Pat was playing a mature masterful game already, and Kenny, his throws now developed, was blossoming into one of the best players in the game. In some ways, however, he was the same player who had run down everything his older brother threw.

Pat King would later remember that what was perhaps his favorite on-field interaction with Kenny came during that season, up at a tournament in Hanover, New Hampshire. King recalls:

> Someone tossed me a soft backhand up the line, near the end zone. My defender tried to make a bid and landed on the back of my legs. I high-stepped for a few strides to pull my legs out from under his body, then looked toward the end zone. Ken was just

finishing a cut to the corner, wide-open as usual. By the time I cocked my arm to throw the goal, Ken's defender closed the gap and I held the throw. Ken sneered at me: "Maybe if you did a little less dancin' and a little more lookin' we might have had the goal!" That kind of pissed me off. So I said, "Fuck you!" and threw the disc to the opposite side of the field, to a place only Ken could reach. He took off, laid-out, caught the disc with two hands, and hit the turf like a ski jumper face-planting on a landing. Ken stood up slowly and turned to me—dirt, blood, and grass hanging from his face. We looked at each other for a second, then we both cracked up laughing.

To King's mind there had never been a receiver like Dobyns: "With Ken if it was humanly possible to make the grab, he made it. Sometimes after an unusually mind-boggling catch, it was easy to believe he could catch *anything*. You had to keep reminding yourself he was only human."

Despite Dobyns's dives and King's throws, their Regionals did not start well, and, despite the name change, it looked like Kaboom! would repeat the Heifers' weak performance of the year before. With expectations high, they fell on their faces, losing to UMass in their very first game and therefore being shunted off into the losers' bracket. Which meant that, while we were winning all our games and getting ready to play the Rudies in the game to go to Nationals, New York would be embarking on a long and torturous course through the losers' bracket, during which they would be eliminated if they lost again. They ended that Saturday in desperate straits, way down to a team called the Tourists, a team they should have beaten easily. With darkness threatening, they launched a mad comeback, but then the game was postponed until the next morning. Granted a reprieve, they came out and stomped the Tourists, then started picking up some momentum. They won the next game and the next and suddenly they were in the losers' bracket finals, ready to play the loser of the Hostage–Rude Boy game.

A s it turned out we couldn't postpone that feeling of invincibility. It was a foggy morning, cool but not too cold. I remember that but not too much else about the Rude Boy game. I know we pulled to them, because, full of until-then-suppressed energy, I sprinted down the field on defense and blocked the very first pass of the game, what had been meant to be a simple short pass from handler to handler. A teammate of mine picked it up, threw it to me in the goal, and we were up 1–0.

Maybe my bad feeling had been misplaced. Maybe what had been surging would continue to surge. Maybe our glorious fall, our great roll, would continue.

But no. It would turn out that that was our only lead of the game.

It wasn't shocking to lose to a team as good as the Rude Boys. But what was shocking was what did us in that morning, what betrayed us, and that was our greatest strength as a team. Our usually sure hands deserted us. I remember that a couple of players in particular had, to put it delicately, "a case of the drops." And so we watched the Rude Boys celebrate, ecstatic that they would be returning to Nationals to defend their title.

We weren't dead yet however. There was still a chance for us to win the number two seed and travel with the Rude Boys to New Orleans. More than a chance really since our opponent in the game to go would be New York's Kaboom!, a team we had never lost to. After their morning spent fighting their way through the losers' bracket, they would meet us in the deciding game. It was only later, after I had played the sport for a decade, that I developed a theory that those losers' bracket finals are usually won by the team that fights their way to them, while the team that waits is less ready. For one thing, as Pat King would later point out to me, the losers' bracket team has been winning just to get there while the other team has just lost. Whatever the theory, in practice we once again had too much time on our hands. I jogged a little, then watched New York win its last game in the losers' bracket. But my bad feeling of the night before returned when I wandered over to the parking lot by the field and saw three or four of my teammates gathered around a car. There was something about their postures, the occasional dipping down of heads and then the rising up and backward, like whinnying horses, that led me to a worrisome conclusion. Could they be using their downtime to snort coke?

I didn't go in that direction but what I did proved equally pernicious. I gobbled down a turkey sandwich, as I did most days before taking an afternoon nap, and I sucked back a beer, just one beer I think, with it. A logginess came over me, and I still felt semi-stunned when we started our game against New York. The whole team played as if in a fog, with a kind of passivity, despite the usually frenetic effects of the drug I suspected some of my teammates had taken. The daring that had been our trademark was replaced by a frightened caution, occasionally punctuated by desperate, ill-advised throws. As things started to slip away I felt the icy fear and cowardice only the choker knows. My limbs no longer operated with the confidence that they had all fall; the magic juice no longer flowed through me.

Unlike today, filming of games was rare back then. Some footage has survived from that game, however—a few snippets that I have glimpsed on and off over the years. The one image that sticks in my mind is of Kenny Dobyns skying over David Barkan in the end zone and then, after catching the disc, raising it in triumph with a kind of matador's flair. My own play was serviceable if uninspired, but my low moment came when Dobyns was covering me. I was throwing a forehand for a goal when he hit my wrist. Since, as I've mentioned, Ultimate is a self-officiated game, it was my responsibility to call a foul. That there had been one was obvious—everyone had heard the clear *slap*—but instead of calling it right away I waited to see if the disc reached my receiver. It didn't but fell short, and by then it somehow seemed too late to yell "foul." New York marched down the field in the other direction and scored.

And so for the second time that day we watched a team celebrate the fact that they would be going to Nationals. We, on the other hand, would be going nowhere but home. The Hostages had been known in our region for rising to the occasion . . . but that day could be called, if not the end of the Hostages, then certainly the beginning of the end. Moreover, that day could justly be seen as the beginning of the rise of New York and Dobyns.

The Hostages had had a glorious fall season, but now that season had ended in spectacular choking fashion. If the world of Frisbee had become my personal mythology, here was the classic fall from grace. I lurched back to Cape Cod in late October, depressed and defeated, an animal back to its lair. The eelgrass had turned the color of wheat and the ocean was gray and frothy. October turned to November, the light died, and the Cape entered a period of what Melville called "suicide weather." There was no longer a reason to drive up to Boston—no more practices or games—and we wouldn't play again until April. It would be a long winter.

6.

My Forever Love

The Hostages were heading home.

The two teams going to the 1983 Nationals from the Northeast were a New York squad led by Kenny Dobyns and a Boston one led by Steve Mooney. That same sentence could be written annually over the next fifteen years. Moons and Dobyns were becoming the story of Northeast Ultimate and increasingly the story of National Ultimate.

Kenny Dobyns was not yet one of the most dominating figures in the fantasy world of Ultimate Frisbee, but Steve Mooney, the defending National Champion, was. The dislike between the two men was still in its infancy and had not yet hardened into what it would become. But already you could see it growing. It was the sanctimoniousness of the Rude Boys that drove Kenny crazy. The way Moons pretended to be above the fray. To see that the two men already disliked each other, all you had to do was watch them on the field. When Kenny approached Moons he always looked like he was about to relive that moment with Pat King and spit in his face. Of course he would have had to have spit *up*. To an almost comic degree, they were physical opposites—Dobyns short and thick, Moons tall and thin—and when they did stand next to each other they looked like a silent movie–era comedy team. They were temperamental opposites, too—Dobyns fiery and surly, Moons reasonable and relatively placid.

You could argue that Dobyns was a short man who played a big man's game, while Moons was a tall man with the skills of a short one. Moons was surprisingly graceful for someone who by all rights should have been all arms and legs. And he was not just the tallest player in Ultimate but arguably the best. It surprised a lot of people on other teams that he was primarily a smart player, rather than a physical one. But while there had been that early moment, famous in Ultimate lore, when David Barkan skyed over him, he would get better and better at using his body as the years passed, and while he never quite became the deep threat that a casual observer of the game might have expected of a giant, he caught everything that came close to him and threw long with the best. Furthermore, he was every bit as fierce as Dobyns, though that fierceness was sometimes hidden under a calmer mien.

The two men contained each other. Dobyns, for all his chest-puffing bluster, was obviously a smart guy, an articulate guy, and, though I never got to know him well, a funny guy. Steve could be funny, too, more of a reactive comedian than a proactive one, but a comedian nonetheless, and despite the fact that many Hostages continued to hate the Rude Boys, like Japanese soldiers hiding out on an island long after the war had ended, I would grow to call him my friend. In the end the ambitions of both Moons and Dobyns did not prove delusional or unfounded. They both have claim to the mythical title of the greatest player of all time. While these things are always subjective, it would be hard to leave either off the all-time starting seven.

A classic Frisbee argument with, from left to right, Nick Donahue, Dobyns, Moons, Pat King, and Andy Borinstein

But if 1983 was not the Hostages' year, then it was not quite yet the age of Dobyns and Moons, either. Three out of the next four years Nationals would be won by Midwestern teams, the only stretch in Ultimate history when the heartland ruled, with the daring throwers of Windy City winning twice, in '83 and '86, and the athletic St. Louis Tunas, the team that had made the finals against the Rude Boys, winning in '84. The Rude Boys, strangely sated by their one National Championship and World Championship, never even made the semifinals again and seemed ready to get on with their lives. Which of course would not do in Steve Mooney's world.

As for Kaboom!, after beating us at Regionals they fell one game short of the semifinals in their first appearance at Nationals. That game was arguably the single ugliest in the history of Ultimate. By halftime the fierce arguments between the New York team and the Dallas Sky Pilots were already the stuff of legend. And then it turned truly ugly.

When the Hostages went to man-to-man coverage against New York, I had always covered Gordon Christmas, who I knew then only as Gordo. Gordo was an athletic black man, about my height, maybe a little shorter, who was used primarily as a goal catcher by New York. The history of African-American Ultimate players was not a deep one at that point, the highlights being the sublime Harvey Edwards, a former hoops player, on the West Coast, and an all-black team, the MOB, from Waterbury, Connecticut, led by a fine all-round player named Jerome Stallings. When New York played Boston in those days Gordo was generally the only black guy on the field. This turned out to also be true when New York played Dallas.

Neither team had ever made it to the semis of Nationals and both teams desperately wanted to get there. Add to this the fact that they were making their own calls and you had a yelling match just this side of a fistfight. "The ugliness started long before the racism," said Pat King.

But the moment of the game that would long be remembered, the one that would live in Ultimate infamy, was after yet another screaming match had crossed the line into a shoving match. Kenny Dobyns, in the unlikely role of peacemaker, suggested to a Dallas player that they both call a time-out that would be charged to neither team, a chance for a cooling-off period.

The Dallas player said no, and then gestured to Gordo.

"You want to get this game under control?" he yelled at Dobyns. "I'll tell you how to get this game under control: get that fuckin' nigger off the field."

It is important to point out that this is a disputed point and that there are those who say that the Sky Pilots have been damned for all time by something that didn't happen. There are also those there who have suggested that these words were yelled by a drunken spectator, but Dobyns insisted that they were said directly to him by a player.

And there it was. Suddenly the Spirit of the Game was no-where to be found. They were a long, long way from TK's Athens.

No one remembers the score of that long-ago game, but every-one remembers the comment. If the Spirit of the Game was alive, it was on life support. Barely hanging on.

Dallas went on to win the game but, happily, they were trounced the next day in the semifinals. Two years later, at Nationals in 1985, Gordo caught the winning goal for New York that elimi-nated the Dallas Sky Pilots from the tournament. As a rule, I don't believe in spiking the disk, but in this case I hope he spiked it.

Only one northeastern team reached the finals of Nationals that fall, and that was the Boston women's team, the Spin-sters, which was made up of many of the same players who had won Nationals with BLU two years before. If Dobyns and Moons would be staples at Nationals over the next decade, so would the best player on the Spinsters. Heather Morris, who I had gotten to know a little on our summer league team, was one of the strongest athletes to play the sport during those early years, man or women. A varsity athlete in three sports at Tufts, she had fallen in love with the Frisbee's flight back in high school where she played, despite her already busy athletic schedule, on the Philadelphia Frisbee Club. She kept this up at Tufts, too, playing with the men's team despite the fact that her field hockey coach often complained when she came back from weekend Ultimate tourna-ments bruised and exhausted.

"You need to choose which sport you care about most," the coach said.

"Okay, I choose Ultimate," said Heather.

"Wrong choice," said the coach.

She kept doing everything at once but was pulled more and more into the world of Frisbee.

"I played the game because I loved the flight of the disc," she later said. "But I also loved the boys."

The boys in turn loved her and during that era a good half of the Northeastern men had crushes on her. Though on second thought that may be too modest a number—maybe closer to two thirds were in her thrall. For her part she reciprocated in a few cases, dating Hostage and Rude Boy alike. If Ultimate were a fantasy world, the position of King, post-TK, was a contested one. Not so Queen.

On the field Heather shared some traits with the Hostages' Gus. They both played with animal grace and had a tendency to make bold throws. Of course this was thirty years ago, a different world, and we would have never said anything like "a tendency to make bold throws." We, and by *we* I mean both men and women Ultimate players, would have used the word *ballsy*. It's understandable that this word has been expunged from proper discourse, given its equating of daring with male genitalia. But it would be wrong to censure it here since it was a word we used all the time, and a word that was, in our world, both oddly gender neutral and a great, perhaps the greatest, compliment. As in "that was a ballsy throw" or "Windy City is a ballsy team."

It was a word frequently applied to Heather. She was generally acknowledged to be not just one of the best but one of the most daring players in women's Ultimate. She had thrown the winning goal at the very first women's National Championship. She had a sense of drama, a sense of bold athleticism, and a sense of fun, even in potentially nerve-racking situations.

While Heather would win many more championships, she, like Gus, never took the game too, too seriously. She liked to party, though only, unlike Gus and me, after her last game. For Heather

Heather Morris

Morris this usually meant the last game of the tournament, and in all the years she went to Nationals she never did *not* make it to the finals, winning five in the end.

In 1983 her Spinsters team lost to a gritty Michigan team called the Fisheads in the championship game. The Fisheads were one of the most dedicated early women's teams, and their motto was "We think of Ultimate. Nothing else." (Their pregame ritual, while not as elaborate as Glassboro State's, did involve the fish-pole, a long stick with actual fish heads attached to it.) On a blustery day in the finals all the Spinsters had to do on the last point was stop the Fisheads from scoring upwind and Nationals would be theirs. But the Fisheads, led by Kelly Green, another claimant for best early women's player, and by Tree Vandenburg and Julia Griffin, worked the disc into the face of the wind and came away with a 12–11 victory.

Heather went over to shake the winners' hands and then had a beer with them. One drink led to another and soon she was out partying with the Fisheads, celebrating a victory in the bars and streets of New Orleans with the team that had just beaten hers. This would not sit well with Suzanne Fields and some other members of the Spinsters, but to Heather it seemed natural. She had played enough *serious* sports with their stupid rules and proprieties, and one of the main things that had drawn her to Ultimate was that it was different. So they had lost in the finals. Why not have some fun?

Heather's decision to celebrate late into the night with the Fisheads would have a couple of consequences. First, it would begin a kind of split between the Boston women, a split that would culminate five years later when two Boston women's teams, Lady Godiva and Smithereens, met in the finals, with Heather's Lady Godiva team prevailing over Suzanne's Smithereens. And, more personally, it would leave Heather with a chip in her tooth that she still has today.

"I'm not exactly sure how I got it," she said. "It was a blurry night. But I was told I fell straight forward onto the sidewalk and didn't put my hands out to stop the fall."

Clearly it wasn't just the Ultimate men who excelled at idiocy.

If this all seemed like it was happening thousands of miles away from me, it's because it was. In those pre-Internet days I sometimes wouldn't find out what had happened at Nationals until weeks after the fact, either through reading the UPA newsletter or through stories told by friends. Later I would nod when I read the following sentence in James Salter's *Solo Faces* about a fabled mountain climber who disdained written accounts of his climbs: "The true form of legend, he believed, was spoken."

Nationals had been held in New Orleans, which was far enough from Boston to begin with. But I, living on Cape Cod, had fewer reasons than ever to drive the hour and a half to Boston. During my career I would have some painful losses but still nothing compares to that first defeat with the Hostages. The megalomania of fall came crashing down into a winter where I came as close to madness as I hope I ever will. Doubt began chewing into my brief, early certainty about what I'd chosen to do with my life, hollowing out my commitment to Ultimate. Why was I wasting my time playing this stupid sport? It was just too painful—the thought of committing again only to potentially be burned, of rising that high only to be slammed so low.

I also felt a lot of shame. By going for it so blatantly, by wanting to win so much, I had exposed myself, I believed, and now I was embarrassed by it. Sometimes, going about my daily life that winter, I would suddenly remember a bad play and curse out loud to myself like a Tourette's sufferer. This would continue throughout my career to some extent, the willingness to be onstage, to throw myself out there followed by a kind of cringing of shame about that same tendency. It also showed itself in my habit of apologizing profusely after my nights of drinking, even when I had done little wrong.

I was not alone in my misery of course. It is a sad fact that in a sport like ours the year ends with all but one team despairing about what might have been. Though I would never again suffer quite as dramatic a depression as that one, any year that doesn't end with a win has a little of that to it. All the training you have been doing is suddenly purposeless. All your teammates are gone until the spring. You have nothing but time, time to think of what you might have done or how you could have played better, and of course if you had any bad plays in the deciding games, they are scorched into your brain, where they are relived, again and again, during the off-season.

It was during this same off-season that Ken Dobyns had a conversation with his brother Brian, who had played alongside Ken on the Kaboom! team that had lost to Dallas at Nationals.

"We're making a mistake setting our sights just on winning Nationals," Ken remembered his brother saying. "Because only one team wins and everybody else goes home disappointed. Why would we do that to ourselves?"

Kenny had just looked at him, mystified. Then he had said, "Because I want to be *that one team*. I'm not worried about all the teams that aren't that team. I'm going to be that team."

It was a philosophical split. During the ugly Dallas game Brian grew disillusioned with the pushing and shoving and, finally, with the racial slur. This wasn't the sport that Brian Dobyns had fallen in love with back at Hampshire College and he simply walked off the field, refusing to return. Brian's was a moral move; he was a conscientious objector. But that was not how his younger brother saw it at the time.

"I thought he quit on us," Ken said. "He said, 'This isn't the game I want to play.' And I said, 'This is the game we are playing.'"

After that the brothers never played together on a competitive team. For a long time they didn't speak. The next year Brian played for the Heifers, not Kaboom!, and the brothers covered each other.

"At one point he caught a disc with me laying out on his back," Ken remembered. "He got up and hit me on the face with the disc. We never covered each other again."

His brother would become one name on a long list of people whom Ken would leave behind as he pursued his dream. People who got sick of practice or showed in other ways that they weren't among the truly committed. There were certain points when people dropped out or were kicked off, when you saw who was committed to greatness and who wasn't.

M eanwhile, in the cold of that unwinterized Cape Cod house I finally began to work on my great novel. It was a clunky thing, a stilted book where the characters acted unnaturally, sometimes even quoting Thoreau to each other. The best parts of the book were those that described the natural world, the trees and beach and ocean that were becoming fused with my inner life. Overall, however, the book suffered from too much ambition, not enough good sense, and it wouldn't be a stretch to say the same about the young author. The only time I ever started to sound like myself on the page was when I was scribbling sentences in my journal while roaming around the beach or bog on mushrooms, which I did twice that winter, and which did nothing to help my overall mental stability. Sunsets started to melt into the ocean and the post oak by the side of the house throbbed. It was a kind of darker version of the way the world had swirled around me the previous fall. That had been Van Gogh at Arles, lots of yellow and sunflowers aplenty. Now I was edging closer to a sky full of crows, and, I worried, to the madhouse.

To add to my overall anxiety, "The Trickle Down Theory" wasn't selling and neither was the second poster I had drawn, "Ronald Reagan: A Physical Examination." As it turned out I actually would finish a complete book that year, though not my novel. In desperation, I drew up something called *Ron and Nancy's Workout Book*, a gag book in which the president and his wife described their workout routines, a parody of Jane Fonda's then-popular books. I floated balloons above Reagan's head and filled them with bits of habitual vocabulary. "Darn it, Mommy, I'm just about fed up with these naysayers and pencil pushers." "Shucks," I made him say, and "dandy," and "doubting Thomas," and, of course—giving his head a charming little bob—"We-ell." Dave Rotman, armed with the book, headed down to New York to try to sell it to agents and editors. In many ways his trip paralleled the Hostages' fall season. There was some real interest, a couple of strong bites, which got us excited, but in the end it was rejected. Which meant not just more depression but that we were running out of money. My long runs had been replaced by long walks on the winter beach, during which I started to question the course of my life. Maybe the fantasy of being an Ultimate player, not to mention the fantasy of becoming a writer, was over. To be honest, I had no idea what I was going to do next.

It wasn't until February, deep in that depressed winter, that the girl called.

Woman, not *girl*, as she would soon teach me.

There is really no need, and no reader could possibly want, for this story to turn even more Oedipal, but I have to say something about the girl-woman before I say anything else. She was an Ultimate player, of course she was, a World Champion, in fact, the same woman I had noticed, and fantasized about, over the previous year or so and the same one who'd played on my summer league team. But Stephanie Kirsch was also something else, or had been recently, and that was David Barkan's girlfriend. It wasn't exactly as if I joined the Hostages and stole the captain's girlfriend, since the two had already broken up. But it wasn't exactly *unlike* that either.

Stephanie called me in early February and on Valentine's Day of 1984 I drove my AMC Spirit up from Cape Cod to her apartment in Allston. Nervous and distracted, I managed to get lost on the way. When I pulled over to ask for directions I saw that a carpet store was having a grand opening and I stopped in to have a couple glasses of champagne to calm myself. Stephanie had called me up out of the blue, or so I thought at first, though that was not exactly right. I would learn that night that she had really called me up because I had apparently professed my ardor for her during a party after our big loss back in the fall, a drunken profession that I didn't remember making. At that same party I'd charged at a small group of Rude Boys only to be fended off by Finlay Waugh, who hit me in the head with a mop. I'd also told her I would give her a call, but never had, so she finally called me. Before she did, she checked in with Hones, who was also her friend, to see if I had feelings for her.

"If you say frog, he'll leap" is what Hones told her.

After we met at her house, I drove us over to the loud dance club she directed me to. We ordered drinks and started to talk.

"You're Jewish, too?"

These were my first significant words to the woman I would spend the next seven years with.

She nodded and asked me if I was, a question I'd gotten often enough due to my name. I told her I wasn't.

"But my whole world is Jewish," I said adamantly. "My best friend who I live on Cape Cod with is. My entire grade school was. My high school girlfriend and the first woman I had sex with. And my roommates, and most of the contemporary writers I read."

The last lines sound a little stilted and may have not been exactly what I said (though I often enough sounded stilted back then), but one thing I know I did say, because she would repeat it when she retold the story of our first date in years to come, was that my chief literary hero was Jewish, too, and that I'd been "weaned on Philip Roth."

Steph just laughed at me. As she should have.

But the dam had burst. Suddenly it was nothing like a first date. We talked about books we loved and I learned that she was a real reader. Emboldened by the liquor and her charming smile and beautiful eyes, not to mention her large breasts, I began to wax poetic about the great book I was destined to write. She in turn told me about her dream of one day becoming a doctor.

Literature and careerism were apparently aphrodisiacal. The next thing I knew we were slow dancing out on the floor, and I, always the subtle one, was reaching down to cup her long-coveted ass in my hands. After that we put on such a strenuous show of making out on the dance floor that the management asked us to leave. We thought the guy who came over to break us up was joking at first but he wasn't. On our first date we were kicked out of a club.

We went back to her house and I stayed over, waking up the next morning on her futon in her octagonal Allston apartment, light shining in through the tall windows. She emerged from below her red comforter looking beautiful: rich brown eyes, short shaved fuzz of hair, sleepy smile.

Over the next seven years we would repulse our friends, particularly the Hostages, with our baby talk. We were that type; we gushed in public. We had names for each other. Mostly cutesy names that bugged our friends when we said them out loud, but one serious one that we reserved for each other's ears. Within about a week we were calling each other our "forever loves."

It would turn out that in our case there would be a time limit on forever. But that first morning, the morning that would lead to approximately 2,556 more, Steph got up and walked across the room naked and put on a Joan Armatrading album. She walked back across the room, not shy but proud. I remember her nipples

looked extremely long and dark. "Like the necks of steamer clams,"
I scribbled in my journal later that day.

But it was her lips, not her nipples, that I first romanticized.
Over the next weeks, beside the drawings I made of her in my
journal, I wrote ridiculous tributes to those lips. "Beautiful and
full, pink and torn," I wrote. "How could anything be so big and
meaty? I'd go broke if I had to pay for them by the pound at a deli."
Even later in our relationship, when the fights had begun and
things weren't quite so romantic, I'd find myself occasionally wish-
ing that those lips were sucking on some part of me, my ear perhaps. Cracked, chapped, perfect, the part of her I desired first.

For the first time in my life I was falling head over heels in love.
Within a week I told her so, though when I did it was in the form of
a mild disguise, by repeating the one Hebrew sentence I knew (the
same one she'd taught me earlier in the day): *"Ani Ohev Otach."* I
was immediately enthralled by what I considered her "exotic" back-
ground, the fact that she had spent much of her early life in Israel.

I drove back down to Cape Cod, but was back up again a day
later. I still remember things from those weeks: her red comforter,
that futon on the floor (all new for me), more Joan Armatrading
on the creaky old record player, the feminist books that crammed
the shelves: *Man Made Language, Fat Is a Feminist Issue, Gyn/Ecol-
ogy, Ain't I a Woman?* We made love again and again, in the usual
rabid manner of young lovers, and afterward I would stare into her
eyes, studying the small green flecks that splintered outward from
the rich brown. We took long walks through Boston and Brookline, bought a dozen bagels at Kupel's and devoured them, every
one, while sitting on the lawn in front of the temple. I couldn't
help romanticizing Steph's appetite. I loved the fact that she was a
strong woman who could break your standard twig-thin model in
half. She ate as if ravenous after sex, ate like a man, almost as

much as I did. At that point I had no inkling that the same appetite would soon turn against me.

During an interview for a TV show called *Amazing Games*, Ken Dobyns described a New York cheer that listed the team's life priorities in order: "Ultimate. Family. Job. God. Girlfriend." Then he amended the list, moving "Girlfriend" up to second place, a correction that didn't placate the woman he lived with, who moved out soon after seeing the interview.

This list of priorities was no joke, or at least it wasn't for Kenny. He had made a decision early on that no woman he was seeing would be more important than Ultimate. Once, when he was leaving for a weekend tournament, his then girlfriend said, "I can't believe you'd rather go to an Ultimate tournament than stay home with me," and he replied, "I'd rather go to an Ultimate *practice* than stay home with you."

"I never really let anyone I was seeing get bigger than the game," he said. "And I was amazed by the people who had important jobs and were married and raising kids—how did they do it?"

"Athletics allows a ballplayer to postpone his adulthood," wrote Jim Bouton, the author of *Ball Four*. During the Rude Boys' run to Nationals Steve Mooney had scribbled this line down in the scrapbook he kept. It was a truth any Ultimate player knew. Most of us didn't lay out our priorities as dramatically as Kenny Dobyns, but everyone knew that as long as winning Nationals was the goal, other things like getting a good job or getting married were not the real priority. A pro athlete might postpone his or her real life to some extent, but since a pro was being paid it wasn't as much of a postponement, at least in the way it was for us. We were not lucky in that way: our passion was not our job.

To be a top amateur can require a greater stalling of real life, though in particular sports some prestige and respect are given to amateurs. Ultimate players are not afforded that luxury. If you told someone that you "played Frisbee seriously," they would understandably regard the phrase as oxymoronic. Once when I was in a doctor's office, the nurse asked how I hurt my shoulder and when I told her, she simply burst out in laughter. This sort of thing happened all the time. "Ultimate Frisbee," you told people. Then laughter and a pause as they waited for the real answer. Part of the problem, of course, was that it really was a terrible name. You almost couldn't have come up with worse. An adjective followed by a silly-sounding word. Like Fabulous Foosball.

You might think this would lead the players themselves to take the game lightly, but it didn't, not at all. Players could be just as nervous before a game at Nationals as an Olympian before a big event. Whether the world had invested or not, they had.

"This isn't a game out here," Kenny Dobyns would cajole his teammates in practice. "This is your life."

He believed it. You weren't about to tell *that guy* that Ultimate was not a serious pursuit.

That was the whole point with Kenny. He was *all in*. I might not have ever liked the man very much, but I loved his commitment. He played the game consistently the way I only played it occasionally and at my best, with a kind of joyous rage. I would come to admire the way he locked in on discs and ran them down. It seemed a perfect metaphor for what some of us were doing with our lives, focusing in on our goals just like we focused in on and ran down spinning discs. And the goal he was now focused on and running down was crystal clear: winning Nationals.

Maybe I was delusional during those years. Or maybe I wasn't delusional enough. Maybe one measure of a person, or at least of their animal vitality, their human flame, is their ability to get obsessed. In a way Ultimate stripped obsession bare, made it its own reward more pure, since it offered none of the traditional rewards of cash or larger fame. Maybe the whole point of obsession is to fill life's emptiness, giving it purpose. Whatever the case, I have seen yellow labs less obsessed with chasing down Frisbees than Kenny Dobyns. In fact, joking aside, a lab is a fine example of letting one thing—the ball, the stick, and, yes, the Frisbee—fill your mind. Though "letting" is not the right word in a lab's case. It is instinctive. Ditto Kenny.

I was not as committed or as tough-minded. One hard loss and I was already backing away from my full commitment to Ultimate. I was learning some lessons and I was learning them fast. It isn't easy to be an amateur; it isn't easy to commit to working at something that the world doesn't give a shit about. And of course it isn't easy to care so much and then *lose*. I could feel myself retreating.

This is something I would come to admire about Ken Dobyns— not just his prowess on the field, which was considerable. No, it was his willingness to commit fully despite hard losses, and despite the world's general mockery of the thing he had dedicated his life to. "Whoso would be a man, must be a nonconformist," wrote Emerson. Say what you want about Dobyns—he was a fanatic, of course, and hardly a healthy, balanced individual—but in the end he would fulfill Emerson's definition of a man. He was going to stick to his crazy goal no matter what the world thought.

About a month and a half after Steph and I got together, I moved into her Allston apartment. Her roommates, who were Ultimate players too, were understandably dubious. Even before I moved up they had been a reluctant audience, courtesy of

Ken Dobyns goes up and gets a disc.

the thin walls, to our frequent, explosive fights, and then, as a bonus, they got to listen in on our loud makeup sex. But we made earnest vows about how we would no longer fight (no vows about the other thing of course), and Steph even brought up a practical benefit: they needed the money and if I paid a quarter of the rent, it would significantly reduce each of their payments by a third.

Money was quickly becoming more than a minor issue for both of us. Steph would gradually move from working in daycare to taking positions in medical labs in Brookline, as she edged toward her deeper ambitions. My path was less direct. Dave had made one last trip to New York to try and sell *Ron and Nancy's Workout Book*, but that had failed and, worse, the payments from our fall loan were coming due beginning in May. My father made it very clear that co-signing that loan was the last help he was going to give me.

I was desperate for anything and when my Hostage teammate Roger Gallagher suggested I come work for his carpentry crew as an apprentice carpenter, I jumped at it. Though I could barely pound a nail or screw a screw when I started, and though I really didn't improve that much, I would work as a carpenter in Boston and on Cape Cod for the next couple of years. I disliked my job but had no prospects for another. I was poor, and what little writing I did dribbled out in a weak stream. In his essay "The Crack-Up," F. Scott Fitzgerald wrote of his own twenties: "Life was something you dominated if you were any good. Life yielded easily to intelligence and effort, or to what could properly be mustered of both." My experience was the opposite. Life was easily dominating me. Though it is ugly to say it directly, I was, by my own standards at least, a failure. I knew no other writers and I didn't yet understand that I was undergoing an apprenticeship, not just as a carpenter but as a writer, nor did I know that writing apprenticeships can last many years.

As usual it was left to Ultimate to provide what writing couldn't. Working at a job I wasn't good at and trying to write alone at the little red desk in the corner of Steph's apartment, I felt, quite frankly, glory starved. Glory, as my old teacher Walter Jackson Bate had said, is the attempt to "fill the minds of others," and so doesn't exist without an audience. I wanted to be known to everyone but, outside of Ultimate, I was known to no one. No one cheered me on while I sat scribbling at that stupid little desk or smashing Sheetrock with a sledgehammer.

Ultimate gave me the juice I needed. Playing Ultimate at a high level is a little like having a secret identity allowing Ultimate players to strip off civies, don cleats and uniforms/costumes, and become someone else. I have been stressing that my life was in shambles after college but I don't want to overplay that card. There was much that was good, too. I was working year round to stay in top shape and loved nothing more than ripping around a field in my cleats. My best weapon was my forehand, which I could throw end zone to end zone. But my favorite, if not most trusty, throw was my overhead. The overhead was where the disc was thrown upside down, like a spear, before, hopefully, turning back over and dropping into a receiver's hands. When my overhead was cocked I, like my old teammate Nathan, had a notion.

If my throws could be erratic, there were things I could trust. Jumping and catching a disc was something I knew I did well, and no one could tell me otherwise. I always felt that anything up in the air was mine. Felt that I could go up and get it and do so in the most *direct* way possible (which may have occasionally involved collisions with other players). A direct line from what I wanted to what I got, so unlike the other areas in my life. I had read my transcendentalists in college and what was this if not transcendent? The moment of leaving the ground—leaving the earth behind! The unthinking moment. Of uncertainty, of risk and reward.

The best I felt during those early years was when I was deep in the Hostage zone. As the deep, I played a kind of centerfield position, hanging back and guarding against the other team's attempts to huck. For once in my young life, I was in command, standing back there, daring the other team to throw, even baiting them to throw. Certainly there were taller players and better jumpers, but I defended my turf with rapacity. It was my responsibility after all. Other people—other *Hostages*—were depending on me.

Since I was behind everyone else on defense, my position also served as a kind of command center where I could call out and tell other Hostages where to go. I loved the feeling of mastery, of seeing the whole field and moving my teammates around like chess pieces. The deep in the zone is very much an individual position— and that suited me—but just as important as being an individual was the feeling that I was *part* of something. When we were playing really well it was as if we were all part of a vast network or nervous system, connected not just verbally but synaptically. I could yell to Neal to dive right and suddenly he had a block, or Jimmy, at side middle, could warn me that someone was running deep on my off side. At our best we were like one connected whole, a single being.

In retrospect, I can't help but feel that our loss at Regionals tore our heart out, and the Hostages would never again make it to Nationals. But we still had our moments. In our own little world, for instance, the annual Purchase Cup once qualified as a pretty big Ultimate tournament, though to me the only tourney that really mattered was Regionals, since it was the gateway to Nationals. Maybe that was part of the reason I was so loose on that fall day in Purchase, New York, in 1984, that and the fact that we were playing with our usual ridiculously small numbers, nine or ten people for that tournament, I think. In contrast, most of the teams were getting larger in those days, some with as many as twenty players so they could sub and stay fresh. But we liked our team small, or at least told ourselves we did, since we were a tight brotherhood, and that way everyone got to play a lot. Too much that day, as I recall. After we won the semifinals, we were exhausted and it didn't seem like we would have much of a chance against Static, a much larger and deeper team from Washington, D.C. Given that, we did what Hostages usually did in those situations. We started drinking.

It may seem odd to swill beer before spending two or three hours running, but it came naturally to me at the time. I'd had about three Bud tallboys before the game even started, and nursed another couple along the sideline during the game for hydration. It is true that there are times when this can be a recipe for disaster, but this was not one of those times. In fact, this was one of those rare occasions when the combination of alcohol and sunshine and sweat and the glory of being in great shape combined in a perfect primal way. *First be a good animal?* We were all good animals that day. Our passes were linked as our arms had been, and though some of us barely came out of the game to rest, we seemed strangely able to keep up with the fresher players from the other team.

These days I suspect every competitive Ultimate game is filmed on someone's phone, but the tape of the finals of the Purchase Cup is the only full film of a Hostage game. As such, the boxy videotape was a coveted item back in our twenties and was passed among us and watched repeatedly. We look good on the film, really good if not quite as good as I see us in memory. But when the tape first arrived a few months after the game, and we watched it as a team, drinking beer and razzing each other, there was one thing missing. I spent the early part of the film secretly waiting for one long pass from Tommy Conlon to me—one that I had run down and pulled in a second before it hit the ground—only to find that it had not been filmed. Why? Maybe the cameraman had taken a break to smoke a joint. Maybe the play had never really existed anywhere but in my imagination. But if I can be calmly philosophical about the missing film now, I wasn't at the time. I have typed a lot of embarrassing sentences as I tell my Ultimate story but none more than this one: when the film ended I stormed out of the room in tears, angry and devastated by the omission of my best play.

I have watched the tape in calmer moods since and what is clear to the adult me is how well we *all* played. Even now watching the tape I can get a little nervous about the outcome but it always ends the same way: with Billy Mac catching the last goal and throwing the disc in the air and us winning by one. Soon there we are shaking hands with the Washington team, and then we retreat to our sideline to slap each other on the backs and crack beers. The last thing the camera shows is the tournament director holding up the Cup we have won and calling for us. But we don't respond, at least not immediately. We are happy just being with one another.

Gradually we did walk across the field to where the Cup was presented to us. We filled the trophy with beer and swilled from it and lingered at the field until dark. It was a truly joyous evening, as happy as any I remember. It didn't hurt that my old Harvard teammates had been watching and were now coming up and congratulating me. But it was only the Hostages that mattered in the end, and we sang each other's praises. My ride home was with my teammate Bobby Harding and we stayed at the field until it grew dark. We were the last to leave.

To listen to a bunch of drunken Ultimate players after a tournament they have won is like listening to a boasting session during a gathering of ancient Yoruba kings. But the best case is if you have a teammate to do your boasting for you—"Remember that great play you made?"—and you in turn recall his outstanding plays. True to form, Bobby and I would spend the whole ride home telling each other how great we were.

By almost any objective standard my life was in shambles. I had no real career, my writing life hadn't begun, I was in debt, and I worked at a relatively menial job, long hours for poor pay. And yet I felt great. At least here, on the Frisbee field, I was happy. Here I could make things happen. Here life really was something you dominated if you were any good.

Winning the Purchase Cup was nice, but cracks had begun to show in the Hostage foundation. In some ways we never really recovered from the big loss at the '83 Regionals. We would actually win a couple more tournaments, but were never again a real threat to get to Nationals. We'd always been jokers, sardonically mocking our own sport, but over the next year we became pure clowns, pretending not to care. We drank more at tournaments and though we still won some big games we were never the same cocky bunch again.

But we were still very much a team. We rented a Winnebago and drove down together to a tournament in Washington, insulting each other all the way in our usual junior high school manner. We began playing games that had nothing to do with a Frisbee, one with the simple name "paper ball" in which we threw a crumpled-up piece of paper, the official size being one 8½-by-11-inch sheet, into a pot or basket and then all switched seats for the next shot in the manner of the basketball game Around-the-World, continuing like this, and keeping track of how many we made or missed, until we had completed a circle. Another game was Topics, in which we threw out a broad topic like "States" or "Hit Songs" and went around in a circle until someone choked, freezing and unable to come up with an answer. (As the game continued the topics would become more esoteric like "Things that bum Hones out" or "Topics we've used before.") It was around then that we all started calling each other "Dude," something that began with mocking the UMass team's tendency to do the same, but then quickly hardened into habit. Soon barely a sentence was spoken without a "dude" appended. As in "Nice catch, dude" or "Dude, grab me a beer."

This was also around the time of the tournament where we spent the whole day singing bad '70s songs (think "Delta Dawn," "The Night Chicago Died," and the song that would become my particular favorite and party standby, "Brandy"). Oh, and we also invented the Frisbee alley-oop, which looked almost exactly like a hand-off (it wasn't) and drove our opponents crazy. One of us would line up in a sort of fullback position and take the near

The Hostages hang out between games.

hand-off over the middle, toppling into the end zone. "That's illegal," they would yell. "You can't hand off the Frisbee." But then we would show them that we actually let go of the disc a millisecond before the fullback-like receiver covered it up, which, we claimed, made it legal. We loved riling up those who took the sport too seriously. Once we forfeited a game in the finals of a tournament to Kaboom! because we wanted to watch a Celtic playoff game at a nearby bar, and Kenny Dobyns went apoplectic. "You can't do that!" he yelled, veins throbbing in his neck. But we could do it, and we did.

The next fall in 1984 we beat the Rude Boys at sectionals and went into Regionals seeded first again but then immediately fell on our face, losing to two teams we should have beaten. I have to think that those losses grew out of fear of once again playing (and failing) in the big game on the big stage, which really meant fear of the pain of losing. After that, most of the early Hostages began considering retiring, content to look back on the 1981 and 1982 seasons as the peak of their athletic lives. The Rude Boys managed to fight their way through to Nationals, though their play there was uninspired, not even making the semis, and it looked like they were done, too. The great burning Hostage–Rude Boy moment was over.

The failure of Kaboom! that season was even more dramatic. They would lose not just the chance to go to Nationals but their co-captain and sparkplug. This was the year Kenny Dobyns ruptured his kidney while diving for a block on defense. He kept playing, despite coughing up blood, until someone convinced him to go to the hospital. Dobyns could easily have died and for most people, of course, that would have been it: no more Frisbee, thanks, it's important and all but no sense risking my life. As should be obvious by now, Kenny Dobyns was not most people. After two weeks in the hospital he was advised to spend three more months in bed, but he declined and accompanied Kaboom! to Regionals. He would soon be playing again, bad kidney or not, though for the next year he would wear a flak jacket when he played.

His father, for one, was unimpressed with his heroics. Lloyd Dobyns—the smart, ambitious NBC reporter who had been the cohost, along with Linda Ellerbee, of one of the first late-night news shows, NBC News Overnight—had a face scarred from childhood acne and a nose broken from too much time in the boxing ring at military school. He would have no chance of being a news anchor today, and it was a wonder they let him on the air back then, but he made up for his superficial detriments with a profound asset. He could write and rewrite better than anyone else in the newsroom. A distant father, according to Kenny, more a provider than a presence, he spent countless hours at his desk revising not just the nightly news reports but also the scripts for the documentaries he was then making for the network.

His interest in his son's one great passion, Ultimate Frisbee, was nil. He had gone out to see his son play a grand total of one time, though to his credit he bought a case of Pabst Blue Ribbon for the team at that early-season tournament in Purchase, New York. He was not there on the fateful day when Kenny dove and ruptured his kidney, but he did visit him in the hospital. Kenny remembers that during those first days in the hospital it looked like he might lose the kidney, which for him meant the worst of all possible fates: no more Ultimate. Lloyd Dobyns was horrified, too, by the prospect, not of the end of his son's sports career but of his life. When the kidney was saved, he said to his son: "So that's it with the Frisbee stuff, you're done."

Ken looked at him and just said, "No."

His father considered this.

"I will never visit you in the hospital again," he said.

He didn't add "—for Ultimate" but it was implied. A year later Kenny would mangle his knee and have to undergo a massive reconstruction. During the operation at Lenox Hill Hospital his leg became infected and he had to stay in the hospital an extra week, a period of time that included his birthday. Lloyd Dobyns proved true to his word and stayed away. Over the next decade, as his son was winning championship after championship, Lloyd never once went out to watch or mentioned the words "Ultimate" or "Frisbee."

It was another hard winter. With Ultimate gone until spring, Steph and I fought more. We had little money and found plenty to argue about. Our different religions, a division that we had seemed breezily above at first, began to loom larger. She didn't dare tell her Israeli grandmother about the existence of a gentile boyfriend.

As she began to think about what she really wanted to do with her life, Steph's interest in Ultimate began to wane. She had been swept up in Ultimate culture, had even won a World Championship, but really wasn't as passionate about the sport as many of the best players. If I dreamed of winning Nationals, she dreamed of moving to Europe, or even back to Israel. Her other dream was of becoming a doctor, which would be hard without an undergraduate degree. Uncertain about what to do next or even where to live, she would soon take her first concrete step toward the medical field: going back to get her undergrad nursing degree at Northeastern.

All this swirling uncertainty was building and that spring it burst. In April Hones and I drove down to another tournament in Purchase, New York, in my AMC Spirit. About a half hour into the drive I realized I'd forgotten my Barbarians.

"Fuck," I said, or something to that effect. "I forgot my cleats."

After apologizing to Hones, I drove home and walked back up the three floors to our small apartment.

I found Steph lying naked on our futon next to a naked man. I would learn that this was her Norwegian cellist "friend" who she had mentioned to me in passing. I knew he was spending the term at Berkeley, majoring in musical composition, and, as I now discovered, minoring in Steph. I had no idea how to respond. My only models for how to act in that situation came from macho songs and movies, but despite my occasional inclination toward the violent I had no interest in challenging this stranger to any sort of duel. Instead, saying nothing, I marched across the room, picked up my cleats, then turned on my heels and walked straight out of the bedroom, out of the apartment and down the stairwell. Before I reached the second landing Steph caught me. She was naked, her face a blazing red, tears coming up in hard, pulsing throbs.

At that point my head was already numbing over and I didn't

yet have recourse to anger, then the most potent of my emotions. It wasn't until later that the betrayal of trust would really register, my fury pouring forth. Meanwhile, I let Steph drag me out onto the small porch that belonged to our neighbors, while her man, the musician, still half dressed, made his way hastily down the stairs. There I sat on the neighbor's ratty old couch while Steph, still naked, curled around me, sitting in my lap with her arms around my neck. To me she looked helpless and pathetic, less like a woman than a newborn, red and crying and gripping on to me as if her life depended on it. Between sobs she tried to apologize. But the sobs were coming so hard she could barely speak, and strangely enough, I suddenly found myself worrying not about my own considerable troubles, but about *her*, frightened that the stress might set off one of the migraines that tortured her. I knew that I was supposed to be screaming with rage, but sensing that she needed me—*yes, this is true!*—I cradled her tight as we sat there on the neighbor's landing. She remained in my lap with her arms around me. Finally, between compulsive sobs, she was able to speak. Her words came in spasms.

"It means *nothing . . . nothing . . . nothing*, David, *nothing.* I can't explain it to you, but it means *nothing. . . .* The whole time I knew I was doing something terribly wrong. I know you can't believe me . . . but it made me think about how much I love you. . . . It was all so empty . . . so meaningless . . ."

I said nothing but held her tight. I think that I already wanted to believe what she told me. She curled like an S around my body. I dabbed a small tear from her cheek and patted the fuzz on her head, all the while feeling my own skull growing cold and small and dull.

7.

Defending Champs

The spring of 1985 marked the end of the Hostages. For most of my teammates, and for Hones most emphatically, it had come time to call it quits. He would put his cleats in the closet and vow to never take them out again.

But I wasn't done. I still had a quest to fulfill. I wanted to win the National Championship, something no Hostage had ever done. Soon after the Hostages disbanded in the spring of 1985, our old rivals, the Rude Boys, hung up their cleats as well. As expected, many of Steve Mooney's teammates were finished with the sport, off to careers and law school and families. Moons, meanwhile, was busy making a new team, gathering together the best remaining players in the Boston area.

I joined that team though at first I felt uneasy lining up next to Moons. After all, wasn't he just a big phony, like the Hostages had always said? Moons was clearly the authority figure on the team, and from the start we had a kind of father-son tension between us. I wanted the team to be called the Primadonnas, mocking the fact that we were a kind of handpicked all-star team, but Moons prevailed with Titanic. On Titanic everything was more structured and less relaxed than with the Hostages; for instance, some of my teammates frowned if I sipped a beer before or during a game. Rigidity replaced wildness, and, reacting to this, I dusted off my old role of rebellious son to Moons's strict father. It was a part I would come to perfect. For the next five years, when not fighting beside Moons in an effort to win Nationals, I would fight with him in my role as the team's resident adolescent. In keeping with Hostage tradition, I would excel at idiocy.

As it turned out it was that year, 1985, my first with Titanic, that Ultimate found itself getting something it had never gotten before: media attention. Suddenly you could hear the famous adenoidal voice of none other than Howard Cosell as he droned on about Ultimate at the end of an episode of *Wide World of Sports*.

"This is a sport no school ever dropped, no scandal ever tainted," he would tell the world, laying it on thick:

"Last weekend, in the shadow of the Washington Monument, over three hundred men and women came to compete in the National Championship of that sport. And yes that's a Frisbee they're tossing. But don't confuse this with the games you play on a summer day. This is known as Ultimate Frisbee. And it's played seven to a side and combines elements of football, soccer, and basketball. Unlike those sports, however, you'll find no referees. All players are honor bound to call their own fouls. And the ultimate reward for their time, money, and effort? Nothing. Nothing save the joy of competition. A refreshing reminder of what sport was meant to be and still, on rare occasions, can be. The ultimate winners? Well, they were all winners."

That year ESPN would also give a nod to Ultimate for the first time, though it would be another year until a young Chris Berman would say of the Frisbee, "It ranks right up there with the wheel for inventions in our time." Every mention of the game would contain some variation of Cosell's "Yes that's a *Frisbee* they're tossing!" as if nothing could be more absurd than the fact that a sport was played with a piece of plastic and not some sort of leathery ball. Usually the announcer threw in a demeaning reference to the beach or dogs or hippies. You couldn't miss the *Can you believe it?* tone, as in, *Can you believe this is really a sport?* Still, we couldn't complain. Attention was attention.

Cosell's wouldn't be the only famous voice that would be heard talking Frisbee in 1985. Another voice would chime in, this one equally distinct but notably more upper crust, with an arch almost-English accent that—as was thematically appropriate, it turned out—was a musical clash between Boston Brahmin and old New York.

"Like everyone else I thought Frisbee was just a game of catch played by two or more people at the park or on the beach," George Plimpton intoned nobly, staring directly into the camera as *Quest to Be Best* began. "But for several thousand athletes around the world Ultimate Frisbee is a demanding full-time sport of nonstop running, accurate throwing, and all out diving to catch that plastic disc."

He then held up an old Frisbie pie plate and, after giving a brief history of the Frisbee, launched into a summary of Ultimate that ended, "When played well, Ultimate is just that, the Ultimate sport, combining the passing and scoring of football, the cutting and guarding of basketball, and the nonstop field movement of soccer."

The film, narrated by Plimpton, would give the game more attention than it had ever gotten before. And, best of all from my point of view, that attention would focus on us.

Us in this case meant the rivalry between Kaboom! and Titanic, and, more specifically, not just the fight between New York and Boston, but the clash of two specific adversaries. "There are many talented players in the sport," Plimpton announced to the world, "but two of the most outstanding are New York City's Ken Dobyns and Boston's Steve Mooney." Of course! As so much of the meager attention would in those days, the film would revolve around Kenny and Steve, the short and the tall, the angry and the calm, the New York and the Boston. It annoyed the rest of us that it always came down to those two. Someone like Pat King had a particularly good case for grievance, since he was every bit as important to New York as Dobyns. But something about the Moons and Dobyns storyline was irresistible. Media people were no more able to resist then than I am writing now. In the first shot of Kenny—"Kenny's life is Ultimate Frisbee," George tells us—there's a bandage across his face and he glares at the camera, jaw jutting, like Churchill glowering from a rooftop during the Battle of Britain. This is when he stares into the camera and utters the immortal line: "What drives me is an insane hatred of losing. Especially to Boston." In our first close-up of Moons he winks at the camera, but later, wearing the famous sweater, looks almost prim and proper. It was a contrast made in television heaven. Good versus evil, or at least nice versus mean. The two men, separated not just by a foot in height but by an ocean of temperament.

The show followed New York and Boston's seasons and it is obvious that the producers' dream result would have been New York and Boston meeting in the finals. But that was not to be.

We both made it to Nationals, which meant I was going for the first time. Titanic had beaten Kaboom! at Regionals and we headed to Washington, D.C., as the top seed, though we would soon begin to fulfill the prophecy of our ominous name. I flew down on a plane with Jeremy Seeger, aka God, now all grown up and my teammate, and a few others, when weather forced us to circle the airport and finally land in Baltimore. By the time we got to our hotel it was four in the morning and we played groggily the next day, losing 19–18 to a bold Chicago team that featured several bold throwers and their great receiver, Joey Giampino, one of the few players who could sky Jeremy. We won our next game but the next day lost again, 19–17, to a Flying Circus team. We didn't even make the semifinals. Howard Cosell was wrong: we were not all winners.

Moons would later regret the interview he gave after our loss. In it he looks not just stunned but anesthetized. Shuttled off into a room and facing a camera, he has obviously had time to don the button-down oxford and blue sweater, but he has understandably not recovered from the loss. His sentences wander: "Hmmm, it's tough losing . . . part of the reason why I'm here is to win. It's not the only reason. . . . I have a lot of friends. . . . Not everybody can win. That's the beauty of Ultimate. The tournament isn't over. I'm not going home, I'm going to talk to friends, so I really look forward to that."

This was the sentence that would so enrage Dobyns when he watched the interview later. What Moons was doing was simply trying to keep the old good-great arête TK spirit alive, but Dobyns thought it appalling. To lose like that, to underachieve, and then to claim it was all okay.

"It's not win or go to the party," he would say later. "It's win or go home."

He would never forget that image of Steve in the sweater. That was exactly what he never wanted to be.

Kaboom!, meanwhile, held up their end of the bargain, making the producers happy. They had never done any damage during their two previous trips to Nationals and they had limped their way through the season, but suddenly, as Mr. Plimpton was only too happy to tell us, they started playing their best Frisbee when it mattered most. They won their pool and in the semifinals they faced the Chicago team that had beaten us.

"Early on the game was tied," George narrates, "but Windy City surged ahead to take a three-goal lead."

On the voiceover, Plimpton had not much earlier given the obligatory nod to the lack of refs, intoning, "This concept, known as the Spirit of the Game, is so sacred as to be written into the rules." But it didn't look particularly sacred as Chicago and New York players took turns screaming at each other.

At one point in the film Dobyns calls a time-out and scolds his team for being distracted by both the arguments on the field and the heckling from the fans, and, possibly, from the camera that is nudging its way into the huddle.

"The point is that we focus our energy on the field," Kenny exhorts his teammates. "What they do with their energy we don't give a shit about."

The point is simple. Don't buy the hype; we've got to win this game.

Sure enough, Kaboom! focuses in and surges ahead, going up by one and receiving the pull to win. But on the last goal the producers got their money's worth. The first pass goes to Pat King, who turns and throws to Dobyns. The pass is high and Kenny goes up and snags it. It is, he will say later, a catch he has made a thousand times before. But this time as he lands he hears a pop and his knee blows out. He goes to the ground screaming and writhing in pain.

Dobyns has torn his knee apart in three places, and will have to undergo major reconstruction, the operation that will lead to infection and the long hospital stay during which his dad will not visit him.

Later that afternoon will be the first time that a team from

New York will play in the finals of an Ultimate National Championship, but they will do so without their sparkplug and best player.
Predictably, they go down early to Flying Circus and it looks hope-
less. Kenny had been carried off on his shield the day before and
his knee cartilage is in tatters. But he can't stand to see the season
end this way and can't stand not to be part of the team's first
finals. Also, there are cameras out there.

It is perhaps on this day that the Dobyns legend truly begins.
Okay, maybe not since he had already come back to play after
nearly losing a kidney, but at least it can be said that it is on this
day that the Dobyns legend starts to get officially narrated. That
narration told the story of a new breed of Ultimate player—a long
way from TK and the golden hills of California—a win-at-all-costs
modern player but also one with an old-fashioned vision of glory.
Someone who, like Churchill or Teddy Roosevelt, and like the old
generals and sea captains, believed that life really came down to
either Death or Glory. Someone who had the ambition, smarts,
and lust for conquest of a Roman emperor.

Is it any surprise that this same someone was soon climbing off
his shield and trying to play despite having no cartilage left? Sure
enough, the camera shows him taking off his shirt and pulling on
and then lacing up his flak jacket. With one kidney not function-
ing he will die if he loses the other. So what? There is a chance for
victory. Next the camera shows him pulling on a large and awk-
ward knee brace, a bulky contraption that looks like something
from the 1940s.

This seems mere heroic gesture, but it's a gesture that helps
rally the team. It would be too perfect, too cliché, for the film's
purpose if Kenny led a dramatic comeback, yet sure enough that's
exactly what happens. The film shows him diving and making
blocks, despite the fact that, as George Plimpton reminds us, "he

was in great pain." It's no use, however. Kaboom! closes to 20–19, then Circus scores the next point to win by two. It's all over.

The final on-field image of Kenny is of him staring straight ahead, arms crossed, looking at no one and shaking no one's hand, disbelieving and seemingly enraged. Oblivious to everyone else around him. It is, by anyone else's standards, a preposterously heroic showing. For Kaboom! to make it to the finals would seem enough; to push himself off the bench with a torn-up ACL and have an impact on the game would seem more than enough. But it is not enough. He doesn't hold himself to anyone else's standards. Once again he has lost. Once again he faces a long off-season, an off-season of vowing to get better and training even harder, and this time he is facing major knee surgery and rehab. One thing is clear: he won't be putting on a sweater and telling anyone it is okay to lose.

The truth is that while the camera focused mostly on Kenny, it was Pat King who had almost lifted New York to victory, playing one of the best games of his life. King would grow used to Dobyns grabbing the headlines over the years. He was not just one of the game's best players but articulate, charming, smart, acerbic, a musician and writer of children's books who also worked for *Sesame Street* and Public Television. In any other sport, or on any other team, he would have been a feature article waiting to happen. But King knew that, playing with Kenny, he would always be on the edge of the spotlight, not at its center. Over the years Pat would sometimes roll his eyes at Kenny, but he also knew how much he benefited from playing with him. Much later, in a letter supporting Dobyns's nomination to the fledgling Ultimate Hall of Fame, he would write the following about his teammate:

> Ultimate, for Ken, was as much theater as sport. He created a
> mythical character and constantly added to the myth. Every

tournament was an opportunity to write another chapter. And page by page, the legend grew. Blocks at game-point to win championships. Insane catches that sparked impossible comebacks. Speeches that pulled teammates back from the brink and whipped them into a victorious frenzy. Life-threatening injuries. Miraculous recoveries. I saw it all. Ken played every second of every game like the camera was focused on him and he always delivered the highlights. Some people hated The Ken Dobyns Show; most people couldn't get enough. Either way, it's hard to dispute that Ken hosted the most exciting show in town.

My own Nationals didn't end with a stunned interview or a heroic attempt at a comeback. What I remember best from that year, 1985, was Titanic's last game of the tournament, a game that was essentially meaningless after our two losses. It was held on the grassy commons in front of the Washington Monument, and, getting psyched for the game, I wandered over to the Museum of Natural History. I had nibbled on some mushrooms back at the field, and inside the museum I was captivated by an exhibit of a Neanderthal hunting with a spear, a figure that reminded me not just of my old teammate Nathan but of myself, or at least of how I felt at that moment. With that vision still vivid in my head, I returned to the fields and went out and threw a half dozen overheads during the first half. If the results were, again, erratic, the feeling inside me was consistent. For a brief period I felt ecstatic, confident, and strong. People on our sideline were already drinking beers and egging me on to throw even more overheads and I complied, throwing nothing else the rest of the game. The game didn't mean anything after all.

But it *did* mean something. From that point on there were two

Ultimates for me. One was in the spirit of Kenny Dobyns and Moons, what would become from then on my biannual quest to win Nationals. But the other Ultimate was something different, something wilder, something pure, something that would become important to me and to my writing, and that would creep into my books. It would be ridiculous to call it the Spirit of the Game and it had nothing to do with that sanctimonious honor code. But it was a kind of spirit, a spirit of wildness and creativity.

It was a spirit that I still thought of as a Hostage spirit, and though many of the Hostages had quit playing, we still hung out together and were still, at heart, a team, a tribe. That spring, a couple of months after the Washington Nationals, our tribe reunited to travel down to the April Fools tournament in Washington in 1986, calling our reunion team Hostage Classic. We had a blast, filmed the entire thing in the spirit of the Merry Pranksters, and much to our own surprise, won the whole tournament, beating a good team named Spot in the finals. We played the tournament with the same sort of loose, comic, primitive spirit I'd experienced after my trip to the Natural History exhibit at Nationals, and for the first two-thirds of the finals the Hostages seemed to have rediscovered the long-lost magic dust. We admittedly tightened up near the end, and it was only through the grace of a bad call that we pulled out the win. But win we did, and when it came to celebrating we had few peers. Once again Bobby Harding and I spent the ride home, this time ten hours of driving, praising each other and boring our girlfriends to death.

Later that spring the Hostages held a reunion out in California, in Mendocino, that included the gobbling of mushrooms followed by a wildly strenuous biking trip up a mountain, beers drunk up top, and a ride down the trails at top speed despite the fact that some of us, myself included, had never mountain biked before. I remember flying down the trail and being shoulder to shoulder with a red-tailed hawk and then emerging from the trees and mountains into the fog of the beach where we swam in the ocean despite the cold. And I remember afterward eating crabs and drinking beer at my teammate Jeffy's house back in San Francisco, where he and his wife, Karen, lived on Potrero Hill.

The point was that Ultimate might not be giving me what I expected, but it was giving me something. When it came to Frisbee media, I was no Ken Dobyns or Steve Mooney, but on the other hand I was far from the shy kid I'd been in college. It was sometime during my last year as a Hostage that I began billing myself as "The greatest player of all time—by far." Of course I didn't mean it, well mostly not. It was part Ali-like boast and part parody of the fact that most people in the Ultimate world, their imaginations unimpeded by such things as coaches and a working press, imagined they were much better players than they actually were.

I decided to quit Titanic the next year, 1986. I was finally finding a way into my first novel, though I still hadn't shown a single word to anyone, even to Steph. I told myself that I could no longer serve two masters. To really train and go to tournaments was a full-time job, and so was writing (not to mention my actual job as a carpenter). But if I wasn't going to commit fully to Ultimate, I still needed the wild community I had found there. So my old Hostage friend Bobby Harding and I created a team called the Popes. The Popes featured a few ex-Hostages including Jeff Sandler and Paul Turner, as well as Tufts alums Paul Sackley and Dave Bertonazzi. We wore white painter masks on top of our heads as "Pope hats" during our first tourney, and we built a wooden cross on the sideline. We often referred to ourselves as "The Mighty Popes" and no matter the actual results of the games we played we would insist that we were "undefeated and unscored upon." Joel Silver would not have felt out of place on the Popes, at least in terms of comic sensibility.

The Popes were less talented than the old Hostage or Titanic teams and Bobby and I had to carry much of the offensive burden. Whether the influence of playing on this team was a good or bad one on us would depend on whom you asked. "Air it out" was Bobby's advice to me, and to himself. And so we aired it out with increasingly risky throws. I thought back to watching the Flying Circus at the April Fools tourney when I was in college, the way they played with wild daring. If in our case the results were not always pretty, there was still something about his advice that I liked. *Air it out.* I wrote down the words and taped them above my writing desk. I was realizing that, in part due to the intense pressure I put on myself, there were times I could be a little stiff both on the field and on the page. Unbeknownst to Bobby, he became my unofficial writing coach. I vowed to "air it out" in all areas of my life.

Around that time I read *Snake,* a biography of the Oakland Raiders quarterback Kenny "the Snake" Stabler, which would include an anecdote about the time a journalist read some of Jack London's prose to the quarterback. The lines the newspaperman quoted were these:

"I would rather be ashes than dust! I would rather that my spark should burn out in a brilliant blaze than it should be stifled by rot! I would rather be a superb meteor, every atom of me in magnificent glow, than a sleepy and permanent planet. The proper function of a man is to live, not to exist. I shall not waste my days in trying to prolong them. I shall use my time."

"What does that mean to you?" the newspaperman asked the quarterback when he was done.

Stabler thought for a minute. And then he said, "Throw deep."

If the Popes were not exactly superb meteors, we certainly weren't dull.

More and more my artistic and athletic worlds were converging. I'd sometimes watch the montages from the Rocky movies to get psyched for training, for doing push-ups and running fartleks on the beach, but it was Van Gogh, not Stallone, who began to fire my mental life. I kept his letters by my bed and loved his emphasis on *willing* oneself to be a great artist. Of course I started painting as well, not just in the style of Van Gogh but in that of the Fauvist painters from the early twentieth century, Derain and Vlaminck. The Fauvists, inspired by Van Gogh, painted in vibrant, wild colors. Vlaminck was a personal favorite, as he had been a professional bike racer, and he brought that athleticism to his painting, squirting his paints right onto the canvas. My own paintings, crude and rudimentary, were in this style.

Fauve means "wild animal" in French and I saw Bobby as a Fauvist Frisbee player. He could run forever and throw his backhand from end zone to end zone; he seemed confident to the point of oblivious. He had been a little shy when we first met, but he had shed this, and like me, his fellow former shy person had moved rapidly toward the blowhard end of the spectrum. We would sometimes clash on the field and we didn't do this in a subtle manner, yelling at each other toe to toe, face to face. But we were energized by this, too, by our own Hostage sibling rivalry and by leading a team where restraint had no place and all the old rules were off.

Perhaps the Popes' greatest triumph came at a tournament held at Cornell, where we made it to the finals by employing a defense that was part man-to-man, part zone that we called "the Clam." (A much more sophisticated version, one that evolved independently but had the same name, would become a staple of later Boston teams.) For more than a few of the Popes the tourney highlight had not been our wins on the field, but our performance at the party the night before. There a small band of Popes had stolen the stuffed deer from a diorama in the Natural History Museum, where the party was taking place. They had then tied the deer to the top of their car and driven off in the manner of hunters.

I was twenty-four years old when I joined Titanic and for the next five years my life would follow a simple pattern. One year I would play "serious Ultimate" and try to win Nationals with Moons. The next I would play with a looser, jokey team—the Popes, then the Whistle Pigs, Mighty Tired, and finally with a group of older players called Father Throws Best—where practice wasn't required and I could make writing my novel the priority. Alfred North Whitehead, who had been Walter Jackson Bate's mentor, said that "Art proceeds through cycles of freedom and discipline." I knew what he meant. The Pope years were the freedom, the Titanic years the discipline. While I still cared a lot about Ultimate, I couldn't quite commit to it the way some friends of mine had. For them it was their art, the thing that made their lives special. I felt that, too, at times, but I was now beginning to see, more and more, that it was also the thing that got in the way of my art.

Even after I caught her in my bed with the Berkeley music student, Steph and I stayed together. I'm not sure why. She promised, swore, that that would be the last time. But it wouldn't be. There would be another time, a year later, with an Italian exchange student, I think, and another, later still, with a German gardener. She was a Europhile all right.

I had wanted a hungry woman and a hungry woman I got. Always vaguely dissatisfied, always looking for more, the kind of woman who I—or at least the impotent, oft-enraged I of my twenties—couldn't hope to keep happy for long.

Why did I tolerate it? Why didn't I just leave her? I still don't know, but maybe it had to do with at least partly believing her desperate explanations. After each infidelity she would return to me, just as she had on the stairwell of the Allston apartment, and tell me how deeply she loved me. In her own analysis, her infidelities were tantamount to alcoholism.

"I have an emptiness inside, David, a huge emptiness," she told me one time. "I love you. You know that. I could say that it will never happen again but I don't know if that would be completely true. . . ."

I stared at her coldly.

"It's not about us, David. It's about me—my problem. I need something that tells me I'm okay. To fill up the emptiness. I need to be validated."

"Like a parking ticket," I suggested.

Maybe my reason for not leaving her was simpler. I really did love her and I believed, despite everything, that she loved me.

And we had good stretches. We both loved to read and travel. We were still capable of erupting into fits of baby talk and public affection that would make the other Hostages cringe. I would make vows about the loyal, loving life we would lead in the future, a life that, per Steph's specs, would be set in Israel for at least half the year. Despite those vows, and despite her own occasional trips back, I never visited the country where she had been born.

While I still hoped to win Nationals, Steph was growing more and more bored with Ultimate; the next year would be her last. Slowly she was facing her real ambition of becoming a doctor, but doing so with a good deal of indirection and angst. She had excelled in the Northeastern nursing program and was at the very top of her class, but had ultimately decided that nursing wasn't for her, that she wasn't suited to taking orders for a living. She continued to work in medical labs in Brookline, at first taking care of and clipping the heads off rats, and then in increasingly well-respected and higher paying technical positions. She began to talk more about medical school.

"I spit on the grave of my twenties," wrote H. L. Mencken. *Spit* seems a little strong, but I understand the sentiment. How can we know what we are going to become when we have only recently gotten to know ourselves? It was a process of definition that Steph was undergoing. Nursing school had seemed a sensible solution but it wasn't enough. Her dreams of *more* prodded her. Steph was no Kenny Dobyns on the Frisbee field; you might even say she lacked ambition. But off the field she had plenty.

Ambition was in the air. This was the mid-'80s with Reagan in his full-blown, semi-senile prime. How much was he the catalyst for the spirit of those times and how much was he merely riding the same wave we all were? Americans had lost faith in the political system with Nixon, and then listened as Carter (wearing a cardigan not unlike Moons's) spoke of humility and sacrifice and goodness. Maybe we had bought that line for a minute or two but then we shook our heads, as if coming out of a trance, and ran as fast as we could in the opposite direction. The direction we ran in, the direction that Reagan led us in whether he was a shepherd or a symbol, was back in time, back before all the babble about limits and less.

We ran desperately and we ran toward the bigger. Bigger cars, bigger jobs, bigger houses, bigger goals. And increasingly toward personal ambition and personal gain. Okay, you couldn't control the world—there were terrorists and real hostages and oil crises— but you could control *your* world. "Make America Great Again" had little to do with it. The real slogan should have been "Let Americans Believe They Can Make Themselves Great While

Ignoring Everything Else." This focus on personal ambition was everywhere. We tripped over each other in our race for blinders. The initial reaction to Watergate had been cries for "fairness." But fairness now seemed a concept to roll your eyes at. Winning, and, just as important, not losing, were things to be truly valued. You could feel it creeping through the entire culture. My college roommates had long since rushed off to Wall Street. But Ultimate players, those old part hippies, part iconoclasts, were feeling the lure, too.

Just as in real life, and just as in the popular movies of the time, the center of this culture of SUCCESS in the Ultimate world was New York City. Once again, in 1986, Titanic and Kaboom! had fallen short at Nationals, though this time they had at least both made the semifinals before losing. Windy City got revenge from the year before, and ran Kaboom! into the ground with a team with huge numbers that never stopped moving. Pat King had once been influenced by the tight looseness and teamwork of the Hostages, but now he saw in Windy City a second model, a team with large numbers that ran and trained as hard as anyone but that also had the old chemistry, the magic dust. *That* was the kind of team Pat wanted, a tight team but a team that could win multiple championships and fulfill his early dream of "dominating the sport." He had come to believe that this was something Kaboom!, as constructed, would never do.

King knew they needed to change their team, and change it drastically. Kenny Dobyns was not so sure at first. After all, hadn't Kaboom! made it to Nationals four straight years, with trips to the semis and finals? But Pat King worked on Ken—what if they could truly create a superteam?—and convinced him that it was time to disband Kaboom! Together they convened a secret meeting of three Kaboom! players and three players from Spot, the other New York team (the same one that the Hostage reunion team had beaten in the finals of April Fools the year before). "Spot had talent and athleticism," Kenny would sum it up. "We had the drive and the will." It was later described as the sport's "first mega-merger," and it had the cutthroat markings of just that. They took the best players from both teams, or at least the players that the captains perceived to be the best. This meant ruthlessly cutting old teammates, old friends. It didn't matter. The year 1987, when the world would be introduced to Gordon Gekko and the movie *Wall Street*, would also see the founding of a team known only as New York, New York. It was a team built for one purpose and one purpose alone: to win.

As luck would have it, New York's very first tournament would be April Fools, the same tournament that the Hostage reunion team had won the year before and that we now came back to again. Unlike New York, we were there to have fun, winning being incidental. The Hostages were stuck in the past that way, not keeping up with the times. Some of us still even had shirts with pictures of Khomeini on them, clear markings of an older era. By then we were a whole team full of clown-princes. All through the tournament we bellowed "Defending Champs!" as our cheer whenever we huddled. We drank as we played and goofed around yet somehow we made it to the finals again, despite ourselves, and it was there that we met the newly formed powerhouse, New York, New York.

It couldn't have been a more perfect clash of cultures. It was the past—not the hippie past, mind you, but the *Mad* magazine one—versus the ruthless future. Not the Spirit of the Game *that was so sacred it was written into the rules*, but two very different spirits. The first was the spirit of irreverence and thumbing your nose that had made me first love the sport. The second was the spirit of winning, of excellence without the silly trappings. The second spirit had little patience with the first and it was clear from the start of the game that Ken Dobyns had little patience with us.

You could tell right away that he hated the idea of playing the Hostages in the finals. This was New York, New York's first real test, and they had ripped their way through the tournament, hungry for their first big win, only to come up against a bunch of anachronistic clowns. It took some of the luster off of the potential victory. Dobyns must have felt he was in a time warp. He remembered our past pranks and found our disrespect for the sport irritating if not disgusting. And we in turn found his irritation and disgust amusing.

We even had Gus with us again, the Hostage founding father, our Goose Tatum and Meadowlark Lemon. He didn't disappoint in his role as clown-prince and agent of chaos. We had all been staying at the house of another Hostage, and Gus managed to sleep with a friend of that player's mother the night before the finals. Sleek and catlike in the early years of the Hostages, Gus now sported a significant beer belly. Earlier in the tournament he had tried to chase down a deep throw while playing defense. In the old days he would have closed on the player and leapt over him, but this was not the old days. When he tried to jump, he instead half-fell half-crumpled to the ground, landing in a large mud puddle. That was the moment when we started calling him "Elvis," as much for his current girth as his past glory.

There was no way we were going to beat that New York team, no matter how much magic dust Gus or anyone else sprinkled on. But it didn't really faze us. I'm sure we were singing bad '70s songs on the sidelines and that we tried an alley-oop or two, something that Dobyns would no doubt have claimed was illegal. It quickly became apparent that our old-school team didn't have much of a chance against new-school New York. Only a few of us still played on a high level and were in Ultimate shape, but it wasn't only that. The New Yorkers had introduced a heretofore unheard-of notion,

Defending finalists

strategy, to the game. They were doing things on defense and offense that we had never seen before. We kept it respectable for a little while, thanks to some of the players who still played, like Jimmy Levine and Bobby Harding and the Phillips brothers, but soon enough New York started to pull away. After that our main amusement was to cheer "Defending Champs!" over and over. It delighted us how much this irked Kenny Dobyns.

Though we weren't the world's greatest Ultimate players anymore, we were world-class hecklers. One player in particular, Craig McNaughton, excelled at getting under the skin of players on other teams in an Eddie Haskell fashion. We had watched New York's semifinal game with beers in hand and had not been particularly kind to Dobyns. He was a bulkier, more muscular man than he had been when most of my teammates had last played against him and, making note of this change, a few of the Hostages heckled him from the sidelines with the same cheer that Red Sox fans used back then on José Canseco: "*Ster*-roids. *Ster*-roids." This was a low blow, of course. Kenny had always been strong and the new muscles were likely the result of the weights he had been lifting to get ready for the season. But we were the Hostages; we liked poking the bear with a stick.

The outcome of the finals was never really in doubt, but that didn't stop us from doing what we did best. We were proud idiots and near the end of the game we called time-out twice just to bellow our "Defending Champs!" cheer.

Dobyns was pissed off. He walked over, close to our huddle, and yelled, "Come on! Take this *seriously*."

That was something we resolutely refused to do. We called time-out again to cheer on our very last possession of the game.

"That's your *last* time-out," Dobyns barked.

When we the turned the disc over, New York started to drive down to score and it looked like the game would finally end. Then there was a loud yell, a kind of garbled screaming, and I saw Gus fall to the ground grabbing his hamstring. The Hostages ran over and gathered around our fallen comrade but Gus smiled up at us. He had played in many great games but he would later say that this was one of his very favorites, ranking up there with the Regionals win in '81. He stood up, his injury miraculously healed, and, still smiling, said, "One more time."

"Defending Champs!" we bellowed as one.

That was too much for Dobyns. He lost it, screaming at Gus and racing around the field, waving his arms and ranting about how we were making a mockery of the sport. It was, for us, the perfect way to lose.

With the game over we grabbed beers, then linked arms and let go with one more cheer, the very last as it turned out in the history of the Hostages.

"Defending Finalists!" we yelled.

8.

Howls of Arrogant Laughter

For the fall of 1987 I was all in. There would be no more hedging of my bets or Hostage-style equivocating. I was twenty-six and in the best shape of my life. I vowed that I would not drink or smoke pot for the month before Nationals and this time, unlike my earlier vow to Honerkamp, I stuck to it. I had briefly moved back to Cape Cod and I trained as I never had before: I foreswore even a drop of alcohol, ran the beach and dunes, did countless push-ups, jumped rope, and threw hundreds of Frisbees each and every day. At Steph's apartment in Boston I would jack myself up on coffee and take ten-mile runs around the reservoir, loving the oogly mushroom feeling that throbbed through my body when I finally stopped.

That is not to say I had completely exorcised the Hostage clown in me. I still hated our team name, Titanic, and made up an obnoxious cheer that I yelled out before each game: "Titanic, Titanic, our dicks are gigantic!" People laughed but were also made uncomfortable, which I liked. The fact that the cheer irked Moons was a bonus.

This would be the year when my internal clown would finally have it out with my internal philosopher-king. This was also the year when I spent the night before the semifinals in the same bed with my grandfather and his loaded gun and when our team played Chicago in those same semis in the highest-scoring game in Nationals history, and when we came back from the dead, thanks to a stirring performance by our defense, to tie the game 24–24. Which, you may remember, was the score when I pulled back the disc, cocked it, and let it rip.

This was in other words the moment I had always dreamed of. Now I was inside that dream, the star Frisbee player playing his best in the most important game at the sport's highest level.

In this age of constant sports reporting, there is a whole lot of blather about who is *clutch* and who *chokes*. A kind of mystical sense of it is accepted: as if some players just *are* clutch, and always come through due to something innate in their character. But a lot of people doing the talking have either not been in a crucial athletic situation or, if they have, tend not to be very articulate about it. As a lifelong Celtics fan I can tell you that there were plenty of times when Larry Bird, as great as he was, failed in the clutch. Of course there were plenty of times he succeeded, too. In fact, everyone does both. But we like to make it simple. One player fails to rise to the occasion. Another rises.

My grandfather's old amateur golf rival, Jack Nicklaus, was one of the few who consistently prevailed, and was also one of the few jocks to ever really speak articulately about what the experience feels like. Nicklaus spoke as not just the holder of the most major golf titles but as the sport's leader in coming in second. The difference between the times he succeeded and failed was subtle, and hinged, he thought, not on being cool under pressure or cold-blooded, but on a kind of excited feeling that *this was it, this was his day*. On another day another golfer might beat him but not *today*. *Today*, for some irrational reason based on a kind of inner excitement, he knew he could win.

It didn't always work, of course. Being clutch in general comes down to three things, I think, four if you include raw luck. First and most important is the feeling that Nicklaus described. You can almost see it take over some players when you watch sports, even some players who have previously been regarded as chokers. Second, the players who really do seem to rise up often have an innate sense of drama, blossoming on the stage in part because it is exciting, definitely more exciting than normal everyday life. And third, you needed to be able to check your niggling brain at the door.

I think I can safely say that I had the stage thing going for me, the sense of drama, and as a rule I played much better in games of consequence, certainly better than in practice or early games, where I was often lackluster. And I can also say that I have experienced what Nicklaus described, that sense that *this is it, this is my day and I will not be beaten*. In fact, I had been experiencing just that in the second half of the Chicago game, having shaken off the stupor of a sleepless night with my armed grandfather and joining the rest of the team as we rallied from behind, and was still experiencing it right up until the moment that Bobby Harding called his time-out and play stopped.

Which brings us to the third element. That was where I perhaps had a little problem. I had always been able to get primal and get wild. But I was also the not-so-proud owner of a niggling brain. I had lived with it throughout my twenties, not just on the field but typing at my desk. In fact, I would have put my brain against almost anyone's when it came to subverting my own efforts.

Unfortunately, that brain would take the field with me when we returned after the time-out, the game tied at 24.

I would love to see film of that moment. It might settle a debate that raged in my head for at least the next year. I do know this. After Moons failed to get open and after Bobby threw it to me and after I caught the disc, I saw Jeremy Seeger streaking toward me, and I cocked my forehand and let it go. My throw got there but it got there low. That was the physical result, the external reality of the throw. But there is also something that only I know about that throw, its internal reality. There was a hitch in it. There was, in the middle of my usual forceful downward Barkan-like crank, some hesitation, some tentativeness, a moment when my forehand was not quite *my* forehand, not the one I had crafted long ago during those Cape Cod summers.

And still Jeremy Seeger, the man we had once called God, could have caught it. He was not a Hostage-style chest-catcher and maybe that was best with Joey trying to dive around him. In fact, Jeremy had a kind of unique way of catching discs in front of him that I had dubbed the "waiter catch," his long arms fully extended, his fingers down and thumbs up. He got those hands on my low throw but it binked off. Before we could react Chicago was picking up the disc, hucking it, and scoring, and it was all over.

I didn't and don't blame Jeremy Seeger. The fault was mine. Had I snapped off a firm chest-high forehand, the results would have been different. I suppose you could call it a moment of cowardice on my part. I certainly called it that over the next year as I beat myself up with the memory of that play.

No regrets, people like to say. That is one of the most bullshit clichés of all time. In a larger sense I get it. As the father of a daughter I adore, I wouldn't want to change any part of a life that has led to her. But what about cleaning up a few messy details? I regret not making a better throw at that moment, in fact would put it in the top ten of my life's regrets. I guess that's better than regretting having committed murder, but it is a regret still.

I sunk onto the field. We all did.

Someone came up to me, patted me on the back, and said something nice about how I had played. Someone else, a player I respected, said, "You were a god out there."

Then added, "Until the end."

I saw no reason to reply, possibly no reason to live. But then I looked up and saw what hung from the player's hand. A cooler.

"Any chance I could have a beer?" I asked.

"Sure, man."

It had been thirty-two days without drinking and the beer was cold and I gulped it down. I would like to say I savored it but that would be a lie. I savored it about the same way a dog savors its breakfast. I asked for another beer and he gave it to me and I sucked that down, too. A few more people gathered around, someone broke out a bowl, and I did a hit. And drank another beer. I would continue to drink and smoke over the next hour with a deep aggressiveness, fending off what was sure to be a dismal and depressing off-season.

The one coherent thing I remember doing was wandering over to my backpack and taking off my Barbarians. Inside my backpack was a T-shirt that Hones had given me for just this moment. I tore off my Titanic shirt and pulled on Hones's gift.

"Instant Asshole: Just Add Alcohol," it said.

It's only in retrospect that we see that particular moments are turning points in our lives. Had I completed that throw, I might be telling a different sort of story right now. Rather than singing the tales of heroes, I might have been a hero myself. I could have been a god of the game, a purveyor of arête. But instead I was about to solidify my role as a clown-prince.

Eventually I wandered over to the stadium to watch the finals between New York and Chicago. All season long, to Moons's chagrin, I had bellowed my obnoxious cheer: "Titanic, Titanic, our dicks are gigantic!" Now I was reduced to merely *watching* the finals, a finals that we could have been in had I made a better throw.

I skulked through the stadium, taking a piss on the grass behind the stands. Then I had an idea. Some folks from the UPA were broadcasting from up in the booth near the top of the stadium, and I headed unsteadily up the steps. Outside the booth, I gathered myself, feigning sobriety. Then I opened the door to the press booth, and making sure not to slur, told those inside that I wanted to ask a trivia question. I believe the question was "What player who plays on the current Titanic team also played on the original Boston Aerodisc?" and that I told them the answer was Leif Larson. They thanked me and said they would announce it; but I asked, innocently, if there was any chance I could ask the question myself. Then they did something that no UPA official would ever willingly do again. They handed me the microphone.

I grabbed hold of it and was soon bellowing.

"Titanic, Titanic," I yelled into the mic. And then, in a rare moment of self-editing, as if worried about shocking the few children in the stadium, I continued: "Our Johnsons are gigantic!"

A great roar went up.

The rest of the night was a blur. Steph's team, Lady Godiva, had lost in the finals to the Lady Condors, and a few of my teammates and I piled in the van with the Boston women and rode back to our hotel on the beach. I played the drums on the van's roof and led the passengers in rousing renditions of the usual '70s songs. "The sailors say Brandy you're a fine girl," we howled.

Steph and I, determined not to spend another night at the home of my crazy grandfather, had splurged and gotten a room in the hotel on the beach where everyone else was staying. She had lost, too, but felt little of the anguish that I did. This would be her last Nationals and I think that by then Frisbee was already done for her. Maybe for that reason, or maybe because she recognized the goatlike glaze over my eyes, she decided to head back to the room.

The next thing I knew I was on the balcony of a room on the twentieth floor of our hotel on the beach, swaying too close to the edge, and then one of my teammates, Turbo, I think, was steadying me and leading me back into the room. Around midnight we all headed down to the ocean for skinny dipping. About a dozen of us stripped off our clothes and dove into the powerful waves. I swam far out, hoping to wash away the day. I body-surfed my way back in and must have blacked out, because what I know of the rest of the story comes from its retellings by Turbo and Jeff Williams.

They were walking up the shore, with their clothes back on, talking about the day's tough loss. Then they saw something thrown up on shore, and walking toward it, found me lying naked and unconscious just above the surfline.

As one falls another rises. Dishonored, I played the buffoon, but the hero role was still up for grabs.

In describing that 1987 National Championship I have focused, in keeping with Ultimate tradition, on events that concerned *me*. But there were a lot of other Ultimate players there in Miami, and they were all every bit as concerned with their own internal worlds as I was with mine. About two dozen of those souls played for the New York Ultimate team and their experience that weekend would be every bit as uplifting as mine was depressing. Many people thought this was just a rehashed Kaboom! team, but it wasn't; it was a whole new animal. Kaboom! had been trounced by Windy City the year before. Now, re-formed in just the way Pat King had imagined—a large but tight team of great players willing to sacrifice for a common goal—they returned the favor, destroying Windy City. Chicago, still tired from our game, was no match for this new vision of what Ultimate could be. The New Yorkers might be barbarians, a million miles from TK's Athens, but they were disciplined and deadly barbarians. They beat the Chicago team 21–13.

In fact, New York's win over Chicago in the finals would be their first of six National Championships over the next seven years. Kenny Dobyns's dream was coming true, which was bad news for every other team in the sport. In our world, the world of Ultimate, the reign of the Evil Empire had begun.

It was fitting of course that the New York team had been formed through a sort of a palace coup, which had meant a series of ruthless cuts of old friends, friends who were sacrificed to the larger goal of winning it all. It was ruthlessness that New York practiced both on and off the field, and one that, in that way particular to New Yorkers, they prided themselves on. Their dedication and determination would become legendary and showed itself in a thousand ways. Late one season during their reign Ken Dobyns and Pat King determined not to shower all the way through Nationals as a sign of their grit and determination. For weeks they allowed the dirt of the city to build up on them, playing in rain and mud, their hair clumping and odor growing.

Later, in a dual interview with Dobyns, Pat King admitted that he had snuck in a few showers, though he hadn't used soap. "I had a job after all," King said. "I didn't," Kenny added. He hadn't showered once.

If Kenny was still a hothead, he was now a better teammate. And a leader.

"The reason it didn't work screaming at people when I played with the Heifers is that I hadn't earned the right to scream at them," he said. "But with New York, New York I earned it. Because, number one, I was so committed to the team and making the team great that no one could question it. There were days I hated going to practice but I went and threw myself into it. I never missed a practice, I never missed a tournament. And that's your currency. Your commitment is your currency."

Kenny Dobyns had put all his chips on one square, betting it all on a crazy hunch. He had given up everything most people cared about to be the best Ultimate player he could be. And somehow it was working out. "Simplify, simplify, simplify," exhorted Henry David Thoreau. Dobyns had done just that, paring life down to the bare bones of existence. He shaped himself through his will. He shaped his body, he shaped his throws. He knew what he wanted and he knew how to get it. He wore blinders that kept out the rest of life.

Other players like Steve Mooney were consistently passionate about the sport. But there was one basic difference between Kenny Dobyns and Steve Mooney, between Kenny Dobyns and me, and between Kenny Dobyns and most of humanity. He really didn't seem to care whether he was liked or not. This is a truly rare trait and fairly startling when you come across it. I think that to say that Gus didn't give a shit about what people thought was a little different. He excelled at things that I excelled at: drunken buffoonery and over-the-top humor. That is not the same as truly not caring whether the people around you are fond of you or not, and requires an external element, alcohol.

I imagine that not caring gives you a kind of wild freedom. You no longer have to worry about the things most of us worry about, and focus everything on being the best. Dobyns could regard anything that did not pertain to achieving his obsessive goal as extraneous and in the way, not worthy of his attention. If he was really going to simplify his life down to fundamentals, then things like girlfriends and jobs were mere distractions. And all distractions needed to be pushed aside to focus on what was most important.

Which was winning of course.

The next year, 1988, Steph quit playing Ultimate and I, vowing it was forever this time, also quit playing with Titanic. I was twenty-seven years old; she, twenty-six, and our priorities were shifting. It was time, in my father's words, to "get serious."

As for exactly where Steph and I stood on each other's priority list, that was still uncertain. I had caught her fooling around twice by then, and by almost any standard of morality and good sense, and certainly by my own somewhat macho standards, I should have left her. But I really loved her and was pretty sure that, despite everything, she loved me. Sometimes we would seem to be on the verge of a larger commitment, would even talk of marriage, but then we would swing the other way and know it was right to break up. Through it all we fought, and our fights could get loud and ugly.

I knew I wasn't easy to live with, and that was an understatement. I try to be kind to my young self when I look back, but the character I was was both terribly insecure and preposterously conceited, prone to fits of temper while convinced of my own imminent greatness as a world-famous writer despite the absolute lack of evidence.

During the off-season after our loss to Chicago, Steph moved to Germany for six months in one of her periodic questionings of our relationship. In response I decided to move back to Cape Cod, where I worked a couple months outside as a framing carpenter. It was cold and miserable, and while at work I could never stop moving long for fear of freezing. It was a bad winter to start with and then, in late February, my hand stopped working.

I didn't know it right away but I had a severe case of carpal tunnel syndrome, and could no longer bang nails. My frantic journal notes at the time read, "My hand isn't working! No blood!" Which meant not just no carpentry but no Frisbee, and, more to the point, no writing since I still wrote longhand. Out of money, and still paying off my old poster loans, I needed a job right away. I must have thought something like this: *I love books, so why not work in a bookstore?* It's a trap many young people fall into, I suppose, forgetting that working in a bookstore is about selling books, not reading them.

Since I worked nights, the job allowed me to spend mornings at my writing desk. This time I was going to write a book, I swore. The words came slowly at first, grudgingly, but at long last a plot emerged, or what passed for a plot in my mind. I sometimes managed to work in a reasonable, steady manner but more often the writing came in erratic, unsustainable bursts. The words would gush out, followed by periods of intense doubt. Back then creativity was a lot like drinking for me, the incredible highs followed by the hard depressions.

Isolation was part of the problem. My friends were all Ultimate players, not writers. They suspected, as I did, that if I hadn't already succeeded as a writer I must be a failure. Meanwhile, I still didn't show anyone, Steph included, a word of my writing. I was worried she would think my words, and therefore my self, inadequate. My creative world, like the world of most young writers, was an intensely solipsistic one. There is an insanity to showing one's work to no one, to spending hours whirling around in your own narcissistic universe, an insanity that would build in me over those hard first years.

But then in March of 1988 as my twenty-seventh birthday approached—with Steph overseas and my hand barely working, isolated and cold on Cape Cod—the dam broke. I see now that it was finding a literary form that did it, that allowed me to break through. While my fictional production had been minimal to that point, I had filled more than a dozen journals with notes about nature, with ideas, and with sketches of people, the last often written versions of the caricatures I still drew occasionally for the *Cape Cod Times*. In fact, I often exhorted myself to try to make my fiction closer to my "journal voice." That March I decided to cut to the chase. It was like skying or diving for a disc, right? Why not just go directly after the thing?

In little more than ten days I wrote the whole novel in journal form. The plot, as it was, had long been clear in my head. It followed the relationship of a grumbling cynical political cartoonist and his wild, possibly crazy younger brother named Stefan, who was based on several people I knew, including my brother Scott, myself, and my teammate Bobby Harding. Mental illness proves contagious and the book follows the disintegration of the older "saner" brother. The other main character, it turned out, was the natural world of Cape Cod. Over the previous five years the place had gotten inside me, and I wrote about its beaches, its colors, its trees, its tides, its winds and waters.

At that point I was still not quite ready to show my work to

Steph, but my life in the closet was finally ending. I was coming out. The book wasn't perfect, but I think it stands up today as a potentially publishable first novel. It might not have been a work of genius, but it was something. After five years of banging my head against a wall, I'd managed to put together a book. I still couldn't type so I paid a typist to type it up, made copies, and bound them. Then that late spring, I, like a true beginner, mailed the manuscript blindly to several big publishers. I didn't know any better and had no friends, or community, to tell me that my first move should be to send a cover letter to agents.

The rejections started trickling in that summer. It's unlikely that the manuscript was read by any but the youngest of assistants, those assigned with guarding the "slush pile" so it didn't spill over into the actual office. The rejections were form letters, all except one.

I fastened my mind on the one rejection that wasn't a form letter, the one written by a real editor. I analyzed each word in that letter and can remember it even today. The best phrase was the first: "You are a writer of considerable talent." I had waited five years for a line like that, the only evidence so far that what I'd spent my adult life doing wasn't entirely crazy. You are a writer of considerable talent. *Yes!* Maybe she was just being nice but if she was, then God bless her. I had been thrown a lifeline. That one sentence, and the thought that I was not entirely insane, made the rejection itself almost bearable.

Pat King called Kenny Dobyns a "mythical character" and he was certainly becoming one in the world of Ultimate. But he was also his own fictional creation, both writer and character. I don't think this is overstatement.

When I look back at Kenny's role, and his obsessive devotion to that role, I can't help but think of a book that obsessed me in my twenties, Ernest Becker's *The Denial of Death*. Becker's premise, simply put, was that our highest need is to be heroic, especially in the face of the most basic fact about being an animal: we all die. It is nothingness that makes us try to create something, nothingness that makes us try to be somebody. The desire to be a hero, Becker believed, is revealed in our basic narcissistic nature, our desire to stand out—to be better or more important than others—something that is baldly illustrated by siblings always wanting more, even if it is a symbolic more, than their brothers and sisters. This tendency was also baldly illustrated in the world of Ultimate, with players not just striving to be the best but telling their own stories that framed them in that light. Looked at this way, Frisbee fields seemed populated by squalling infants crying for attention.

Heroism, for Becker, was a way to take this basic narcissism and hammer it into something more. The tendency in modern life is to bury heroism under layers of conventional achievements like "piling up figures in a bank book." But what would happen if we turned away from these false and tinny definitions of the heroic and embraced the real thing? To really create your own symbolic world, to define it and then embrace it, would be a brave act and would, in Becker's words, release a great "pent-up force."

Setting higher, nobler goals would also stand in defiance of modern life and its bland subtleties. This is what I want, you'd say. And I'll give everything to get it. I know I'm going to die, going to be nothing, but for now I will strive to be this particular something.

Was Ken Dobyns thinking this sort of thing consciously? I have no idea. But he was a smart guy, a literate guy, despite being kicked out of all those schools. He must have at least suspected what he was doing was unusual in the modern world. Not just that being an athlete was unusual, but throwing so much energy into being an unrewarded and unappreciated athlete, among a group of similarly unrewarded and unappreciated athletes. You would never say it out loud but maybe Ultimate, rather than being just a punch line for a self-deprecating joke, could be an arena for the heroic.

Whether he chewed over these things or not, it took imagination and verve to keep playing the role he had set out for himself, and he knew a truth that most Ultimate players only suspected subconsciously or half-consciously. He knew that we were entertainers. Our audience might not be large, might often be only our fellow players, but we were entertainers still. Kenny had the skills but he also had stage presence. He wanted to be great, yes, and he wasn't lying when he told George Plimpton he hated losing. But when he yelled in outrage or fell to the ground in defeat or thrust his hands above his head in victory he knew he did so on a stage. And after he laced up that flak jacket, protecting the one good kidney, he knew that his leaps and dives were being seen. From the beginning his role had been an overall heroic one but with a dash of Iago and not a small amount of pro wrestling villain. Somehow he had hit upon the role immediately or at least as far back as when he spit in Pat King's face. But now, during the reign of New York, he was fine-tuning it and perfecting it, and he would play it to the hilt during the next few years. It was true that not everyone believed the role he played with such passion. One Hostage, who had grown up in New York City without much money, didn't buy the act of Ken Dobyns, prep school kid and son of celebrity, as a New York tough. Most of his teammates and opponents seemed to buy it, however, and, most important of all, he seemed to.

Like Kenny, I craved an audience. If not yet for my writing, then for my narrative. I would sometimes curse the way that Ultimate competed with writing for my attention but that seems silly to me now. Without Ultimate my isolation would have been complete. Ultimate gave me an audience, not for my sentences but for myself.

Meanwhile, Moons's role, in his own mind perhaps and in the mind of more than a few watchers of the game, was a more noble one, that of the striving hero and leader of men. His job was to keep those men focused and motivated, their chins up, until through perseverance they arrived at the shining city, a place called winning, but more accurately winning nobly. He had achieved it with the Rude Boys and there was no doubt in his mind he would achieve it again. That he had to vanquish a troll-like creature from New York was annoying, but a champion needed to persevere, and maybe having to beat an evil enemy ultimately made the plot more interesting.

I write this with my tongue somewhat in cheek but I also write it truthfully. Losing made me hate myself. It did not seem to have the same effect on Steve Mooney. At least outwardly he would come back as confident, hopeful, and assertive as ever. Maybe it was having that one championship he had won with the Rude Boys under his belt, but more likely it was just temperament. If not exactly sunny, he was, to use a word that would have made my fellow Hostages cringe, "positive."

"The funny thing is that every year I thought we were going to win," he told me later.

Of course the New York teams vilified Steve, just as the Hostages had before them. They claimed that this tall, handsome entertainer had a flaw and that that flaw had to do with *control*. This actor wanted to write his own script and direct the play as well, and sometimes when others got in the way he became petulant. This was no different from Kenny, of course, except in the desire to be, or appear, different from Kenny. The model was still Tom Kennedy and the arête, but Moons was not TK exactly. He couldn't quite see that his own inner Dobyns was not always kept as hidden as he imagined. He wanted to be the great-good man; he wanted to play within the rules; he wanted to be a gentleman. But, God, did he want to win.

What had driven the Hostages crazy about Steve now drove New York crazy. Kenny himself was not only all in, he was all *out there*. He didn't hide anything. His striving was bald. You could see him as he was, practically frothing, doing almost anything to achieve his goal. The Hostages didn't like that, he was too damn serious, but they respected it. In fact, our old team motto, usually repeated after someone did something stupid, was "You can't be afraid to be yourself." Say what you would about Kenny Dobyns, he wasn't afraid to be himself. In contrast, the Hostages had always been wary around Moons, suspecting he was hiding something, working some hidden angle. There was a sense that they would have respected if not liked him more if he had just come out and said, "I want to crush you fuckers."

As it turned out, this was just the direction in which Moons was evolving.

I wavered about whether or not to play with Moons and Titanic in the fall of 1989. But Steph was done wavering and had put the game firmly behind her. One weekend during that early fall she drove up to a friend's farmhouse in Vermont and brooded over her future. Three days later she returned and announced her intentions. She was finally going to do it; she was going to medical school. It was time to tackle a profession, so why not tackle the toughest profession of all? She plunged into the exhausting process of getting recommendations and completing applications, taking the Stanley Kaplans and MCATs, traveling to schools, and finally sending in the applications themselves. I admired ambition in others as well as myself, and, despite some apprehension about this marking the end of our relationship, I supported her completely, helping edit the essays for the applications and driving her to her interviews.

I kept telling myself that I needed to commit completely to writing, but in the end I couldn't quite quit and rejoined Titanic for one last try at winning Nationals. We had a strong team that fall and Moons ran practices with an iron hand, with an emphasis on doing lots of running, including Monsters and field-long wind sprints. The old days of just scrimmaging at practice were long gone. With each passing year the sport was growing more serious and competitive, New York in particular always upping the competitive ante. The most extreme example of this had been during the first few months after they formed New York, New York. In the old days, in Timba's day, for instance, scrimmaging had been the main way of staying in shape, but New York decided to barely scrimmage at all during their early months together, focusing instead on drills and implementing strategy.

In the Hostage way, I still sort of fancied myself a weak practice player who could rise to the occasion in games, sprinkling on the magic dust, but the truth was that as I got older I had a hard time keeping up with the faster players. If I still clung to some Hostage vestiges, Bobby Harding had almost entirely shed his. He had been reluctant to join Titanic during our early years, and saw playing next to Moons as "selling out." But now he had completely embraced the team's win-or-nothing philosophy and scorned more moderate views. There was a fervor in his eyes that scared me a little, and he would rip into players at practice if they didn't perform to his liking. His concept of "airing it out" had also blossomed into a full-fledged worldview, and both on the field and in conversation he held nothing back.

Bobby and I were close friends by then, and, surprisingly, our third musketeer that fall was none other than Steve Mooney. After practice, the three of us would often head over to a nearby bar in Wayland, where we ate bowls of peanuts and drank pitchers of beer. Our conversation focused mostly on winning, on how this was a do-or-die season, and how we had to win it this fall or quit. All remnants of hippie grooviness had been wrung out, at least in the way we saw the game. We grumbled about players on the team who might be soft and therefore might crack at Nationals. After a couple of pitchers, we would begin a round of toasts that would get at the essence of our philosophy.

"More points!" was one.

"No pussies!" was another.

It was animal farm, no doubt. We were becoming our enemy.

That October we beat New York at Regionals in a fierce, argument-filled game to go into Nationals seeded first. The most dramatic photos and video from that game aren't of great plays but of the two teams yelling at each other. We knew that wasn't the last we'd see of New York, and sure enough there they were in the semifinals of Nationals in Washington, D.C. Another change in the game by that point was that we now usually played in shifts of offensive and defensive players, and I played offense exclusively, my days as defensive specialist long gone. But this morning as I dug up old footage I see that I am there running down the field on our first defensive point. This was in keeping with Titanic's new strategy of dramatically tightening the number of players who actually played, the embodiment of our new, more cutthroat strategy. But there was a problem with this strategy. Up until the semis our philosophy had been not unlike that of a progressive preschool where everyone gets to play and everyone gets a trophy. But now the rotation tightened, and those not playing grumbled. The players on the sideline who weren't in the game seemed lackluster, uninvolved, even wandering off to mingle or flirt with some of the spectators.

There couldn't have been a more stark contrast with the New York team. They were frothing, all twenty-five players on their sideline fully committed. There was a passion, a single-mindedness to the team that still impresses me. "Keep the Shiites on the field!" was their war cry. The Shiites were what they called their defense, and the idea was that if the D kept getting blocks and scoring, and then pulled the disc and scored again, there was no reason for their offensive team to ever set foot on the field. While about a third of our team, the third that wasn't playing, seemed either uninterested or disgruntled, their whole team was united toward a single purpose.

There had always been a martial element to the sport, despite the hippy-dippy reputation, but Dobyns's teams would take this to a different level. I thought of those New York teams recently when I read William James's essay "The Moral Equivalent of War." James wrote, "The earlier men were hunting men, and to hunt a neighboring tribe, kill the males, loot the village and possess the females, was the most profitable, as well as the most exciting, way of living. Thus were the more martial tribes selected, and in chiefs and peoples a pure pugnacity and love of glory came to mingle with the more fundamental appetite for plunder."

My old Harvard teammate Simon Long had come out to watch the semifinal game on the Washington Mall, and he commented on what he had seen after the game.

"They were just faster than you," Simon said. Yes, I agreed, they were, but that wasn't it, or all of it. It was something else, which I can only describe as a sense of purpose. Not individual sense of purpose, we had plenty of that, but an intense psychological unity.

This was the New York team that would beat San Francisco's Tsunami in the finals to win the second of their six titles. It had all come together for them. They were led by Dobyns, of course, who was now in his prime. He might have busted a kidney and mangled his knee but he had lost none of his fight. His reputation has been reformed in recent years, and it is common to hear people say, with some surprise in their voice, that he really was a "good guy." I am here to tell you he wasn't, at least not on the field. Dobyns, at his essence, hadn't changed. He liked to spike discs after he scored, often rendering them unusable. When winning is the only goal and you play a game where you make your own calls, the results are predictable. But while whether or not he was a good person is up for debate, that he was by then a great player was undeniable.

New York also had a new star named Dennis Warsen, a young goofy kid who could jump through the roof and who was known as Cribber. The coming years of Ultimate were the period that might loosely be called the Rise of Cribber, and it wouldn't be going too far to say he changed the sport. The winters I spent playing pickup basketball in the Harvard rec center had given me some perspective on the game I played the rest of the year. I'd always said, "Just put a decent college small forward out onto the field and it's all over." Now that college small forward had come and his name was Dennis Warsen and New York had him. He was listed at 6'4" but looked taller, though he also looked like he weighed about 140 pounds. Though shorter than Moons, he could sky over him, and, all arms and legs, he threw himself all over the field. He quickly developed into a deadly thrower of the "notion" camp, with a whippetlike forehand that could go the length of the field and a monster overhead that could do the same. His target on those wild throws was frequently Dobyns, and often enough Dobyns returned the favor, Cribber becoming his favorite target.

It feels a little wrong to single out the team's stars or individuals, since what New York was about, and what beat us that day, was a *team*. The truth is that, had I not been playing the game, I might have rooted for New York to beat us. We were still an all-star team. They were a single entity, a living, breathing unit.

I played well in the semis but there was one particular play in the game that is worth noting. I caught the disc near the goal line and was forced to call a time-out before I was "stalled" by a New York player. When I returned to the field I had only five seconds to throw the disc or I would be stalled and turn it over. A teammate, I don't remember who, came up to me and said that if it was getting down to the last second, I should just throw the disc and follow through into my New York defender and call a foul. They rationalized this by saying that New York "did it all the time." I am not proud to say that I proceeded to do just that. I had never done this before, and would never do it again. But I did do it then, when the stakes were the highest.

This gives you a pretty good idea of where the Spirit of the Game was at that particular moment in the sport's history. I personally was of the belief that not having referees, far from elevating the game, meant that self-interest ruled, and that the lack of regulation played into the worst, not the best, parts of our nature. Spirit seemed no more than an idealistic remnant, an evolutionary leftover like our little toes.

As far as fair play went, New York had one player who was perhaps the least spirited in the game's history. No one played harder, I'll give him that, but I believe he also was consistently unethical, and when excited he could make Dobyns seem like Gandhi. There is no need to mention his name: the community knew then, just as the community knows now. During that game this player often covered Steve Mooney, who was almost a foot taller, a disadvantage rendered moot by the fact that he consistently mugged Moons, knowing there were no refs to rein him in. He frequently made calls that those watching just shook their heads at. Even his own players admitted this particular player went beyond the rules.

"Some of my teammates did things that were wrong," Pat King would admit later. "And I let them do it. I am tainted by that."

Was the team itself tainted then? It wasn't hard to make the case, but it was even easier to make another: that New York, New York was playing Ultimate at a level that it had never been played at before. It is unfortunate that in pushing each other, they also occasionally pushed. But whatever one's moral qualms, there is little doubt that New York was the best team at that time, perhaps the best ever. Unlike Titanic's oddly matched parts, they were a team that functioned as a unit and had clear leaders. If you dared get in an argument with them, God help you, but in a way that was the least of it. They took an old hippie sport and shook it out, beat it like a rug with a broom, making it into something different, something tougher. They trained as no team had before and introduced all sorts of innovations and strategy. They were steely in the clutch and they had the best hands and some of the best throwers. Which made any complaining you wanted to do somewhat irrelevant, and made any talk of "fairness" sound a lot like whining.

We got in plenty of arguments with them but during my time playing New York I don't once remember a game being decided by a call. Sure, foul calls and traveling calls might have swung momentum in some games. But in the big picture this mattered little. They infuriated me, they pissed me off, they frustrated me. But they also were just better than us. It was that simple really. I played them only during the stretch of time that for me began in 1987 and ended in 1999, and therefore my experience is limited, but they were the best Ultimate team I ever saw and I have no experience of being cheated out of a game by New York.

The year ended with a crash. If what you cared most about was winning, only one team was happy at season's end, just like Kenny said, and during that time period the happy team was always his.

I had played well but it didn't matter. Unlike the last semis I'd played in, this time I felt we had been beaten by a better team. And they didn't just beat us, but beat us soundly. Which is not to say I was not upset. Once again, I had failed at the one thing I was a success at.

After the loss, it was almost obligatory for me to create some sort of scene. If Kenny had his Frisbee audience, I had mine, too. I had left my "Instant Asshole" shirt at home, but that didn't stop me from drinking hard. A small group of us—Bobby, Turbo, Jeff Williams, Tom Watson (a new handler who had played at Stanford and was becoming a good friend), and a couple others—threw a party of our own out on one of the outlier fields, refusing to watch the finals between New York and the San Francisco Tsunami. But gradually we got bored with ourselves and, perhaps sensing the juvenility of our self-ostracism, migrated over to the stadium where the finals were being held. We were sitting off to the side of where most of the fans were, when I noticed something. This time the game wasn't being announced from a press booth but right on the grass beyond one of the end zones, where three UPA officials stood around the mic. A notion formed in my head, which I excitedly communicated to my small band of friends. *I need to get my hands on the mic.* What would I do then? they wanted to know. I would sing "We Are the Champions" to the New York team, now well

Attack on the microphone

ahead and on their way to their second title. But how would I get the microphone? The UPA authorities, the "regulators" as we had begun to call them, knew what I had done the last time with my "Titanic, Titanic" cheer and they wouldn't let me anywhere near it.

A plan was hatched. The end zone where the game was being announced was clearly not a defensible position. There were only three announcers around the mic, so I put together a small war party, made up of Bobby Harding, Turbo, and Jeff Williams, and after a drunken Patton-like speech, convinced them to storm the microphone. Or thought I convinced them. Halfway through my charge I looked back and found myself alone, with only Bobby even close. I could have quit, of course, called off my raid, but what was this if not a chance for another stupid, futile quest? So of course I charged ahead and tried to wrestle the microphone from the announcers on my own.

Three UPA officials tried to fend me off before a policeman arrived and grabbed me and pulled me away. I was not arrested however. Things did not work like that in our Dungeons-and-Dragons world. Instead I was henceforth banished from ever playing Frisbee again in the Washington area, an edict that holds to this day. In the official letter that Steve Goodwin, the local representative of the UPA, sent to Steve Mooney, he charged Titanic three hundred dollars for damage done to the microphone. Goodwin also said that though he understood "that while Steve personally tried to help give Ultimate a clean image," this sort of behavior reflected poorly on the team.

Then he turned his ire on me. Referring to me by my last name—"I know him only as Gessner," Goodwin wrote. "Perhaps it will come as no surprise to you that Gessner was intoxicated at the time." He then handed down his sentence: "Gessner is now *barred* from participating in *any* WAFC sponsored event. I'm sure that this news will be greeted by him with howls of arrogant laughter, and you yourself might think that we're being a little *too* serious. Let me assure you, we have never been *more* serious. *There will be future UPA events in Washington, and it is more than likely that your team will qualify. WAFC will suspend all play at any tournament in which Gessner appears.* His team will forfeit all games. Disappointed players will be told exactly why the tournament was cancelled. We'll show them this letter."

So there it was. Banishment, at least from play in our nation's capital.

Moons went ahead and paid for the microphone damage out of our team dues.

As for me, I wish I could say that I was properly chastised, that I began, then and there, to finally grow up, but I'm afraid the truth is I greeted his letter just as Mr. Goodwin had predicted I would. Over beers, I showed the letter to Hones and my other Hostage friends and we howled with arrogant laughter.

9.

Childish Things

Life in Ultimate meant constant long road trips where your legs cramped on the drive home (usually late at night if your team was any good). It also meant popping Advil like M&M's, and eating everything you could get your hands on before, during, and after a weekend of running. Finally, it meant Mondays when you returned to your job (if you had one) completely depleted of energy, like a wrung-out sponge, after a weekend spent chasing discs in the hot sun or cold rain, a weekend where (again if you were any good) you might have played as many as seven or eight games, each lasting a couple hours. We used to laugh at pro athletes who complained about being tired from their rigorous schedules.

Most serious Ultimate players have spent a decent amount of time in hospitals. Not just due to split kidneys but the full array of lacerations and tears and traumas. Knees in particular tended to snap like rubber bands. It was just part of the game and operations were common in the off-season. I haven't dwelled on my own injuries, but I have plenty of scars from the sport, including the time I ripped my leg open on a field in Tempe, Arizona, and the open wound was infected by the chemicals used on the field, sending my temperature through the roof. I've often thought it would be fun to get together with old Ultimate friends and reenact the famous drunken scene in *Jaws*, the one where Brody, Hooper, and Quint are drinking whisky and comparing scars down in the boat's cabin. I didn't know it yet but my most dramatic scar of all would be earned during the very last week of my twenties. My most obvious injuries, before then, were to my front teeth, which I had knocked out a couple of times while playing. Since I didn't ever have much money or any health insurance I would sometimes go weeks before getting my teeth repaired, which appalled Steph and led Hones to calling me "Backwoods Jack."

After I quit Titanic for good, I played in a tournament with a bunch of older players, many of whom had children, on a team called Father Throws Best. Father had several former Rude Boys on the team, and at the end of one tournament in Amherst they indulged in an old Rude Boy tradition of diving after discs into a big mud puddle. One player would float a disc into the air and another would come running up and lay out for it, "getting horizontal" as it was known, then splashing down and sliding in the puddle. I refused to play along; it was a Rude Boy thing after all, and I, in my heart, was still a Hostage. But then a few of them grabbed me by the arms and tried to drag me over to the puddle. I told them to let me go, that I'd do it, only I'd do it *my way*.

I whispered instructions to one of my teammates, an ex–Rude Boy named Toby Lou, and then began my running approach to the puddle. Toby did what I'd asked him to do, tossing not a Frisbee but a half-empty case of beer into the air. I took off and flew toward the case, getting horizontal, ready to make a spectacular catch. But our timing was a little off, Toby's underhanded beer case toss a little ahead of my dive. The beers were out of reach and they landed and shattered upward just a second before I landed on them. For a second the puddle was a mess of water, blood, mud, and flesh. Then it became clear that a good chunk of my left forearm, a scrag of flesh, was hanging down where it wasn't supposed to hang. Fortunately, we were on the whole a more mature team, and we had our very own doctor playing for us. Dr. Gil immediately set to cleaning my wound and picking glass out of my arm before accompanying me to a nearby emergency room.

It was obviously time for me to completely quit Ultimate and "get serious," the course of action my father had been urging on me for some time. Ultimate had been a big waste, I decided in 1990 as my thirtieth birthday approached, aiding if not solely responsible for my arrested development. As proof of this I had only to look at my college roommate Dan, who was by then making more than a million dollars a year. In contrast, my life was in shambles. Working as a part-time bookstore clerk, I was fortunate that debtors' prisons no longer existed. I could only nod in agreement when my father muttered about how I'd never learned to live in "the real world." There was no choice but to admit he was right: it was time to put away childish things.

A few months after Titanic's loss at Nationals, Steph's letters from medical school arrived in the mail: some rejections, most acceptances. In the end she decided to attend the University of Massachusetts, which was in my hometown of Worcester. What went unspoken but implied during our talks about med schools was that Steph's going away and starting a new life was a logical way for us to end our relationship. That relationship was by then bruised and battered, not just by infidelity but by too many fights. I was hard to live with and not just for the reasons that should be obvious by now. There was also my innate and unshakable sense that to be a great writer I had to live alone, to put writing first, ahead of girl-friend, family, God, job, and, yes, even Frisbee. My drinking was also a problem, especially when mixed with my anger about Steph's cheating. *Instant Asshole* might be a funny thing to have embla-zoned on your T-shirt on the Ultimate fields, where drinking led mostly to buffoonery, but on the home front it was no joke.

Had I been willing to let her go, Steph was ready to fly. But just as with my novel, and to some extent with Ultimate, I wouldn't let go. In fact, I gripped so tight that the next fall I followed her all the way back to Worcester. Why? Maybe because, with my life as a writer not yet begun and with Ultimate now, I vowed, in the past, she was all I had that was real. We moved into a rental house in Boylston, right outside of Worcester, where Steph was soon fully immersed in medical school, and I was fully immersed in nothing. Before we moved she explained that school would have to be the year's main focus, and it was. One of our only dates that year was when she took me down into the bowels of the hospital to show me the cadaver she was working on. In a short story I later wrote, I had the character based on me whine about how the character based on Steph spent more time with that corpse than with me, and it was true. That fall was long and empty, without Steph and without Frisbee, and the more depressed I got the less I saw a way out. To fill my time and make money I worked as a substitute teacher in the Worcester school system, and gradually took a job as a residential counselor at a home-less shelter, mystified that the administrators there allowed someone who had so clearly bungled his own life to counsel others. I also tried desperately to start a new novel, but I found that I kept coming back to the same old material, even the same sentences, wanting to revise my first book and make it perfect.

For the most part I managed to stay away from Ultimate that

fall, but I did drive up to Dartmouth, where Regionals were being held, and played for another Bobby Harding–led jokey team, this one called Mighty Tired. The main thing I remember about Mighty Tired was that before each game the team would do shotguns of warm cans of Budweiser. This would become so entrenched in the Mighty Tired community that one of the players would later bring out several cases of warm Bud at his wedding reception and the wedding toast would be followed by a communal shotgunning. Parents and grandparents looked on bewildered, shaking their heads and searching for the champagne.

As for me, I played pretty well at Regionals and was tempted, after a fall in the grim isolation tank of Worcester, to consider rejoining Titanic the following year for another shot at winning Nationals. One thing that I'd found overwhelming during my depressed fall, working as a substitute teacher in Worcester, was the strong sense of being a nonentity. I might have been known only as "Gessner" in the Frisbee world. But at least I had a name.

Tempted though I was, I stuck to my guns and headed home to Worcester determined to become a writer, not an Ultimate player. I followed Steph's lead and applied to schools. A few months earlier I had mailed out requests for a half dozen applications for grad schools in creative writing, and now I doggedly set to filling them out. I was depressed, sure that I wouldn't get in, but I will say this for me back then: at least I was a relatively active depressive. Feeling desperate, I took action. I filled out all the boxes, wrote the essays, and sent in a section from my novel, my only novel, the obsessive novel of my twenties, the one that proved I was "a writer of considerable talent."

Even where I ended up applying to grad schools turned out to be influenced by Ultimate. And by Steph. Six of the applications were for schools in Massachusetts, including UMass Amherst and a bunch of Boston schools. This would allow me to stay near Steph and, even though I didn't admit it to myself, to return to playing for Titanic and finally win it all. It was the seventh school I applied to, however, that was the wild card. That was the master of arts in creative writing at the University of Colorado in Boulder.

The reason I applied to Boulder was that Titanic had won a tournament there a year and a half before, in July of 1989. Back then the Boulder Fourth of July tourney was as competitive as Nationals and teams flew in from all over the country to play on fields laid out below the foothills of the Rockies. I hadn't played particularly well in our win, but I had been dazzled by the place. As I filled in the application, I imagined what it would be like to live in the shadow of those mountains.

The sport I was leaving behind was quite different from the one I had started to play, and it seemed to be finally finding its legs. Joel Silver's vision was beginning to come true. More than a million people were now playing the sport on college campuses and in various summer and spring and corporate leagues. Meanwhile, the game had gone international, with strong Ultimate cultures sprouting up in Japan and Sweden among other countries. Less often were the words "Ultimate Frisbee" greeted with a laugh or bewildered look, even as the sport moved from using Wham-O products to those of a new distributor, Discraft, and the word *Frisbee* was officially dropped from the name. Pat King might still choose not tell his workmates where he was after he came back from winning Nationals, maintaining his secret identity, but the next generation would require no such secrecy or modesty.

It had been a long time since anyone had played barefoot. The new leader of Lady Godiva showed just how far the women's game had come. Gloria Lust was a tall African-American woman with a Grace Slick hairstyle, a college sprinter who was not just Heather Morris's athletic equal but was clearly better than some of the men. Hers had been another classic Ultimate conversion story. On top of running track and field at Cornell, Glo, as she would become known in the Ultimate world, was rowing crew, and it was while out on a five-mile run with her rowing mates that she saw Frisbees flying out on one of the playing fields. After the run she went over and explored, and ran into Tiina Booth, who was one of the earliest women Ultimate players and later would be a legendary coach of both men and women's teams, and the next thing she knew she was hooked. After college she moved to Boston to play Ultimate, but didn't like the rigidity of the roles on Smithereens, the team that Suzanne Fields led.

"I wanted a team that had more flow, more dynamic movement," she said. A team that was, in short, more Hostage-like. So she quit Smithereens, and, along with two teammates, Donna Sue Levine and Meca Lynn, formed Lady Godiva. Though Godiva lost in the finals during the first year of their existence, 1987, the next year they would beat Smithereens to win their first title. While Glo would move away after the first two Nationals wins, to play for a West Coast team called the Maine-iacs that was Godiva's chief rival, the team she left behind stayed strong not just for years but for decades. With the infusion of a brilliant strategist named Peg Hollinger, and better athletes like Christine Dunlap, Laura Orlando, and a division 1 soccer player named Molly Goodwin, Lady Godiva took the game to new heights, winning nine championships in all. The official Ultimate history book summed it up simply by saying that they were "the best team that has ever played the game."

On the men's side, another pretty good team, New York, New York, was in mid-dynasty mode. Nineteen ninety would have been

Gloria Lust goes up for a disc

the year that brought New York's third championship, and what I saw when I watched them play at Regionals was a very fast, very disciplined team with many players, most all of whom subbed in specifically for offense or defense. In other words, the game was becoming not just better but more specialized. The wild west of my Frisbee youth had been tamed and the result, on the field, was impressive.

From the outside New York looked like a slick modern Ultimate machine. But it wasn't that simple. They had won the last two years I had played (in Miami in 1987 and Washington in 1989), but in 1988 they had briefly slipped off their pedestal. In fact, it was a brutal loss during that year that would spur them to win five in a row. After their Nationals win in 1987 they pretty much felt like they would never lose again, but the next year they grew complacent. At Worlds they stayed up all night partying before playing a Swedish team in the semifinals. No U.S. team had lost to an international team in world competition at that point but the Swedish team had been training hard and instituted a regimen that included hundreds of sprints, strict diets, and no alcohol. Worlds is known for its parties but the Swedes had been going to bed early, gaining a reputation as party poopers. They didn't care and as the semis began it became clear why. They came bursting out of the gates and took a commanding lead. New York was caught off guard but not too worried. At least at first. They figured Sweden couldn't keep playing at the level they began at and that soon enough the New York machine would crank itself up. The way it always did.

"They'll choke," they told one another. "They'll choke."

This wasn't as cruel as it sounds. It wasn't based on some intrinsic flaw in the Swedes' characters, but on something very real in sports and particularly strong in Ultimate: the pecking order. It is very unusual for a team to suddenly break out of its rank, out of the position it has always occupied. A team that usually loses in the quarterfinals seldom jumps up and wins a tournament. Often when a team is on the verge of breaking out of their spot in the pecking order, a player will make an egregious error, assuring that the team ends up back where they belonged. This even happened at the sport's highest levels.

For Sweden, beating a U.S. team, and not just a U.S. team but a New York team with players like Ken Dobyns and Pat King, players they had read about and seen on film, was something beyond the reach of most of their imaginations.

And yet as the game went on, they kept rolling.

"They'll choke, they'll choke," the New Yorkers kept saying, but the Swedes weren't choking. And then suddenly it was game point and Sweden was up by 2 and had the disc to win and there was a player open in the goal and the throw was good and . . .

. . . the player dropped it.

At that moment New York woke up and, simultaneously, the Swedish dream ended. Sweden might have thought they were still in the game but it really was already over. New York scored quickly and then got two blocks against the increasingly nervous Swedes.

New York had pulled it out, barely, and the pecking order had been restored.

But the next fall they were not the same team that had won Nationals the year before. They lost to many teams they should have beaten. For one thing they only occasionally had Pat King who, having fulfilled his goal of winning it all, had turned more to his music. When he told the team he would not be going to Nationals, however, Kenny started working on him and, in the end, convinced him to play. The problem was that Pat was out of shape, and on top of being not physically ready he was not mentally ready. The team itself was softer than the one that had won the year before.

Despite this, they made it to the semis against the San Francisco Tsunami. Now they would surely rise up and become themselves again. Just like they had against Sweden. But they didn't.

Pat King in particular has nightmarish memories of that game. "I just wasn't battle ready," he remembers. "We all choked but I led the choking."

In the months after the loss Pat fell into a real depression, plagued by constant doubt and a sense of failure. He might have thought he was ready to leave behind the childish game, but apparently not. He certainly wouldn't be going out this way.

For Pat King, that failure was the main building block of what would become the New York dynasty, and it was that one loss that would lead to all the winning.

"In some ways it was the best thing that ever happened to us. We just never wanted to feel that way again. We all knew how much it hurt to lose. And that we *could* lose if we let up. We were never going to let that happen again."

The loss had another less positive consequence, at least for Pat

King. After the first Nationals win he had felt elated, his long-held dream finally realized. But in the coming years, as the Nationals victories piled up, he was never able to retrieve that first feeling. After the big loss in 1988 he was driven mostly by the dread of defeat.

"It was actually kind of grim," he said later. "I never felt elation. Just relief."

Kenny Dobyns had a similar reaction to winning. He later wrote, "I vividly remember the feeling immediately after we first won in '87. It felt completely hollow . . . like, is this all it is? Really? After shooting for it for all those years it just didn't really feel all that special. And we absolutely crushed everyone except for our very first game. We won the semis by ten and the finals by eight. We rolled through the tournament, and it just seemed easy. And who gets excited about that?"

He continued: "Losing the next year, in 1988, was crushing without question, so for me, winning in 1989 was the closest I ever came to elation. . . . I really think it was because it was the last year semis and finals were played the same day. That semi against Titanic was brutal. Clean game, but physical, with a lot of very familiar matchups where the line between success and failure was razor thin. The field was ringed with spectators and the energy was so intense. I remember sitting on a bench afterward and wondering how I would possibly summon the energy to play another game. And then we did. You just did. The finals wasn't as clean a game, nor as fun, but we had that great comeback, and then held on at the end. I remember game point after a timeout and a throw to Skip on the restart, it was clear that nobody but Pat and me were going to touch the disc. Something about that feeling, being on the field with Pat and just knowing there was no way we were going to lose. Yeah, that was as good as it ever got for me. Everything after that was just relief. There was never joy after that, just relief."

I was ready to graduate from Ultimate and begin a heathier, saner life, but, as it turned out, Ultimate wasn't through with me yet.

In December, after mailing in the applications to grad school, I drove back to Boston to play basketball with some of my old Titanic and Hostage teammates. During the last game, I was kneed in the balls and fell to the court. This was normal enough, but what wasn't normal was that the pain lingered for the next few weeks.

Over Christmas I visited Simon Long in New York City, where he had a big apartment. It was always a blast visiting Simon because he was rich and would pay for everything. We played racquetball at a fancy New York sports club, followed by a feast of dim sum in Chinatown, and then drank our way all over Manhattan.

If it was fun, then Simon irritated me, too, and not just because his lavish lifestyle reminded me of my relatively impoverished one. It irked me that he didn't take my attempts to become a writer seriously. Like everyone else, he would only start to consider my preoccupation "real" later, after I was published.

Here is how I knew he didn't take my writing seriously: I had finally begun to attempt to share my work with people and six months before my visit to New York I'd sent Simon the revision of my novel. He had given no indication he had read the book and as we sat in his living room doing bong hits I finally got up the courage to ask him about it. He put down the bong and gestured toward the right-hand front corner of the couch. I looked down to where the missing front leg should have been, and there was my fat manuscript, doing a serviceable job of holding up Simon's couch.

This pissed me off, of course, but after another hit I forgot about it and started to tell him about the pain in my groin. That was when Simon redeemed himself.

"You've got to get in and see someone," he said in his usual loud and intense voice. "You don't fuck around with things like that. You need to get in there."

I did when I got home. And so found myself in the same UMass hospital where Steph spent most of her days. Of course I didn't expect much from the visit, certainly didn't expect that I would be told I had cancer, and that in less than two weeks I would have my midsection sliced open. But that is what happened.

In short, Simon saved my life.

I took notes during that first meeting with Dr. Cuokos and here is what he said to me after examining an ultrasound:

"The way I see it, David, we have two options. One, we can make an incision in your lower abdominal wall and pull the testicle up using the spermatic cord. Then we can pop the testicle out and examine it. . . ."

I didn't hear the rest. *Pop it out?* I stared intently at him.

"Or we can wait another couple weeks, do another ultrasound, and take it from there."

That was what we did. During what we would come to call my "waiting period" Steph would be both my nurse and sparring partner. I mostly just hung around the house though near the end of that time, waiting for the second ultrasound, I drove to Wellesley in my old LeBaron station wagon to deposit sperm at a cryopreservation clinic in Wellesley.

"It's in your best interests," Dr. Cuokos had said. "An investment in your future."

As Dr. Cuokos predicted, the second ultrasound still showed a mass, and just two days later I headed into the hospital for my operation. Steph drove me in and walked me to the elevators. "See you soon," she said, squeezing my hand. I knew the next time I saw her I'd be lying flat on my back under the glaring lights of the operating room. When Cuokos had learned that Steph was a medical student, he'd invited her—if it was okay with me—to don scrubs and mask and observe the operation. "As a learning experience," he added. He had also agreed to waive the cost of the operation as a professional courtesy since I was the significant other of a medical student, which, along with the fact that I was poor enough to qualify for free health care in Massachusetts, meant I wouldn't pay a penny.

I remember a moment of happiness as I was wheeled into the operating room. Steph bent down beside me and said, "Hello, David." I reached out and gripped hold of her hand. For all the strangeness of having her there with me, for my half-castration, I knew I'd made the right choice. I was glad not to be alone.

"Keep an eye on things down there," I said to her. "Don't let them get carried away."

"I'm watching out for you," she said. "I have a vested interest."

I would remain awake for the whole operation. During the routine pre-op testing, it was discovered that I might have a condition known as "malignant hyperthermia." The doctor had explained that due to this they would give me a local anesthetic instead of putting me under, a spinal of the sort women are given during childbirth. That meant that my straight-ahead view for the next hour was of a sheet that covered my lower half. I had some vague awareness of the goings-on behind the sheet and could hear various murmured voices—one I was quite sure was Cuokos's—and the clinking of metal. If, instead of looking forward, I looked up and back behind, I could see my anesthesiologist's face looming above me, his features close and distorted like a reflection in a bathtub faucet.

I'd never been much of a stoic and when things got really painful, I let those around me know. During the worst stretch—the actual period of searing pain when my testicle was dislodged from its resting place of almost thirty years and the spermatic cord was reeled in—I squeezed Steph's hand with a grip that could have crushed rock. It felt as if a thin line of acid was being dripped along my abdomen. I moaned and groaned while Steph, as if watching a tennis match, glanced back and forth between me and the other side of the sheet. Despite her efforts to hide it, an anxious look began to spread over her face. Her forehead crinkled, and at one point I looked up and thought I saw some rather unprofessional tears forming in her eyes.

Once the worst of the pain passed, I heard a minor commotion down by my feet. Then I saw Cuokos leave the room, presumably carrying a part of my manhood along with him. It seemed terribly strange to watch him amble away with what, for as long as I could remember, had been my own private property. He was off to the pathology lab, and from that point it was out of his hands as well as mine. He would stand by while the pathologists sliced up my now public privates like so much deli meat. I imagined these lab-dwellers as giant insects, pincers for hands and goggly eyes. I saw their thin, bony limbs bent over their microscopes as they peered down and analyzed my tissue. . . .

When Cuokos returned his pace was still steady, but slower. I understood right away that the news was not good. If it had been, some minor celebration—a handshake, perhaps—would have been in order.

"What happened? . . . What happened?" I mumbled to Steph.

She disappeared behind the sheet to confer with the others. I felt panic rising through the fog of the drugs, and when she came back I looked into her eyes. This time I was sure I saw tears.

I woke the next morning in pain, not able to climb out of the bed. Never had I needed Steph as much as I did over the next week and never did she acquit herself so well. Bristling with efficiency, she took control of the situation. She was there by my bedside when I woke up and had already questioned Cuokos the night before. She knew, as my father liked to say, "the facts."

"It was a small tumor, David," she said. "The smallest Dr. Cuokos has ever seen." I nodded. This was good.

"They have to do a full biopsy down at the lab now. That will determine what sort of cancer it is. Because of the weekend it will take four or five days." I nodded again. Over the next week nodding would become second nature, my head starting to bob up and down on its own.

"You're going to stay here until then. Dr. Cuokos has prescribed some painkillers. And some Valium to help you relax."

The reason I needed to relax, I would now learn, was that not only was "the kind of cancer" to be determined in the UMass laboratories but my fate as well. Yes, *fate*. If the word reeks of melodrama, so be it. Steph, who in a fortnight had transformed herself into something of an expert on testicular malignancies, laid it all out for me.

The best case, she explained, would be if the cancer was a seminoma. That would mean I'd undergo a month of radiation therapy and my odds for a complete recovery would be upward of 90 percent.

"And the worst case?" I asked.

"That would be if the cancer is 'mixed,'" she explained. "Different types of cancer. Choriocarcinoma, embryonal carcinoma, teratoma, yolk sac tumors."

She rattled off the names while I imagined a kind of nauseating tapioca spreading like goo inside of me. What the doctors were worried about was the possibility of the cells metastasizing. Movement.

"If the cancer is mixed," she said, "they'll cut your stomach open and look for more."

I winced. But I appreciated Steph's dual roles as caregiver and lover.

My parents, meanwhile, didn't visit during that week, deciding not to fly up from their new home in North Carolina. Why not? I have come to think that they were disarmed by my joking manner. I know I made a lot of ball jokes that week (and laughed out loud when the intern came in offering the possibility of a prosthetic testicle). But for all my joking, I was terrified.

I don't want this to turn into one of those stories where the parents bear the brunt of the child's complaints. I can't say it didn't hurt that my mother didn't come up. As for my father, our relationship was, as always, complicated. Certainly there is plenty to blame on him over the years, as there is with any parent, but the truth is even then I would have rather had no one else for a father. I hated him at times—for his toughness, his sarcasm, his judging eyes, his irrational rages—but I also loved him. There was another side of him that I have not dwelled on enough in these pages: he was smart, funny, and he *cared*, loving me as much as he, fatherless himself as a child, could. I quickly forgave him for not coming up, at least on the surface. I rationalized that maybe his not visiting was just a case of his being squeamish. He hated hospitals and had already been operated on for bladder cancer. I remembered visiting him on Cape Cod, a few summers before, and seeing the toilet bowl water turn bright pink with his blood, the sides of the porcelain stained as if from a weak watercolor. He was a blunt, tough businessman, but when it came to cancer he was what my mother had once called him over the phone: a scared little boy. As it would later turn out, there was a very good reason for him to be afraid.

Whatever his reasons, he stayed down in North Carolina. So there were no touching hospital scenes with father at son's bedside. When that scene finally did play out, three years later, it would do so in reverse, with me taking care of my father, not the other way around.

But while my blood family did not come through, my Hostage family did. Hones took a day off from his job at the Ski Market Warehouse, where he was the last Hostage standing, and drove out to Worcester. He brought with him a mocked-up copy of the book *Brian's Song* with our names taped over those of Gale Sayers and Brian Piccolo's. After I opened the present and laughed, he gripped my hand and we acted out the deathbed scene right there in the hospital.

Ultimate had meant, for most of us, a continued postponement of adulthood. The sport itself seemed intent on the same sort of postponement, refusing to grow up. This would come to a head over the next few years when Jose Cuervo, the tequila company that had helped make beach volleyball a popular, televised sport, tried to sponsor some Ultimate tournaments. Dee Rambeau, a great Ultimate player in his own right, had been involved as an announcer and promoter in the early days of beach volleyball, and he now helped set up a series of Ultimate tournaments for Cuervo with cash prizes and the hope of real TV coverage. But many of the players rebelled, balking at wearing shirts with numbers on them while smoking joints on the sidelines. At the party after the tournament the sponsors foolishly offered the players free tequila for an hour and then tried to close things down. Players started climbing over the bar and pouring themselves shots, while the sponsors looked on, shaking their heads and deciding, perhaps right then and there, that Ultimate wasn't ready for prime time. It was crystal clear to Dee Rambeau: the players didn't want to grow up and neither did their sport. "If you can't sell the sport to a tequila company, who can you sell it to?" he asked.

Despite a deep craving for legitimacy, there had always been an equally deep ambivalence among Ultimate players about the possibility of the sport becoming more popular. For one thing, real legitimacy would mean better athletes, which would leave many of us shit out of luck, more Cribbers meaning fewer of us. For another, many of us reveled in the way things were: beers drunk and joints smoked on the sidelines, clownish uniforms without numbers or with ironic numbers.

It's easy to look back from the heights, or depths, of middle age and say of both the sport and myself, "Thank God you have finally grown up." But while perhaps it shows my own persistent immaturity, I can't help but see something beautiful, some genius, in the wildness of early Ultimate. One definition of wild is "self-willed" and in this sense Ultimate was so much wilder than accepted professional sports. Can you imagine a high-stakes football game where the players suddenly decided to start the game later because of the weather or where the players subbed themselves in or where the players made their own calls? Maybe Gus, drooling on the trophy, understood something fundamental about the game that even TK did not. Perhaps the real Spirit of the Game was not the sanctimonious sense that we were nobler than other people and other sports, but that we were wilder and funnier and had more fun. We didn't wear uniforms or do the bidding of corporations (even Cuervo) or listen to coaches or referees or sponsors. We decided who would play and how we would play, and we weren't going to leave behind our sense of humor or our nonconformity.

There were always those who argued insistently that we *had* to be less wild. Why? To be more *successful* of course. Successful in what way? Well, you know, to be on TV and make money and have people not laugh and say, "Is that the thing you do with dogs?" when you told them what you'd dedicated your life to. And, okay, sure, it's only natural to want that. *But guess what?* If you get all those things, you won't be the one playing; you won't be the one getting them. Because you were at best a good high school athlete and guess what kind of athlete will be taking over when TV money and attention come to the sport?

This was the game's deepest conflict, maybe even deeper than, "Should we have referees?" since the referee thing was subsumed by the other. It was a psychological battle that raged, even when people didn't know it was raging, the whole time I was playing. And it was a battle where I, like so many others, fought on both sides. Yes I wanted to win Nationals, maybe more than anything else in my life at the time, but I also wanted to lose and drool on the trophy. I understood the desire to make the sport bigger. I was attention-starved after all and hadn't gotten even a page of what I considered my real work out into the world. So when I was suddenly appearing on a show George Plimpton was hosting, it felt good. I'd been noticed by the unnoticing world! At the same time a big reason I was hooked on the sport was because of its wildness. I like the fact that we refused to grow up and that the game was really only understood by my band of brothers and sisters within it. A part of me even liked when the outsiders asked if it was played with dogs (even as I hated it) because then I could smirk and laugh with my Hostage brothers about the moron who had asked the question.

Finally, there was this. We really *were* the men in the leather helmets. We were the pioneers in uncharted territory, and pioneers know a freedom that later generations never will know. Players who come later can be better but they can't be first. Ultimate players now are better as a whole. They are well coached and the game is a better product, better *branded*. But we had the thrill of being first, of making it up as we went along. We were idiots at times. But we were proud and joyful idiots. We were not afraid to be ourselves.

For me the loss of a testicle would be a metaphoric as well as physical loss. I have already brought up the word ballsy, and I know it is not a popular word these days, and perhaps it shouldn't be. But, it was a quality that I valued during my twenties. I loved when I made daring throws, for instance, and I also admired this in others. I admired the way Kenny Dobyns took chances and rose to the occasion and I was not at all surprised when a later incarnation of his New York team took on the name Cojones.

I had always admired my father's ballsiness, too, the way he gambled with a glint in his eye and the way, I imagined, he must have driven hard bargains as a businessman. Now, as I approached thirty in a hospital bed, my father was more mystified than ever with his seemingly aimless son. What I couldn't see then, and what I can see looking back with a kind of avuncular attitude toward my younger self, was how much more daring my own life choices had been than my father's. Despite his gruff exterior, in some ways I was the tougher of the two David Gessners. He was at heart a lover of words and books, a history major with a passion for writing and delivering speeches who sometimes fantasized about being a writer, or perhaps a professor, himself. Instead he had taken the safe course and gone to business school and returned to what was, despite its having been abandoned by the Gessners for a generation, the family business of textile machinery. He had in other words played it safe while I was doing anything but. I had instead hucked my life deep while hoping someone as determined as me would catch it. As of the week of my thirtieth birthday, my gamble did not seem to be paying off. But, as it turned out, my luck was about to change.

On Tuesday of that week I had a CAT scan and finally managed to shuffle to the bathroom to piss. The Valium helped, and I didn't worry as much about my fate as you'd think. In fact, on Wednesday Steph and I started planning out my birthday party.

In a year of drama here is some more: exactly a week after my operation I would turn thirty. The operation would neatly bisect my life into a *before* and an *after*.

Standing by my bed, Steph asked me what I wanted to do for my thirtieth birthday, which was on Saturday. I said I wanted a party.

"Should it be small?" she asked, concerned.

"Big," I said.

And then on Thursday, after almost a week of waiting, I finally got the news. Dr. Cuokos came into my room, walked right over to my bedside, and fixed his eyes on mine. He placed his hand on my shoulder. Then, when his thin lips curled slightly upward in what was unquestionably a smile, I understood that he had come to tell me just what I most wanted to hear.

I sat up straight.

"A seminoma?"

"A seminoma, David."

"A seminoma!" I punched my fist in the air. "A fucking seminoma!"

I pushed myself off the side of my bed. This caused a small stab of pain in my groin but I didn't care. I knew how to play with pain, and I was tired of lying around. Right then what I wanted was to waltz Cuokos around the room, though I contented myself with pumping his hand and showering him with thank-yous. Then I danced a little shuffling dance, while he stood off to the side with his arms hanging in front of him, one hand gripping the other wrist. For a minute he stood there, the smile still on his lips, nodding slightly and steadily like a wind-up doll. Finally, he congratulated me one more time and backed around the curtain, while I continued my celebration. *A seminoma!*

Ultimate Frisbee is famous for its parties—crazy, wild, loud, late-night parties—and the party that Saturday night was historic. I was turning thirty and it looked like, with some luck, I might just eventually turn forty and fifty as well. The house was packed, people driving from Boston, New York, and Connecticut. Most of those in the crowd were of course Ultimate players or former Ultimate players.

Hones was downstairs grilling with Bobby Harding, and I joined them and we toasted to, what else, the Hostages.

"May our passes be linked as our arms are now," we said in unison as our toast, though in fact only the tips of our beer glasses were touching.

The party also marked the beginning of a change in my relationship with Steve Mooney. He came through that night and he would come through for me in other ways, and I would begin to see what a good man he was. We would no longer be teammates but we would start to become friends, and I would start to understand that the Hostage prejudice was just that, prejudice. We reflexively sneered at authority figures and in a sport like ours Moons was one of the few available to sneer at. At the time I didn't think much about the fact that he annually managed to wrangle twenty men with big egos into fighting units. Or the fact that while my Hostage teammates' main way of addressing me and my attempts at writing was by insult, Moons had always been a supporter of mine on the field, just as in coming years he would be one off it. Later, when I gave readings from my first book in Boston, few Hostages would show up but Steve would always be there. In fact, as I get older, I've started to think that "always being there" might be the best thing you can say about someone. Earlier I had seen him through Hostage eyes, but now I began to understand how dedicated and loyal he was.

If during the previous fall I had tried to "get serious," telling myself that Ultimate had been a big waste of time, aiding if not solely responsible for my arrested development, I now felt something different. Yes, it was time to put away childish things, but maybe my time in the game had not been entirely worthless. Looking around the room that night, I felt better about all the time and energy I'd thrown into the sport. Maybe it hadn't been, as my father contended, "a colossal waste of time." Not only had Moons and the Hostages come, but so had players from other teams. While I hadn't achieved my purported goals in Ultimate, I'd gained something else while I wasn't paying attention. I had become part of a second family, part of a tribe, and now when I needed them most, my tribe was rallying around me. While my real family remained in the South, my Frisbee family was coming through.

For the sake of this book I could say that it was that night that I started to see how much the sport had given me, that it was then and there that I learned the true meaning of Ultimate. But it would be more accurate to say that during those years and in the decades since I have only gradually come to see the enormous role that the sport played in my life. *Frisbee* may be a silly word—like *testicle* in that way, come to think of it—and the sport may not have been taken any more seriously than tiddlywinks. But that didn't—and doesn't—matter, not to me at least, not anymore. It's not the object of the thing so much as the passion poured into it. What's more, I had gained the strength of working long and hard at something that others thought ridiculous. It was like writing in that way. Something we tend to forget, or belittle in our corporate and connected age: that certain muscles can only be built by *going against*. So what if no one knew what the hell Ultimate was? When NBA players said they "love this game," as they did constantly in an ad from that time, they also meant they loved the money, the attention, and the perks. I loved Ultimate *despite* the fact that it had nothing like that to offer. I loved the pure play of it, the great moments, the camaraderie, the stories we told after. As silly as it sounds, it is true: I had begun to form myself through Ultimate. Frisbee helped make me.

"You're lucky," Steve Mooney would tell me later. "You have goals."

Well, yes, a little lucky, though a little cursed, too. The whole time I played I was not unaware how superficial, not to mention silly, it was to put so much energy into striving to be the greatest player of all time (by far). It was unreasonable and absurd, a dream, as Walter Jackson Bate liked to say in the spirit of Samuel Johnson, of "filling the minds of others." But it also provided me with excitement. With energy, with *juice*. If ridiculous, it was also fun. Perhaps my goals were overblown, vainglorious. But they kept me going in the face of what at times seemed a pretty desperate reality. If my goals were impossible, that made them less dull. Much later I would read, in Donald Hall's *Life Work*, what the sculptor Henry Moore said when Hall asked him what the meaning of life was: "The secret of life is to have a task, something you devote your entire life to, something you bring everything to, every minute of the day for your whole life. And the most important thing is—it must be something you can't possibly do!"

But I am getting too highbrow here. There was more singing at the party than quoting from great books. I made a lot of testicle jokes. And perhaps retaining some residual bitterness from my week in the hospital, I tacked up a large poster that I called "The Wall of Hate." On the poster there were a hundred blank spots where partygoers could write in their nominees for the most hated human beings. This was 1991 and notable write-in candidates for most hated humans included Dick Vitale, Garfield, Nixon (still and always), Bill Laimbeer, Yakov Smirnoff, Sinbad, the Blonde Poseur who played guitar on *Saturday Night Live*, Judas, and, of course, "One-Balled Guys Who Sing at Parties for Attention."

Simon Long had driven up from New York and I thanked him profusely. Simon had never been an easy friend to have but as much as I owed Dr. Cuokos, I also owed Simon. Without him pushing me to see the doctor, I might not have gone in and my story might have had a very different ending.

The party was, as Ultimate parties tend to be, a wild, drunken affair. Still not recovered from the operation, I tried to bluff through as if I was. I pooh-poohed any cancer talk, one beer after another sliding down my gullet. Then someone started passing around the tequila.

Suddenly I was a million miles away from the hospital, a million miles away from a grimmer diagnosis. Another Hostage, Paul Turner, had given me a K-Tel tape called "The Greatest Hits of the

Seventies." We sang along with "Delta Dawn" and "Having My Baby" and "The Night Chicago Died." After Steph brought out the cake I got the whole room to sing "Brandy." We roared out the climax:

Brandy used to watch his eyes
When he told his sailor's stories
She could see the ocean fall and rise
She saw its rage and glory.
But he had always told the truth
Lord, he was an honest man
And Brandy does her best to understand.

I don't know why "Brandy" affected, and still affects, me so; I only know that it had become the closest thing I had to a personal theme song. I sang it sarcastically for years but that night it seemed suffused with real emotion. After we finished singing, I told people it was the song I wanted played at my funeral (and please note, friends who are reading this, I still do).

It was a night full of the usual stupid drunk things: people fought and made out and I put my arms around friends and told them I loved them and danced and maybe even took off some of my clothing. As best I can remember I didn't wear a lampshade, but if I did, it wouldn't shock me. Of course it was asinine to be carrying on like that just a couple days after being released from the hospital but there it was. I can sit here and pretend to have completely changed from the young person I've been writing about. But I am not so different. Even today partying—with its forgetfulness, fun, silliness, relief—does not seem such an insane response to the predicament that is life, a predicament that ends with dying and rotting.

I even danced with Steph that night and told her I loved her and thanked her for standing by me in the hospital. There were two reasons for telling her this. One, I was feeling magnanimous. And two, despite everything we had been through, I really did still love her.

She could see the drunken sheen over my eyes, and maybe feared where the night could go, but she either hid her concerns or was simply caught up in the resurgent spirit of the night.

"I love you," she told me, and I'm pretty sure she did.

At one point I went out back and took a leak into the bushes while staring at black-blue clouds skudding across a moon that looked like it had been chipped out of soap. It was accident that had guided my story, just as accident guides all our stories. So what is the deeper meaning? I don't know. Maybe there is no deeper meaning. Maybe life is the only meaning, and not-life the only other meaning.

Most of the insights I gained from my illness came long afterward, once I'd had enough time to digest what had happened, but there was one brute fact that I understood right away: *I was alive.* Not through any virtue of mine, of course, but through sheer dumb luck. For me life was as simple as a kick in the balls during a game of pickup. Had I not gotten hurt playing basketball or had I had a less sensitive doctor my condition might not have been caught. I would have gone about my days, worrying about writing my next book and whether or not I should keep playing Ultimate, while the cancer swam happily into my lymph nodes. I would have found out about it eventually, but it would have been too late.

The party went deep into the night with Simon Long gloating about schooling some of my old Pope teammates in Scrabble in the TV room. Their game wouldn't end until 4:00 a.m. when Simon fell asleep, drooling right on the board. These were the same

Pope players who had once stolen the stuffed deer from the Natural History diorama at Cornell. Now, before driving off, they took the Scrabble letters and spelled out SIMON IS A GREASY WANKER on the board where Simon slept.

Meanwhile, Hones, Bobby Harding, and I sat in a circle in the living room passing around a bottle of tequila, a beer, and a joint. Each of us would take a hit of whatever was in front of us and pass it along. Sometimes someone would mutter "cannonball it," the Bill Murray line from *Caddyshack*. It was crazy to be doing this right after being cut open and losing blood but if crazy, it was also an appropriate way for my twenties to end. Forget that I still had weeks of radiation ahead or that the prospects for both my health and career were uncertain. For one night it didn't matter. Spring was only a week away and it looked like I wasn't going to be dying any time soon. In fact, within a week I would be walking out at the reservoir, within a month running. This was spring at its most pagan then: Persephone gone to Hades and returned from the underworld.

And on my thirtieth birthday my cause for celebration was the most elemental of all. I was a strong animal. *And I would fucking live.*

10.

Benediction

A good friend of mine once said that our bodies are like credit cards: we get the bills later on. I am over fifty now and have been paying my bills lately in the form of varicose veins, arthritis, and a torn rotator cuff from my years playing; I've become like an old sailor who can feel weather coming in across the ocean in my bones. Not long ago, on a particularly achy day, I said to my wife, "If I were young again, I wouldn't play that stupid sport." She looked at me the way she does sometimes. "If you were young again," she said, "I'd give you a beer, toss you a Frisbee, and you'd chase after it like a border collie."

The spring after my operation I did not play Ultimate once. Instead I endured a month of radiation, during which my insides burned and gurgled and smelled like rotting tarpaper. All April long I would march into the radiation lab and lay below that awful gantry, in a Frankenstein posture, my arms stiff at my side, my body raised five feet off the ground on my slab, a sci-fi ray beam pointed at my middle. I waited, however, not for a lightning bolt to spark me to life, but for the dreaded noise that signaled, once again, that the cells within my abdomen were being cooked into extinction.

But there was hope now and it was in the midst of my nauseating month of radiation that I got my first hint of a new life, that hint coming through the mail like a letter from my future self. Before the ray of light came darkness: rejection letters from UMass and Boston University and all the rest of the grad programs I'd applied to. Except one. This last letter would be the deus ex machina of my Worcester year, delivering me. It was an acceptance into the graduate writing program at the University of Colorado in Boulder. The other writing schools I'd applied to had been within an hour's drive of Worcester, since I was still operating under the illusion that Steph and I would continue living together (and, secretly, that I might play again for Titanic with Moons and finally win Nationals). But this new turn of events made the fostering of that illusion more difficult. If I did decide to go to school, it would be hard to commute from Worcester to Boulder.

Despite this, I still wasn't ready to leave Steph. Also, going west meant leaving behind the security of Cuokos and my other doctors, doctors who I was scheduled to see regularly for follow-ups over the next months and even years, as well as giving up, in all likelihood, my free health care. But at least leaving Worcester and Steph were now possibilities, possibilities that I fed off of.

Gradually, as the radiation ended, I turned back to the business of being a good animal. That fall I'd vowed to never play Ultimate again. And I would stick to that goal, I swore I would, at least as far as playing *serious* Ultimate went. But during that irradiated spring I decided I needed a goal and that I had to play in at least one more tournament. In fact, being in good enough shape to play Ultimate became a private mission, something that would be a secret sign to myself that I was whole again. I didn't want to throw myself fully into the sport. But I did want to test myself, to see if I could do it.

I began to jog out by the reservoir, wearing the old Frisbee quiver I'd fashioned out of a Dunlop tennis racket cover. Soon the jogs turned into runs during which I sprinted through the woods in random fartlek bursts, crunching over leaves and acorns. The movie *Rocky IV* had come out earlier that same year, and, unable to drag anyone (and certainly not Steph) to see the film, I'd gone alone. I was well aware that it was a very stupid movie overall, but I loved the training scenes in the movie version of Siberia (read Colorado) where Stallone, dressed in a leather jacket, ran through the snow, helped a villager right his topsy horse-drawn carriage, tossed boulders into a chute, chopped wood, climbed mountains, and engaged in an overall primitive workout in stark contrast to his opponent Drago's high-tech ones. After the movie ended I'd somehow gotten into a footrace outside the theater with a twelve-year-old boy, both of us full of the movie's energy. I might have let him beat me in the end though I don't remember for sure.

In the Wachusett woods I lived out my own montage, diving into my own primitive workouts. Despite my still-burbling stomach, I was recuperating faster than anyone expected. At Wachusett I'd sometimes see a great blue heron or listen to loons laughing out on the water or, as happened one night at dusk, be caught unawares by the great horned owl who came flapping down by and then in front of me, her wings whisper still. We might have been only ten miles from the city but here birch trees grew diagonally out of the banks, here there were tracks of rabbit and coyote, and here high ridges and promontories jutted out into the water like ship's bows. You could feel like you were a million miles away from Worcester or like you were back seeing Worcester before the city was built, back when the Nipmuc Indians roamed this area and the woods were full of bear and moose and wolves. Thoreau wrote that Wachusett Mountain symbolized the West, and when he saw it from certain hills in Concord, it would set his thoughts traveling westward. Two summers before, Steph and I had hiked and camped in the mountains of Colorado after the tournament in Boulder, and so I knew Wachusett to be a relatively puny hill. But there were times, especially when I heard the train running through Boylston, letting off a particularly plaintive Wolfean whistle, when the mountain seemed positively Western and I would look up at it and imagine a life beyond my Worcester life.

School was still all consuming for Steph and I had begun to daydream more and more about an escape to Colorado. In this way we staggered into summer, maintaining the illusion that these were not our last days together. In early July we took a train together out to Boulder to look for an apartment. For *me*, of course, not for *us*: she would continue living in Worcester.

Despite the state of our relationship, it was a romantic trip: we hiked up Mount Audubon, saw our first coyote, camped in Rocky Mountain National Park, made love in the tent. One evening I stood on a huge rock behind our campsite and watched the darkness come in slowly in waves. I tried to concentrate, catching the subtle gradations, the move from light to dark, darkness coming in like the tide. The mountains became a hulking presence and the outlines of trees and rocks oddly human. Something strong and strange welled up inside me. "To be alive on this earth," I wrote in my journal. "Sometimes it seems like this is something. That this is enough."

It was my first glimpse of what would be my new life. With Steph's help, I found a funky blue cabin to rent below the spectacular cleaved canyons of a town outside of Boulder called Eldorado

Springs. The cabin's owner, my roommate to be, was a tall dark-haired woman who, I would soon find out, loved astrology and heavy metal. She had bought the house and come there to live alone and recover after a divorce. From the room I would be renting I could look out the window at the mountains and hear the burbling of the creek. A perfect place for recovery, I thought. And for writing.

I was in Boulder to find an apartment, and I was there to scout out my new turf. But I was also there to play in an Ultimate tournament. It was the July Fourth tourney, the same one my Boston team had won two years before. Boston wasn't playing that summer so I wandered the fields hoping to pick up with a team, something that players do sometimes but that I had never done before since I had always played for either the Hostages or Titanic.

Were it back east I might have picked up easily with almost any team. But here a lot of the teams were from the West or Midwest, filled with players I didn't know and, more importantly for my purpose of securing a team, who didn't know me. But at the far end of the fields there was one team that knew me and that I knew well. I went up to that team's captain and explained my plight.

It would be my last tournament, or so I thought at the time, and I would be playing it with Kenny Dobyns and New York, New York. After I asked if I could play with them, Kenny went over and huddled up with his team. He came back and told me to put my cleats on. None of us were unaware of the irony of the situation.

All in all, it would prove a bizarre experience. I thought I had run myself back into shape around the reservoir in Worcester, but that level of fitness didn't translate to the rigors of Ultimate or the altitude of Boulder. Only two months removed from radiation therapy, I was less myself than I thought.

In one of the first plays of our very first game someone threw it long and it looked like Cribber would pull it down. But the disc got batted around and fluttered through the air, and there I was muscling my way out of a crowd for the rebound. It was what I did: I was what I caught. And so I dove and had my fingers on the deflected disc, but it binked off my hand. I swore loudly at myself. *If you can touch it, you can fucking catch it.*

Dobyns came over to me on the sidelines after the play, and put his hand on my shoulder.

"When it went up I said, 'That's the kind of shit Gessner always gets.'"

Not that day, not that weekend. Our team steamrolled through the tournament, but I contributed little, reduced to playing mostly defense, one of the lesser Shiites, a role I couldn't fill very well even *before* I'd been irradiated. The best part of the tourney, for me, was talking on the sidelines to Andy Scheman, who had often covered me when Boston played New York. My old nemesis turned out to be not just a great player but a great guy. The New Yorkers didn't know I was recovering from cancer, but I told Andy. I also expressed my worries that I would never be the same, and not just as an Ultimate player.

I didn't contribute much in the finals, which we ended up winning. On one of my few decent plays, I poached and caused a turnover, and Kenny yelled from the sidelines, "Great job, Gessner!"

It was a funny moment for anyone who could really appreciate it and as it happened there was someone in the crowd who could.

"Great job, Gessner!" someone yelled sarcastically from the sidelines, mocking Kenny's encouragement.

I turned around and saw that the heckler was none other than David Barkan, who now played for San Francisco.

It was strange but fitting that I was going to play my last

Ultimate game for New York. If the old Hostage cohesion lived on, it did so in that team. True, they were better and bigger and more fit than the Stooges had ever been, but what Pat King had seen back at that '81 Regionals, with not just Gus and Barkan playing out of their minds but the entire team becoming one living, breathing unit, parts of a whole, had now been incorporated into a vision that had become New York, New York.

That was something that Pat took pains to explain whenever he described the phenomenon of the New York dynasty. To the casual viewer, and even to most of the players on the teams they played against, it was the Kenny Dobyns show, co-starring Pat King. In this way it was a kind of echo of David Barkan and Gus with the rest of us as the Hostage-ettes. But that wasn't what New York, New York was about, Pat knew. What they were about, at least when they were at their best, was team, which meant the full commitment of twenty guys not to individual glory but to something more.

That was why Pat sometimes got irked with Ken and even thought on an occasion or two that the team would be better off without him. He remembered warming up with him once before the finals of Nationals, just throwing the disc back and forth, when suddenly a man with a TV camera appeared and Kenny threw himself to the ground and let go with a kind of primal scream as if psyching himself up. Then, as soon as the cameraman left or the red light on the camera went off, Kenny stood up and went back to playing catch.

Pat had initially recruited Kenny for Kaboom! after he had been cut by the Heifers, because he knew that New York Ultimate could not win without all its best players. Kenny of course was still one of those best players. But there were other people on the team, such as Skip Kuhn, Dave Blau, Andy Scheman, Karim Basta,

Walter Vander Schraaf, Mike Nevins, and Ben Usadi, who were equally important if not always as flamboyant. "I believe Ken Dobyns was a giant without equal," Pat would later write of his teammate. But he could say that and believe it while still believing something that sounded like its opposite: Ken Dobyns was nothing at all without his team.

W hen we got back east, perhaps freed by the desperation of sickness, I finally had the courage to contact my old professor, Walter Jackson Bate. I wrote him a long, honest letter, telling him how much he and his books had meant to me over the years, how I had struggled to begin to become a writer, and how I would like to visit him. He responded by inviting me to his home in Cambridge.

The visit went well and afterward we wrote letters and spoke on the phone a few times. Then later that summer, right before I left for my new life in Colorado, Walter Jackson Bate called and invited me up to the mythic farmhouse in New Hampshire. It had taken almost ten years, but I had finally achieved the same status as my college roommate Jon.

It was early August when I made the trip to New Hampshire. On the first afternoon we toured the property in his old Jeep, just as he and Jon had done. I had to bite my tongue to keep from crying out as we bombed down dirt paths, through briars, and across farmland. Here was my old professor wearing a pair of flip-up sunglasses and smiling with delight at the speed and rushing wind. I'd heard stories about his charging around campus on a motorcycle as a young man, but I'd never before been able to imagine Walter Jackson Bate as daredevil. This was a new twist.

After dinner that night, he poured us drinks. We drank several

"Italian kisses," a mixture of red and white vermouth, then small glasses of Madeira, or "old Maumsby" as he called it—"The liquor that Richard the Third had his brother drowned in," he muttered. I nodded as if I knew the allusion.

That night his talk was varied, ranging from cattle to religion. The first subject came up because it turned out he'd owned a small dairy farm "after the war," the second when I, emboldened by liquor, asked him if he believed in God.

"Oh, yes, I suppose," he said. He pointed out through the plate-glass window. Rain poured down hard on the flower beds and mist rose above the rolling hills. "I have to believe that there is something behind such a miraculous world."

I was surprised by his statement, even more surprised by the adamancy of my response.

"I can't believe in Heaven," I said. "Heaven seems the worst case of wishful thinking. Like believing in Santa Claus."

He studied me.

"I said I believed in a God who created the universe," he said. "I never said I believed in an afterlife."

He stood up and excused himself, and I wondered if I had committed a grave faux pas. But he returned a moment later with a book in his hands.

He sat down and, without introduction, began to read from T. S. Eliot's "East Coker." He began in a near monotone, but then his voice started to quaver, becoming more dramatic, and his hand—the wonderful right hand I remembered from lectures—fluttered and rose off his lap. Throughout the poem he held his hand up by the side of his head. It trembled slightly like a dry leaf as he read:

Home is where one starts from. As we grow older
The world becomes stranger, the pattern more complicated

Of dead and living. Not the intense moment
Isolated, with no before and after,
But a lifetime burning in every moment
And not the lifetime of one man only
But of old stones that cannot be deciphered.
There is a time for the evening under starlight,
A time for the evening under lamplight
(The evening with the photograph album).
Love is most nearly itself
When here and now cease to matter.

Old men ought to be explorers
Here and there does not matter
We must be still and still moving
Into another intensity
For a further union, a deeper communion
Through the dark cold and empty desolation,
The wave cry, the wind cry, the vast waters
Of the petrel and the porpoise. In my end is my beginning.

He sighed as he finished, cupped wrinkles drooping below his eyes. At that point in my life his reading was the most dramatic thing I'd ever heard. I had no idea what to say.

"Thank you," I managed.

"Thank *you*," he said. "It's been years since I read poetry out loud. The last time I read this piece was at Eliot's memorial service."

If I had not already been transported to some other mythical literary stratosphere, this last bit of casual name-dropping sent me there. The poetry, the liquor—"Old Maumsby"; here even the booze was poetic!—and Bate's presence intoxicated me. Of course I should have let the moment settle, should have savored it, but that wasn't my style. Before I could stop myself my lips began to flap and words spilled out of my mouth.

"I don't really know how to tell you this, or even if I should," I blurted. "But I feel I have to. Since I first heard your lectures I've tried to write the book I mentioned in my letter. For seven years now I've been writing it and rewriting it, but I can't stop. No matter how I try I can't get it right. You see I want it to be a great book but . . ."

I carried on in this vein for a good ten minutes, my words becoming more and more tangled. I tried to explain how I had begun a new story, about my cancer, but I didn't feel it would be right to start the new book until the old, the book of my twenties, was finished. Wasn't it logical to finish the old and put it to rest before starting the new?

When I finally finished my confession, I stared down at the floor. I had no idea what to expect, but wouldn't have been too surprised if he'd walked across the room and slapped me.

"A tar baby."

I heard the words and looked up. His chin rested in one hand while the other rubbed his eyes.

"What?" I asked.

"A tar baby. That's what we used to call it before the word became unfashionable. A tar baby. You put your hands on it, get stuck to it, caught on it, never get away from it. I've seen the same thing happen to friends and colleagues. Seen it ruin careers."

He paused to sip his drink.

"They say that knowing too much about a historical period makes it impossible to write historical novels. Maybe you know too much about your book. Maybe it's time to stop for a while, to put it aside and work on other things."

"But I feel I have to finish it. If I don't, the last decade will be a failure."

"Of course you feel that way," he said sharply. "If you didn't, it wouldn't be a tar baby. But despite how you feel, you must put it aside. Keats had the right idea when he refused to further revise *Endymion*. He wrote: 'Let this youngster die away.'"

The next two days passed quietly. We read, walked, talked, and toured the property in his Jeep. I took notes in my journal, a Boswell to his Boswell. During those days Bate spoke of many things but never mentioned my outburst over my writing or his response, and I thought perhaps he'd forgotten about it since we'd both been a little drunk. Our conversations grew less literary, often revolving around domestic affairs.

"The one rule is we don't let the cat out at night. If we do, a fox might get her. You've got to be careful. She waits by the door and then—zip!" With the last word he shot his finger and whole arm forward with surprising speed.

Another day passed and I imagined that I was perhaps overstaying my welcome. I decided to leave a day early. The night before my departure Bate left me in his study as he headed up to do his nightly reading. Once he had gone upstairs I took a copy of his own biography of Samuel Johnson down from the shelf. On a whim, I skimmed forward to the front pages. According to the title page, Bate had been born in 1918. I checked that date against the date of publication of his various books. Despite being obsessed with Johnson, Bate had not published his first book about him until 1955, at the age of thirty-six. He published the Keats biography eight years later, at forty-four, and hadn't produced his great life of Johnson until 1975, at fifty-six.

There was something comforting about those numbers.

I hadn't yet experienced the exhilarating feeling of rebirth and regeneration I'd feel the next year while writing my new book while living in a cabin in the Rockies, but perhaps it was then, in Bate's study, that I got my first hint of it. "Without hope there is no endeavor," Johnson had said. I put aside the books and turned off the light. That night, for the first time in many nights, I fell asleep comforted by a feeling of hope.

At Bate's New Hampshire farmhouse, of course, I still regarded the thought that I might one day publish an actual book the way a dying skeptic regards the possibility of a miracle cure, hoping but unbelieving. My infatuation with Bate was still in full bloom: I saw him as my Merlin, my Obi-Wan Kenobi. If this sounds mythic and overdone, it was. But also somewhat fitting. Recovering from cancer, coming back from the dead as it were, I was about to move to the West into a new life. And, now, how could I fail? I had the benediction of a wizard.

We took one final Jeep ride around the property on that last day—the last day I would ever see Jack Bate, as it turned out. I had spent the better part of the morning thanking him, but before stepping into my car, I extended my hand for one final "thank-you." To my surprise he clasped my hand tightly and then laid his other hand on top of mine. His voice was gentle.

"I've been thinking about your book," he said. "The more I think of it, the more I think you must be done with it."

He let go of my hand.

"You understand?" he asked as I climbed into the car.

I nodded.

"There are plenty of other things to write. You can always go back to it. But for now be done with it. Let it die away."

I nodded again, and he turned and began to walk the cobbled path back to the house, the cat running in front of him. He didn't turn around as I pulled out of the driveway, but threw his right hand straight up above his head in a final backward wave.

Colorado was like a whole state full of Ultimate players. Almost immediately I felt like I had found my lost tribe.

Following Bate's advice, I left all my old writing behind when I headed west that late summer. During those first weeks in Eldorado I scribbled down notes about the wonder I felt at living on my own in that strange new place—notes about the birds, plant life, and weather. "How could I not be happy here?" I wrote in my journal. To survive I took out student loans so that for the first time in my life I could write without work or worry. I started running up the canyons, having to stop every hundred yards at first, my lungs bursting from altitude and exertion. I pissed outside at night watching moon shadows on the cliffs and breathing in the smell of wood smoke, and I began to learn the natural history of the place. After mornings of writing I would hike up through the canyon and rebaptize myself in the creek. At my favorite spot, the spot where the torrents came down silver over the flat rocks and the cottonwood tree and tamarisk bushes blocked the outside world, I would strip off my clothes and edge into the frothing frozen creek, dipping in three times minimum. And then I would climb out and loll in the sun against the red sandstone slabs while dragonflies buzzed by and the tamarisk blew gently; I felt reborn in those waters—yes, reborn, there is no other way to say it—trying as I was to wash off the cancer and the Worcester year.

Of course no sooner had I washed off the Worcester year than I returned to it, the way writers do. During my dips I felt the first stirrings as the year I'd just lived through began to gradually transform itself into art. One morning in September I typed these words:

*To lose a testicle is to lose a friend. At least those were my senti-
ments at the time of my de-balling.*

After that I attacked my new cancer book every morning, writing the first draft straight through. I missed Steph achingly, but I
also felt stronger than I ever had. "The hero was the man who
could go into the spirit world, the world of the dead, and return
alive." I taped that quote from Ernest Becker above my desk.

All my writing efforts before had been halting, but now I finally had a story to tell. I wrote in my journal: "I feel like ripping
off the top of my brain and writing, painting, drawing, and walking until I drop dead from exhaustion." Soon painting and drawing fell by the wayside and just writing remained. The novel came
out pure and fast, what my old hero Thomas Wolfe used to call
"taking a book off the brain." I began to type as if taking dictation
and I didn't stop, the words pouring out.

While I typed, I let my hair and beard grow, and I smoked cigars
and drank coffee, my heart taking off like a racetrack rabbit. Still
prone to excess, I was now at least steadfast and consistent in one
thing: my work. I had my first real story to tell and I would tell it.

Then after class one day, on my way back home to Eldorado
Springs, I pulled over at the bargain theater and took in a matinee
alone. The film was called *The Doctor* and starred William Hurt.
I still have no idea about the filmic merit of this story, and maybe,
to people who have not been through an illness, it comes off as
sappy, a tearjerker. All I know is that that afternoon, with no one
else in the empty theater, I had the most affecting and profound
film experience of my life. From the first it was just too much, too
familiar. The initial diagnosis of the tumor, the doctors, the tests,
the operation, the life-and-death period, the recovery. Sobs started
to heave up into my chest after the first five minutes, but I fought
them back. I finally broke down about halfway through the film,

and then kept it going right up through the credits. I had forgotten how much crying can be like real laughter, how it rises up and takes over your body in great convulsive waves. My thoughts were reduced to caveman basic: *Every life is important.* This simple idea struck me with the force of revelation. Then, another: *I don't want to die.* Followed by more senseless blubbering. I came out of the theater red-eyed and splashed my face with cold water in the restroom. I was at once embarrassed and aware that what I'd just experienced was a good, old-fashioned catharsis.

After that my love for Eldorado Springs deepened. It was like living inside a painting: at night the moon would set over the strange gorgon-like rocks of the canyon, and in the morning lambent light would pulsate through the leaves and play shadow games on my futon. The mornings were cold and full of birds; I took my coffee up the trail behind the house and watched green swifts darting low over the rash-red sumac. And eagles too, and falcons and canyon wrens and towhees and bluebirds, and a great blue heron stalking fish in the always-gurgling creek, and then deer and coyote, and even a rare ringtail scampering up a scree pile. The Chinook winds blew down through the canyon and the creek lit up silver in the fall light while my story poured out of me. I wrote and wrote and wrote.

Which would make a neat and happy ending. Our hero, having finally grown past his immature obsession with Frisbee, has now left his old life behind and begun his new. Perfect. Except for the fact it didn't happen that way.

Ultimate had served its purpose, you might think, and it had; believe me, it had. During those first weeks in Colorado it seemed I'd finally managed to put aside childish things. There was a small problem, however. To get to school from my home in Eldorado canyon I had to drive past the high school playing fields where the

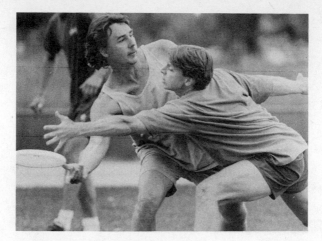

The author in Colorado with Lou Burke

Boulder Ultimate team, called the Stains, practiced. During those days of hard denial I had no way of knowing that I would play Ultimate "seriously" for six more years, soon numbering some of my Boulder teammates among my closest friends. And I had no way of knowing that I would have a Frisbee afterlife, that while I no longer had the Hostages as my tribe, soon I would have the Stains.

For a week or two I didn't give in, driving by grim-faced, thinking about my novel, trying to ignore the plastic discs that described parabolas or the people running up and down the fields. But by the third week I had a notion, and the notion couldn't be stifled. On the way back from school I pulled my Buick over at the fields and dug my cleats out of the trunk. I walked up to the fields casually, cynically even, sure that I wouldn't be suckered in again.

I don't remember which of my new teammates threw me the Frisbee, but I do remember that they overthrew me.

I chased after it like a border collie.

11.

A Frisbee Afterlife

The next years were a dark time for Steve Mooney. While others, like Bobby and me, had quit Titanic, he would keep going. Of all the Boston players remaining from the old days, he was the only one to have won a National Championship, back in 1982 with the Rude Boys, but that was almost a decade behind him and he was now, if possible, even hungrier to get the title back. Despite all the losses, some fairly close, he kept pushing. He might still be able to let loose and be silly at tournaments like April Fools or Solstice, but when fall came his demeanor changed. Fun was fun but winning trumped fun. The fact is he had long been a type A athlete trapped in a type B sport, and he now drove his teams through endless running drills until a common sight at Boston practices was of players bent over, hands on knees, gasping for air or retching. And if he was hard on his teams, he grew even harder on himself, often continuing to run hundred-yard sprints once the squad was done. His wife, Mary, who he understandably called "the real athlete in the family," was a world-class sculler who'd won both the Head of the Charles and two national championships in rowing. From her Steve adopted a tradition that crew jocks had long endured if not embraced: running stadiums. Moons, over the next decade, would keep pushing himself up the concrete steps of Harvard Stadium, ascending the old crumbling stadium until he could stare out over Cambridge and the Charles, before taking a deep breath and descending for another rep.

None of the training seemed to make any difference. For the next four years New York, New York would continue to beat Boston. Boston would change personnel, would change its name—from Titanic to Big Brother to Boston Commonwealth—but nothing worked. They always lost. And New York—and Kenny—always won. As Pat King once said, "We had Boston's number."

During this time Steve Mooney grew his hair long, fully in his Ichabod Crane phase. Though maybe the more apt literary comparison would be Ahab. While New York held the sport in its death grip, Moons would struggle on, obsessed with getting his second ring. Boston had become the sport's Buffalo Bills, always coming up short, but rather than simply taking his lumps, and one championship trophy, and calling it a career, Moons persisted, and would continue to persist. What I would come to admire most about him was how he continued to work during those years of losing. To drive all year long toward a goal, only to fail, leaves a pain that lasts for months. Many players, stinging from the pain, withdraw from the sport. Sometimes this withdrawal is subtle; they continue to play but commit less wholeheartedly, sporadically, afraid of being burned again. Total commitment in the face of failure is an impressive thing. For the twelve years after the Rude Boys' great victory Moons would commit all out and lose, banging his head against the wall without success.

Boston lost to New York in the finals 21–14 in 1991, the fall I moved to Colorado, and 21–13 the next year. After New York won in 1993, the *New York Times* ran an article on champions of unheralded sports in which Ken Dobyns talked about the fact that Ultimate becoming better known would be a "double-edged sword."

"If Frisbee was more popular than it is today," he said, "a lot of guys might not be able to play because better athletes would likely take their place."

But even within an article about sports that are slighted, Ultimate managed to sustain a slight. Joe Durso, the then-eight-time national handball champion, was quoted as saying, "I'm not taking anything away from Frisbee, but it's a very limited sport and very narrow skills are required to play it. Handball, on the other hand, is a very difficult sport to master, let alone be great at."

The truth was that by the next year, 1993, Ken Dobyns and his teammates were tired of playing a sport that got no respect. They had won four in a row, five overall, and they were exhausted from the effort. Cracks were forming in the great wall that was New York, New York, and it looked like this would be the year that Boston would finally break through. That fall New York teammates fought each other in practice and some team members vowed they would no longer play with certain others. Boston had beaten them several times in the fall season building up to Nationals, and it seemed clear that they were at least their physical equals if not their superiors. They had also added Joey Giampino, the great Chicago receiver who had moved to Boston, and he had convinced the team that they needed to fight fire with fire and not just beat but out-tough New York. The way to beat a bully, Joey preached, was to punch him in the mouth.

There are those who believe that if Boston had played a clean game against New York at Nationals they might have won on talent alone. But that hadn't worked for the last decade and they didn't trust it would now. It was at some point early on in the game, during one of the inevitable arguments, with Kenny doing his blustery thing and bumping up against Moons, that Moons pushed him with two hands in the chest. Kenny fell backward but then jumped up and started chesting his way up to Moons when from off the sidelines Jeremy Seeger began sprinting. With a full running start, Jeremy plowed into Kenny and knocked him to the ground again. A brawl ensued. For Boston, years and years of frustration came pouring out.

Later Pat King reported that he couldn't help but laugh at what he was witnessing. "Boston's whole world view was collapsing," he said. He had a point. Until that moment their only claim to superiority over New York was a moral one, and now they had lost the high ground. It was the ugliest game of Ultimate since the famous Kaboom!–Dallas Sky Pilot game eight years before.

Boston had also inadvertently given New York the game. "Play your game," good players tell themselves, and the corollary: "Don't get taken out of your game." Fisticuffs was New York's style, not Boston's. When the fight started, the game had been tied but now New York pulled away. The next day New York, New York routed Double Happiness, the San Francisco team, in the finals 21–13 for their sixth title.

Having spent all these chapters on Boston Ultimate, it is not fair to squash Colorado Ultimate into a few short pages. But, as my father always liked to remind me, "Life's not fair." I set out here to write a Frisbee memoir, to map the wild territory of my strange twenties, and those twenties were over by the time I arrived in Colorado. The next six years of my Ultimate life were calmer ones, my Frisbee obsolescence, and while some of my new teammates might have still thought of me as something of a wild man, I knew mine to be a comparatively tame wildness.

The Colorado team at Nationals

I loved my life in Colorado. Loved the mountains and loved learning the new flora and fauna and the classes I both took and taught, loved the way I was starting to write every day, and loved the way my body gradually returned to its old self after cancer, and then, training in the mountains, turned into something stronger and better than its old self. And I loved my new teammates. How lucky I was to land in a new town and suddenly be part of a *team*. Imagine it: to move to a new place and instead of feeling alone suddenly having twenty new friends: Ian, Zeke, Bobby, Rob, Big Dave, Juancho, Buzz, Randy, Kargs, Ted, Louie, Captain, Mikey, Jim, Paul, Steve, Jerry, Emery, and yes, even, God bless him, Renzo. I felt like a changed man: my beard had grown in and I wouldn't shave it for many years. I even had a new name in my new place, one that came about by a mangling of the pronunciation of my last name. I was no longer Gessner, but Gersh.

Having never lived outside of Massachusetts before, I never knew how regional Ultimate was. There was, it turned out, a world beyond New York and Boston. In a sport where the stories were communicated not through the TV wires, but by the spoken word, many of these players had never seen Turbo dive for a disc. Which meant that I wasn't exactly greeted with open arms, but instead had to prove myself. This wasn't easy at first since I still was not fully recovered or used to the altitude. And if they hadn't played against Turbo, I had never heard of players like Bob Pease and Ian Hutchinson. Bob, a strong handler, ran the team with a natural confidence and efficiency that reminded me of Moons. As for Ian, he was simply one of the best athletes I had ever encountered. I remember once early on going up in the air against him. Both of us got our hands on the disc at about the same time and, to my surprise, he yanked it away from me. *As if I were a child*, I thought later. That didn't happen back where I was from.

One difference between this team and the Boston teams I'd played for, especially the Hostages, was that everyone on it was so *nice*. There was always a kind of cruelty to the eastern teams, a certain junior high school meanness. Sure, we still gave each other shit in Boulder, but it was such gentle shit. They would never do what I had done to one of my Hostages teammates—who was himself kind of a dick—the time we had been tripping and I said to him, "We all pretend to not like each other. But with you it isn't pretend."

No, this was a new world and it seemed to me, a better, kinder world.

My life improved in Colorado in many ways. Even the first and most historically intense of my personal relationships, that with my father, got better after I moved west. It was funny but it made a huge difference to him that I was now in school. Somehow the fact that I was getting a graduate degree in writing changed things, sanctioning and making official what had until then seemed to him to be my vague plan to "become a writer." My decision to try to write had always felt wild and unstructured, but the stamp of school gave it, in his mind, structure and form. What I had been doing before scared him. School he understood.

For the first time my father and I even took a trip together, just the two of us. In December of 1991, after my first fall in Colorado, we traveled to the town of Aue in what until two years before had been East Germany. It was the ancestral home of the Gessners, and just a month before they had changed the name of the town square back from Karl Marx Platz to Gessner Platz. My father's goal was to purchase his great-grandfather's textile machinery company, Ernst Gessner Textilmaschinen, and he would do so in January of 1993, becoming one of the first foreign owners of a once-nationalized company in the recently desocialized state. Throughout the week my father spoke his *Berlitz* German, which to my ear sounded blunt, slurred, and guttural, a little like Klingon. But watching him in action as he outnegotiated the Germans in their own language, sighing, jabbing, grunting as he went, I became vaguely aware of an alien sensation bubbling up inside of my chest. It took a while, but by the time the week was over I recognized it as pride. It was an important time for us. I had always thought the whole problem between us was that my father didn't respect me and what I was doing, but it occurred to me that week that until then I hadn't always respected him. From Germany I flew back, not to Colorado, but to Boston, and from there I drove out to Steph's new apartment outside of Worcester. It was great to see each other again, and we had a fine reunion. We made love and told old jokes and called each other familiar pet names. To me we didn't seem any more or less "over" than we had before, though Steph did say with certainty that after medical school she now wanted to live in Israel. I carried on in my usual oblivious fashion, suggesting that after I graduated we could live half the year in Israel, half the year in the States. I would not go down easy.

On the last day of my visit we took a walk around Wachusett reservoir. I remember the sky was gray and the ice on the water creaked like the song of a whale. That afternoon I drew a picture in my journal that I still have, a picture of a small plant encircled by ice like a ballerina's tutu. We were halfway around the reservoir, near the cove where I sometimes saw the great blue heron, when she said it.

"I need to talk to you, David."

I understood the phrase was trouble as we had already been talking, as best I could tell, for over an hour. She took a deep breath and told me how much she loved me, the same thing she had always told me after I caught her cheating.

"I love you so much but we just can't do this anymore," she said.

"What do you mean?" I asked, dense to the end. "We can make it work. We can live in both places. Israel and here."

"It isn't about places," she said. "I've always loved you but it's over."

And it was.

After we had finished bawling a while, we walked back to the car, together but apart.

The next day I flew back to Colorado, officially single for the first time in almost eight years.

Even then our relationship wasn't dead. Though Steph and I would not see each other for close to a decade after that walk around the reservoir, we continued to play roles in each other's lives. When I returned to Colorado that winter after our breakup, I worked out as I never had before, lifting weights and doing push-ups and running the trails, fueled by the pain of her rejection and vowing I would "crush her like a bug." A month and a half later, on the Valentine's Day that would have been our eighth anniversary, I got together with a woman named Greta. Greta was and is a wonderful, smart woman, and I felt lucky to be with her. But our timing was bad. One morning, when my new lover and I were lying in bed together, Steph called. When I heard her voice I brightened and said instinctively, "Sweetie," as poor Greta listened and cringed.

Not long after that Steph called to tell me she was engaged to an Israeli doctor. They married in September, just nine months after we broke up. Soon after they moved to Israel.

In 1994 my new team, Boulder, made it to Nationals for the first time. Boulder played well but failed to make the semis. But something else happened at that Nationals, something that would signal a seismic shift in the sport. The tournament that year was held on a horse farm in Kentucky, and as I remember it, I was returning from watching the Boulder women play when I strolled over a hill and came upon the men's semifinals between Boston and New York. I walked up to the sideline near the end of a very tight game, though I don't remember the score. There was Moons and there were some of my old teammates, though many of the players were new. At that point, New York had won six Nationals, five in a row, and the year before had ended with that ugly brawl. No Boston team had won one since 1982 when Moons and the Rude Boys prevailed, and it seemed amazing to me that Moons was still playing. As a newfound believer in daily consistency, I admired his dedication. (Little did I, or he, know that he would still be playing at the national level almost a decade later.)

Boston had taken a lead and looked like they might finally break through. In fairness to New York, this was not exactly the same squad that had won all those titles; they had lost some of their stalwarts, including Pat King, who had retired, and their defensive star, Jon Gewirtz, who was now playing for another team. But the new team still had Ken Dobyns and Cribber and other great New York players. The team was called Cojones, and from what I saw they were earning that name with ballsy throws and great diving catches that were keeping them in the game.

As it happened I was there to witness the moment when Boston's dark night of the soul finally ended. The exact moment that broke New York's back and ended their reign came when Boston was working the disc upwind. In any kind of strong wind an upwind goal is precious and they were advancing it carefully, nervously, even tentatively, it seemed to me. There were all sorts of new stars on this Boston team—including Jim Parinella, Alex de Frondeville, and Chris Corcoran—but it was an old player, not a new one, who would make the throw that made me, and perhaps their team, believe that this year might be different. As I watched that very player, a man who had once been the boy who Simon dubbed God, caught the disc on the far sideline. I would learn later that Jeremy Seeger had been hobbled that season by an ankle injury and hadn't played his usual dominant role on the team. But now he had the disc and now he was pulling it back in that long-armed way of his and now he was ripping it forward and there was nothing tentative in the throw that sent the disc launching deep. It flew far and true and over the heads of all the New Yorkers until it reached the opposite end zone and rested in the hand of Billy Rodriguez, a great Boston player.

There was still plenty of game left but Boston was fired up now, and, riding blocks by two of my old teammates, John Axon and Lenny Engel, they pulled ahead to win. Steve Mooney threw the winning goal and New York, even if it really wasn't New York, New York, was finally vanquished. It was more exorcism than mere Frisbee game. The Boston players howled with relief and joy. It had taken many years and many losses but they had done it.

"We were no longer the kid brother trying to match our mean older brother," said Jim Parinella, who was so overjoyed he couldn't speak after the game.

The next morning Boston would play Double Happiness, a team from San Francisco, for the title. I only saw the beginning of that game since I had to catch my plane back to Denver, but I remember it was a cold, windy morning, and that the San Francisco team was all covered up in Lycra and warm-up suits while most of the Bostonians wore shorts and T-shirts. Based on those sartorial choices alone, I liked Boston's chances. Whether that really had anything to do with the results I don't know, but that morning a Boston team finally won Nationals again, the first since the Rude Boys. All through the next winter Jim Parinella, instead of hitting his desk and yelling "Fuck!" about another opportunity having slipped away, would clench his fist and celebrate, yelling "Yes!"

Steve Mooney had gone twelve years between championships, and he would later say that the second championship felt more "professional" than his first one with the Rude Boys and that he experienced less "pure joy." Which is not to say it wasn't deeply satisfying. His work and persistence had paid off. At long last he was a champion again, his quest fulfilled.

By my second year in the writing program I began to have some small victories of my own as I started to finally get my work published. The first essay that I *almost* got published was about my trip to Walter Jackson Bate's cabin in New Hampshire. Even before I'd left New Hampshire, I already knew that I would follow my Boswellian impulse and write an essay about the experience. Of course I would. That weekend had been one of the most thrilling occasions of my life. I would do what almost any writer

Steve Mooney, triumphant

would do: I would record it. What I didn't know was that Bate would react with indignation to that essay, which I thought a tribute, ending its chances at publication along with our friendship.

As any sophisticated reader knows, these mentor/ disciple stories rarely have happy endings; they follow a fairly standard arc from infatuation to worship to disillusionment. My story was no exception. I wrote my essay during my second year in Colorado. I wrote about Bate well, I think, and sent it out to a prestigious review where it was accepted, my very first acceptance as a writer. To be polite I also sent the piece to Bate, sure that he would appreciate the admiring, even loving, spirit in which it had been conceived. What he saw instead was a caricature of an enfeebled, senile old man. He called the editor of the review and raged, and the editor promised not to run the piece.

Due to the miracle of what was then modern technology, I got the news of my first acceptance and subsequent rejection within seconds of each other, both singing out to me from my answering machine. I had been away for a weekend of cross-country skiing and had come back home, my face flushed from the outdoors and exercise. My fine mood got better as I listened to the first message on the machine, accepting my essay. I was in the middle of a celebratory dance when I heard—and was crushed by—the second.

Bate sent me a scathing letter, along with a marked-up version of the essay. He particularly objected to my description of his over-active hands, saying they made him look crazy, like something from "Hogarth's pictures of Bedlam." The essay's pages were filled with his scrawled notes: "Too much fluttering of hands!" "Hands again!" "Do you have a mania for hands?"

Reading the old piece today I agree with him, up to a point. The essay verges on caricature, but my admiration for my subject— why call him anything other than my hero?—comes through. At the time I was decimated. Wasn't this the man who embodied magnanimity and empathy? I sent a letter of apology, but Bate re-fused to respond either to it or to my phone calls. I wrote again, promising never to publish the piece.

But I would publish it eventually, breaking that promise. I did so much later, five years after Bate died. By then I had heard sto-ries of Bate's occasional irrational rages, how he once threw his ashtray against an English-department wall, for instance. At first it didn't sit well with my image of the kindly, wise professor, but later I was a little more inclined to believe it.

Of course it isn't big news that heroes have faults. For all that we pained each other, Bate remained my greatest teacher, an in-spiring guide whose voice I still hear and who helped me define who I am. What I choose to remember about him is that he was heroic in the Johnsonian sense, struggling to manage his own imagination, disciplining it toward empathy and the creation of art. That that imagination might have been a bit more unruly and irrational than I first believed is no longer cause for despair or bitterness, but hope and reassurance.

While the Bate piece was not published immediately, an essay about my trip to Germany with my father was, as were a couple more pieces. *Wormtown*, my novel about my cancer, was rejected by a couple dozen publishers, but I immediately started working on another book and it was that book that garnered some real interest. It was a nonfiction account of an off-season on Cape Cod, full of the nature descriptions I'd collected in my journals over the years, intermingled with a memoir of my father. I published a couple of the chapters from the book in literary magazines, and then even went as far as taking the unprecedented step of mailing two of the pieces to my father. He admitted to liking one of them.

Then, during the first week of April in 1994, twenty-two years ago as I type this, I began dating my wife, the writer Nina de Gramont. When Nina came along it was right. She was beautiful, with a radiant smile, and despite some fights at the start, it quickly became clear that we fit together in a way I never had with anyone else before. "You've met your match," said Ian, my teammate on the Stains, and I had. Artistically, sexually, personally. Another friend said that we contained each other's secret selves: I could be loud and brash, a big ham, but valued my quiet, creative time, while Nina, who seemed quiet at first, was full of humor and took delight in all things fun and wild. As a bonus I knew from the start that I wouldn't be walking in to get my cleats and find her naked with another man. She was loyal and what's more, she needed me. Early in our relationship, when we were camping in New Mexico, we were fording a river when the force of the water began to sweep her away. I picked her up and carried her the rest of the way across the river. But more and more she was the one carrying me. She took me and my writing very seriously, and she saw me as larger and better than I saw myself, making me larger and better. In her eyes I was not a clown-prince but something else, possibly something heroic, an artist, and that was a large part of the reason I would eventually become one. And I like to think I gave her a little of the same gift back, that I knew she was a real writer before she did.

We would grow together but our first months were rocky, and this was at least partly due to a strange and brutal fact. During the same week that we first got together I got a phone call from my father. He told me he had lung cancer.

Nina would never meet my father. He would die only three months later at the age of fifty-seven, an age I am closing in on now. I spent the last month of his life with him at my parents' home in Charlotte, North Carolina. During that time I often found myself thinking back on our trip to Germany. For the first thirty-two years of my life I had played the child to his adult, but during his last weeks, when he was restricted to his hospice bed, our roles were reversed. I became the parent, helping him to the bathroom, emptying his urinal, hand feeding him grilled hot dogs (the one thing he could stomach after chemo), finally lifting his emaciated form off of the bed so that we could change the sheets.

Both of these phases had the disadvantage of unevenness, of one figure being relatively powerful and the other relatively help-less. But what I'm thankful for today is that there was another phase, a phase that began on that trip to Aue, a time when we were as close as we'd ever get to being on equal footing. Sometimes when I get melancholy I imagine what might have been: a period of years, not months. But if that time didn't last long enough, I'm thankful to have had it at all. Thankful to have been, however briefly, my father's equal, or at least his near-equal, and, for a short while, something like my father's friend.

The fall of 1996 was my last season playing Ultimate Frisbee. I was thirty-five years old. Boulder made it to Nationals, after an exciting but rough ride through the losers' bracket at Regionals in Las Vegas, but once again we did not make the semis. Boston fared

The author playing for Boulder

better, winning their third title. They had a creative defense and a cold-blooded offense with players like Alex de Frondeville, Paul Greff, and Jay Watson who seemed untroubled by heavy winds that blew through the tournament. Most of all they had an air about them, an air of certainty despite the field of chance. Having been forged against the great New York teams, they would never wilt under pressure again. The little brother had become the big brother.

They also had Steve Mooney, version 6.0, the long-haired elder who was closing in on forty. If Steve's reputation had taken any hits back during the days of losing to New York, or of starting fistfights, it was once again fully burnished. The evil troll had been vanquished and all was right in the land. If this Boston team, called DoG (or Death or Glory) had too many argumentative types to be a re-creation of TK's band of great-good men, then they were a hell of a lot closer than New York had been. They didn't spike the disc after scoring and at World's one year they won the award for good spirit along with the championship, just as the Rude Boys had at the very first Worlds. That year in the finals Steve Mooney's Boston team would beat the Seattle Sockeye, 19–16. That made three Boston wins in a row, halfway to equaling New York, New York's six.

In the end Boston would end up matching that number, giving Moons himself seven National titles. Moons was now known not just nationally but internationally in the Ultimate community, not just as the game's biggest winner but as a good sport. While my Hostage prejudice wouldn't allow me to swallow this entirely, I began to see something in his Ultimate career, more than in Kenny's and certainly more than in my own, that proved a model and a mirror for what I was trying to do with writing. Not that I won championship after championship. Hardly. But that persistence in the face of failure was my greatest strength as a writer. And that, oddly, like Moons, I would go into each book the way he went into each season: sure that it would be this one that was the best, the one that, despite past results, would break through.

Ken Dobyns and Steve Mooney would win thirteen national championships between them, seven for Steve and six for Kenny, and they would captain the only two true dynasties in men's Ultimate history. A fun armchair game to play during that period, and since, was to wonder which team would win in their primes. Since quite a few of the Boston players were already in their primes during New York's reign, and since Boston didn't win until at least some of the key New York players split from the team, the answer might seem self-evident. In fairness to the Boston teams, they would add some players, and a whole new system of both offense and defense, and that complicates the question. But for me it was hard to imagine any Ultimate team taking down New York and the frothing hordes on their sidelines. They had my vote as the best.

Meanwhile, after I quit playing my Boulder team moved into the Masters Division, where they won two National Championships

under their new AARP-approved name, Old and In the Way. That
meant that two teams that I had played for had won national titles
soon after I left. Which allowed me to joke that whenever I left a
team it was like throwing off ballast, the team immediately rising up
like a hot air balloon.

The package arrived in the mail in March of 1997, the winter
after I stopped playing. Since I had never won it all, winters
usually carried a tint of failure, but this one would be different.

It came in a simple UPS box and even though I knew what
was inside the box I didn't think it would affect me like it did. This
was no big deal after all. Being on the cover of the *New York Times*,
winning some big prize, having your face on the cover of a magazine. Those were the things that real writers were supposed to
glory in. Not this.

And it wasn't a surge of glory that I felt as I unwrapped the
package and looked down at my first book. Hones had taken the
cover picture, a beautiful beach scene of some birds over the sand
flats in Brewster. (I didn't think it wise to tell the publishers that
he had been tripping, as had I, when he took the photo.) I held the
book in my hand and felt something profound rise up inside me. It
was not the blood lust of a Frisbee conqueror spiking a disc on the
field, or the exhilaration I would feel at the birth of my daughter.
It was something much quieter. Something calm and deeply satisfying. My face flushed with pleasure. I had the sense that I had
finally accomplished something, something that it seemed I had
been trying to accomplish forever.

But, then again, at the same time I had the opposite sensation.
The sense not of finality and achievement but of promise. The feeling that, after many false starts and much stumbling, I had begun.

Epilogue

This Is the Modern World

Over the next few years I drifted away from the sport. In 1998, after I had published my second book, I briefly came out of Ultimate retirement and returned to play with the reigning champion Boston team, not so much as a player as a reporter. My idea was to write a George Plimpton–style book about the game, from the inside, and maybe kill two birds with one stone and win Nationals. I played one spring tournament with the Boston team, during which we beat Ken Dobyns and New York in the finals, and then I raced home to start typing up my notes. I loved the idea that I was going to take the stories from the game's oral tradition and put them on the page. And as an added bonus there was this: I might finally make people understand that Ultimate was not a joke but a real thing, a great thing.

I sent a sample of what I was working on to my agent, who was also excited. She didn't reveal this to me, but I heard through a mutual writer friend that she thought she would be able sell it for big bucks. And sure enough there was interest in the Ultimate book from New York publishers. I drove down to New York to attend meetings, thrilled to think that I would finally be published by a big publisher and that the subject of that book would be Ultimate. From my journal at that time, I know that my wife and I had less than fifty dollars in our joint bank account.

It was close, my agent told me later; they *almost* took it. Why didn't they? I asked. In the end, no publishers would buy the book, mostly because the marketers and publicists were afraid no one would know what Ultimate Frisbee was. *Isn't that the thing you do with dogs?*

It was perfect in its own cruel way. Once again my Rodney Dangerfield of a sport had gotten no respect. I had been interviewing Ken Dobyns for the book and he put my failure in terms I could understand. Ultimate is like that bad girlfriend, he told me, the one you keep going back to who keeps screwing you over.

It would take almost another twenty years until I finally decided it was time to write a book about the sport that had swallowed up my younger years. In the late summer of 2015 I left my new home in North Carolina and drove north with two stops in mind, one in New York and one in Boston. In rural Pawling, New York, I visited Ken Dobyns, and we sat on his back deck and sipped a beer in the near dark as deer nibbled around the edge of the property.

At the age of fifty-three Ken's life had changed significantly, his wife having just given birth to a daughter, his first child. But we didn't talk about that. We didn't talk about *now*. We talked about the old days.

"I can say honestly that I never questioned it," Kenny Dobyns told me. "There was never any doubt about what my priorities were."

"What about your father?" I asked. "Did he come around after you won all those titles?"

"He never did. He never mentioned Ultimate."

I found this astounding, and even more astounding, to me, was

Ken's lack of doubt in the face of his father's indifference. My own father had been dead twenty years and it was now hard for me to reimagine, to re-*feel*, what a looming figure he'd once been in my psychic life. I apologized to Ken for getting Freudian, but asked him to elaborate on his relationship with his dad.

"You said your father ridiculed Ultimate," he said. "Well, ridicule is one thing but a total rejection of the notion that it was something worth appreciating was pretty tough. As much as I denied the notion that his approval was important to me at the time, ultimately it was. He's my dad."

Ken Dobyns is a smart man, a funny man at times, and a gifted writer. But what still fascinates me is his certainty, his unwavering belief. The fact that he determined, at about the age of eighteen or nineteen, that the most important thing in life was being a great Ultimate player and playing for a National Champion, and that he then clung to that goal, tenaciously, ferociously even, unlike most of us, and achieved it. Of course obsession is at least in part about control. If I do this, if I throw all of myself into it, all of me, then I will succeed. We are taught as a culture to respect those who are driven, and I do. But the word *driven* implies someone else is doing the driving. Does a lack of doubt make a commitment unthinking or does it make it pure in the way more wavering souls will never understand?

"I'm also enough of a realist to laugh at what we were back then," he said. "We were over-the-top and I was probably the most over-the-top of all. But at the same time I wouldn't take any of it back."

Before I left I asked him if he had ever made peace with his old enemy, Steve Mooney.

"Not really. I haven't ever really had a chance to chat with him. I'm not sure it would matter anyway. The intensity has faded with time but we still don't like each other."

The next night I visited Moons in Brookline, Massachusetts. We went to the park and tossed with his teenage son, Ben, and then came back to the house and drank beers and talked about the old days. We had a great night, and I felt a deep fondness for Steve. But at one point I felt compelled to bring up the accusation, made by Hostages and New York alike, that he could be a phony.

"We're all human," he said. "You don't win any National Championships without being fiercely competitive. So I'm in absolute agreement that my goal was to win. I tried to do it with the highest degree of integrity and occasionally was unable to hold it together. But the phony thing. It's hard to understand that."

He admitted that during the dark years of the New York–Boston rivalry lines had been crossed.

"If you want to win, you are going to cross the line every now and then. I don't take anything away from what New York did. They were awesome. As for the other stuff, they didn't need to do it. That is the frustrating part. We did it a little, they did it more. In a perfect world you wish we had done it the same amount. That the ref or whoever would even it out and we'd just be out there playing."

He told me a story of a moment during halftime of a finals game sometime in the middle of their run of National Championships. They were in the huddle and one of his teammates was yelling, "It's about desire!" The huddle broke and Steve was walking back to the sidelines when some random spectator said quietly, as if to himself, "It's not about desire, it's about will." And Steve thought, *This guy is right.* That's it. Willpower. The payoff of desire.

In the long haul, Steve's career had been a sustained act of will. From the early success with the Rude Boys to the dark days of losing to New York to his run of six championships in a row. There was a final elegance to it all. Year after year he had shaped his career with willpower and ultimately made it conform to his will.

The training, the stadiums, the strategy, the leadership. You could take off for style points if you were of the Hostage mind-set, but you couldn't criticize the effort.

"In the end it's not all about winning," Steve said before we called it a night. "It's about trying to win."

As talented as Moons and Dobyns were, it was really this ability to recommit, this character of mind, this persistence, that was even more impressive. They had focused on a thing and never lost focus. They could handle the pain and potential embarrassment and keep on going.

I made one final stop on my way back to North Carolina. You could say it was just a parking lot, but for a parking lot it was pretty wide-open and fieldlike. A creek ran off to the left in a gully, and while it was garbage strewn with a cinder block and Sprite bottles it was still a creek. On the right, the other side of the lot, was a humped-up hill with train tracks on it, where the New Jersey transit ran. Mourning doves cooed and trash dotted the thistles and while it was semi-fieldlike I suppose nothing really distinguished the place from other parking lots, nothing except for the rock near its entrance with a circular plaque that read: "Birthplace of Ultimate Frisbee. Created by Columbia High School in 1968."

This was it. The very place where Joel Silver had played, predicting that Ultimate, his baby, his invention, would one day conquer the world. Had it? Maybe not, but in that summer of 2015 there were more than a few glimmers of possibility. Millions of people were playing worldwide; there were pro leagues where some of the top players were paid $50,000 a year. And best of all, earlier that summer the International Olympic Committee had announced that Ultimate was a contender sport for the Olympics. This had led to a media flurry that included reports on NPR and in the *New York Times* and *The New Yorker*. *The New Yorker* noted that disc sports were now played by "7.5 million people in more than ninety countries around the world, including 4.5 million in the U.S." and wrote that the reason for the IOC recognition really came down to several things: "the spirit of the game, gender equity, global growth, youth appeal, and, most of all, how fun it is to watch."

As I walked across the Columbia High School lot, I realized I didn't have a Frisbee with me. I hadn't planned on stopping and had nothing to throw. Discless, I felt unarmed, and so like a beachcomber I skimmed through the trash at the edge of the lot hoping to find something round and throwable, like the lid to a plastic tub. But while there was plenty of plastic, that substance without which Ultimate would not have come into being, none of it was the right shape. A Big Gulp cup, gallon jugs, white spoons, soda bottles. Finally I came upon a pizza box and opened it, hoping there would be one of those circular cardboard inserts inside, but all I found was a scrambling cockroach. It seemed wrong, if not sacrilegious, to not huck a disc the length of the sacred lot.

In November of 2015, nineteen years after I'd last played at Nationals, I traveled to Dallas and the National Championships. I was an anthropologist beamed into the future. During the decades I'd been away I'd always vaguely wondered what the game, my old girlfriend, had been up to. Now I would find out.

When I first walked onto the fields, after showing my press pass to the cop at the stadium gate, I was struck by how *clean* everything was. There was a grubbiness to Ultimate in my era, an era not just of gray cotton sweats and cases of beer on the sidelines but of lots of dirt and blood on fields that sometimes looked like a battle scene in *Game of Thrones*. There was still blood and beer, though the latter was sold at a concession stand, but there was also something that, to my archaic eye, seemed antiseptic and commercial about the whole thing, a festival still but a less spontaneous one. I walked past a series of tents along the end zone where, along with discs and programs, a whole line of cute and stylish Ultimate clothing was being sold. In my day most of the spectators were other Ultimate players who didn't happen to be playing at the moment, and while that didn't seem to have changed much, the fans were now far back from the field in the stadium stands, not gathered on the sidelines right on the field. Since my old Boston teammate John Axon had secured me an all-access field pass, I, after buying two beers and pouring them into my water bottle, got to watch the game the old-fashioned way: right on the sidelines.

By chance the first game I saw was the semifinals and the sideline I was standing on was Boston's, which sent me down the rabbit hole of memory. They were playing Seattle in the semis, and it turned out they were losing to Seattle. *Losing in the semis.* Ah, yes. I remembered it well. Later that night I would go by the hotel and try to interview the Boston players, but they were too busy with the hard and obsessive work of reliving their loss, drinking, and regretting. Again, I knew the feeling. Frisbee had, in its own way, taught me about loss. Though losing a tournament couldn't compare to losing a testicle or father, there is a way in which a loss in sports is more vivid and direct, more obvious, than the gradual losses of real life. You have the sense of failure, of something being snuffed out, that you rarely get with more quotidian failure. As Dobyns had long ago pointed out, if winning is your goal, then only one team heads into the off-season happy. For the rest, for the young Boston team, it would be a long winter until spring broke and brought back hope of winning again the next fall.

My first thought was that the game looked *good*. Thin, tall athletes who knew what they were doing. Lots of fakes and fore-hands and not too much stoppage of play for arguing. It seemed like everyone had good throws, not just the best players—or as John Axon put it, "even the guys who can't throw can throw"—and both teams had huge rosters filled by mostly clean-cut men who all wore numbered uniforms. There wasn't a small grubby Hostage-like team in sight.

It was all pretty impressive but then something started to change while I watched, and the game became less clean and controlled as a new element of uncertainty was introduced. This was the same element that had always been able to change Ultimate games, the same element that had so vexed Steve Mooney against the Hostages back in the early '80s.

As the wind picked up there were more drops and throwaways, and the sport started looking more like the one I knew. This was clear during the men's semifinals and even more during the next game I watched, the women's semis between Colorado and Boston, where the wind turned the game into a sloppy turnover fest. The skills in the women's game had made even more of a jump than the men's, however, as I learned the next day during the finals when the Boston women's team won it all. After the game, which had featured layout dives and skying of the sort that matched any men's game, I gave my field pass to a dad of one of the players, a guy who had played during my era, and I teared up as he ran out and hugged his daughter after the win. I found myself wondering if my daughter would ever play Ultimate. In fact, the second-generational aspect of the sport was one of the most moving things about the weekend (and, mathematically speaking, for my group of players, a third generation isn't far behind).

What I saw on the field was the same sport but a different sport. A stubborn adolescent grown into adulthood on its own terms, though also having made some concessions to the real world. Had Ultimate made it? Well, what is the *it*? It is the same *it* it has always been, the thing that many players have hoped for and just as many have feared. It is the same *it* as in other professions, despite the protestations. To be noticed, to be known, to be acknowledged as worthy. And what will be lost if the unknown becomes known, if people nod with respect instead of laughing when you tell them that you play Frisbee. Will it become "just like other sports," whatever that means? Does being on TV or wanting to be known suddenly detract from the purity? Does anyone really still believe that? Did they ever?

At Nationals I learned that the Spirit of the Game lives on. The morning before the Boston women's finals I'd talked to Will Deaver, the managing director of Competition and Athlete Programs, and the longest tenured employee, for USA Ultimate. We stood on the sidelines and watched the coed finals, while he gave me a state of the Spirit report. All the games at Nationals now had "observers," sort of semi-referees who made some of the calls. This innovation had begun in my time, though much less formally, and I told Will about a friend who had observed an important game while tripping.

"They don't trip anymore," he said with a smile. "They are trained. Well trained."

I asked if observers weren't just referees by any other name, an attempt by Ultimate to eat its cake and have it too.

"No, not really," he said. "Observers make all the calls that a player can't possibly make. Like whether he or she is in or out along the sidelines. But players make the calls where they have a better perspective and that they are involved in, like fouls. Then, if they can't resolve it quickly, the observer is called in. We are trying to set up a different dynamic. Not a dynamic where you are trying to get away with something or you're trying to convince a ref that something happened that didn't. We are asking the players to take responsibility and sometimes it works. We've created a sport that is exciting to play and watch, and with different expectations about sportsmanship and how you follow the rules."

I retained my skepticism, but I had to admit that the current game moved a lot more quickly and was less argument filled. But could there ever really be a sport on TV without referees? Could McEnroe have made his own calls at the U.S. Open? I have always thought it preposterous, but the observer system has its advantages in that it gives players the opportunity to do the right thing. But why? To prove that Ultimate is different, that Ultimate players are a higher life-form than regular athletic schmucks? Or because there really is something ethical and maybe even inspiring about the idea that the job of the athlete, the embodiment of arête, the excellence, is to be honorable, not to try and convince or fool a stripe-shirted policeman?

I watched the finals the next day. The clear star was a former University of Colorado player, a kid from Alaska named Beau Kittredge. A decade earlier Beau had won the Callahan Award as best college player, and had already won Nationals with his team, the San Francisco Revolver, as well as twice being MVP of the pro league. He was 6'4" and extremely fast. During his off-season training his numbers were comparable with other elite athletes, including a 400 time of forty-six seconds, less than three seconds off Michael Johnson's mind-blowing world record (and incidentally, two seconds faster than Rude Boy Finlay Waugh's time back in the early '80s). It was a time that would have *been* the world record halfway through the twentieth century. But for all his speed he didn't play like a stop-start sprinter, or burst from a standstill the way Kenny Dobyns had. Instead he cruised around the

Beau Kittredge, a thoroughly modern Ultimate player, skying.

field sharklike, in control, and then gradually took his speed up a notch, and then another. He owned anything in the air, though even there I had a sense that he was in control, explosive in a relatively subdued fashion, if such a thing were possible. Would he have skyed over the best receivers of my day? Probably, though Joey G. and Cribber could have won their share of battles with him. A more relevant question might be, could an NFL cornerback break up a pass thrown to him? The obvious answer is yes, but there are complicating factors. Cornerbacks aren't usually all that tall and discs don't drop from the sky the way balls do. They hover. It is less about intercepting the angle than going up and getting the thing.

Watching Beau led me to imagining what it would be like if the very best athletes, say a LeBron James, were going up for a hovering disc. He would come swooping in, first slowing down and then exploding upward and reaching, snatching the disc from where it hovered at, what, say eleven feet in the air or so.

And that was the thing. Coming back, watching after all those years, that was what I noticed: it was a beautiful game. You could squabble about particulars—the Spirit of the Game or whether players were "selling out" by turning pro—but what you couldn't argue about was the game itself. The physics of it. The way a disc hovers above the ground before landing so that a player can snatch something that looked impossible to catch when it was thrown. The way a player can time a leap in the air and grab a disc that seems to be sitting up there, hovering like a kestrel or an osprey. And the way a disc can carve above or curve around in a way that a ball never could. Bend it like Beckham? Try a throw that can go out of bounds 20 yards on one side of the field and then boomerang back to the opposite corner of the other. Add the world's best athletes to this and what you would have is a kind of wild ballet, a game full of moments that seem improbable, crazy even.

By the way, I watched the men's finals in the stands with the Boston women. Not in a creepy way, mind you; I was aware that I was old enough to be a grandfather to some of them. But it was fun to watch their jubilation, an end-of-the-season feeling I had never experienced myself, and they half-watched the men's game and half celebrated, hugging each other and crying, and drinking and gobbling down the pizzas they had had delivered right there in the stands. They had had *their* glory, but the highlight for me came when someone threw a mini-Frisbee into the stands and I shot up my right arm and snatched it between two fingers. The crowd cheered. That might have been my greatest athletic achievement in close to two decades. I felt unjustifiably proud.

The Boston men were there in the stands with us, too, but while they tried to enjoy the buzz of the women's victory, most of them couldn't quite shake the loss in the semis the day before. And they wouldn't shake it, not right away, not in fact until a year later, on October 2, 2016.

For Steve Mooney that second day in October would be a nerve-racking one. Like many Americans, he would spend that Sunday watching sports on TV, but unlike most, he wouldn't be watching football. Instead he would watch the Ultimate National Championships on ESPN 3. Boston would make both the men's and women's finals, with the outcomes of both games coming down to the last point. Moons found himself jumping up out of his seat and yelling as if he were there. I had an additional rooting interest. A few of the Boston players had played for the Harvard team that had made it to the finals of College Nationals the spring before.

The conclusion would prove satisfying for Moons, and for me. Boston won both squeakers, which, combined with their win of the coed category earlier in the day, meant a rare sweep.

Boston was back on top.

About halfway between San Francisco and Los Angeles, San Simeon Bay is the first significant bay south of Monterey. It sits in the shadow of Hearst castle and the beach, with its peeling eucalyptus trees growing down to the eroding hump of dirt above the sand, is also named after the long-dead newspaper mogul.

In April of 2016 I found myself on Hearst Memorial Beach throwing a collector's item, an actual Frisbie pie tin with the words FRISBIE'S PIES imprinted on it, with none other than Tom Kennedy, he of the arête and shining city on the hill. The pie tin actually flew pretty well—you could even throw a forehand with it—and was the same type of disc that the Yale students threw back in the 1950s. Earlier TK and I had hiked to the end of San Simeon point as a bald eagle flew off in front of us and enjoyed stunning views of the bay, where TK often kayaked (and had once been thoroughly soaked and almost capsized by a breaching whale). I'd spent the previous afternoon with TK, a day filled with talking Ultimate, touring his machinist's shop, and hiking to the hilltop of his property in rural Cambria. The highlight had come while I was

Tom Kennedy, back in the day

interviewing him outside his office and a young bobcat strolled by the window. Only after I'd been there a couple hours did he admit it was his sixty-seventh birthday; we celebrated by heading down into town for dinner, then coming back for an impressive bout of partying and Nerf Ping-Pong late into the night

Thinking about Ultimate again, and hanging with Tom Kennedy, led me back to thinking about the old arête-renaissance man ideal. It had been the dream of my twenties, to be a kind of intellectual barbarian. To have my cleats and Frisbees piled up in the corner of my bedroom, but to also have books piled up and a drawing board at the ready. As it turned out I had rarely been able to do all those things at once, but they had, rather, taken turns in my life.

After a while we put the pie tin away and broke out the modern version. We backed up over the sand so that the little tidal outflow was between us, and had a good long throw. TK threw almost all backhands and I threw almost all forehands.

"I have an A backhand, but a B-minus forehand," he said.

He wasn't bragging, just telling the truth. Closer to A plus actually. "He could put that backhand anywhere," said Buzz Ellsworth, my childhood friend who'd played for the Santa Barbara Condors. In fact, it was that backhand that had helped the Condors go undefeated for months, and at one point even *years*, at a time.

It may not have been quite as strong as it once was, but his backhand still flew far and true, and I felt honored to be throwing with him. How many games of catch had TK had in his life? How many had I had? This was where it all started.

We'd built up a good sweat by the time we had to say good-bye. TK was heading home and I was heading up to San Francisco, where I was going to give a reading from my new book that night. The day before I'd toured Santa Barbara and gotten to see firsthand the Mission lawn and Palm Park, with fifty-foot-tall palms swaying in the offshore breeze, the very un-parking-lot-like places where West Coast Ultimate had come into being.

There were a grand total of six ex-Hostages at my reading at the bookstore that night. Afterward we posed together for a picture and then headed over to the Marin Brewery. I spent the night at Jeff "Wheels" Sandler's and Karen Bayle's house in Marin. Jeff had been a great Hostage goal catcher and Karen was a Hostage, too, even if she had never played with us. Over the years I had stayed at their homes in Marin many times and they were always generous hosts. The next morning my old Boulder teammate Ian Hutchinson (née Hue) drove down to join us on a bike ride from Jeff and Karen's house up Mount Tam. Neal Lischner, another fellow ex-Hostage, had recently broken his ankle in a rock-climbing accident and couldn't join us, but his wife, Eileen, did. It was a four-and-a-half-hour bike ride and it almost killed me, but it was a beautiful day and looking out from near the top we saw a bald eagle soaring and beyond it the banks of fog that seemed to stop right at the bridge with the white city still farther beyond. I hadn't told anyone yet but for me it was also a training ride. My old Boulder teammates had invited me to join them the next fall at the Great-Grandmaster World Championships for players over fifty. Old dreams of winning it all were stirring. Despite a bum shoulder and a suspicious hip, I had started training. Maybe it wasn't over yet. Getting my aged self in shape, without breaking that self, would be the challenge.

We were barely back in the house when the first beers were cracked. Neal, on crutches, would be bringing barbecue for dinner. I felt exhilarated by the big ride. Jeff brought out a copy he had of the long-ago letter banning me from playing Ultimate in Washington, and he showed it to Ian. He read it out loud and we all howled with arrogant laughter.

When David Barkan arrived I took a break from the merry-making to interview him about the organization he had founded, Ultimate Peace. Barkan, the former sparkplug (and hothead), had turned visionary and now directed a summer camp in Israel where Jewish Israeli, Arab Israeli, and Palestinian kids learned to play Ultimate. Could the peace of the world hinge on Frisbee?

When I first heard about UP, as it was known, I'd been a little skeptical. Not only of the idea of Ultimate Frisbee solving the problems of the Middle East but of Barkan, of all people, playing the role of peacemaker. I told him this.

"Well, in a way that's where it all came from," he said. "I know that in the old days I was one of the worst culprits as far as Spirit of the Game. I was kind of a dick. It wasn't the players from the other teams that were upset with me as much as other Hostages, especially Gus. And in a way Ultimate Peace began with my own transformation. I took some time off to live in Israel, and when I started playing again on the West Coast I tried to put Spirit first."

Later in my career, when I'd played for Boulder, I sometimes played against Barkan and his San Francisco teams, and I can testify that he was a different player. He never attained the white-heat supernova moments of the Hostages wins in '81 and '82, but he was a more steady and consistent player, and he was much more spirited. Players who knew him only from the West Coast saw him as more statesman than hothead.

After he retired from "real" Ultimate he formed a Jewish all-star team called the Matza Balls. The Matza Balls actually won a few tournaments and in 2005 they were invited to play in an exhibition in Israel. It was on the plane ride back that Barkan had his insight. It had been great to showcase the game for Israeli Jews, but what if he brought in other cultures? What if the same tools with which he had helped transform himself could transform others?

Four years later he organized a one-day camp in Israel, and the next year, riding on the success of the first year, they held a week-long camp. A key moment was when they teamed up with the Ministry of Culture and Sport in Israel. The idea was to recruit Jewish, Arab, and Palestinian kids and mix them up on different teams, and use Ultimate, and the Spirit of the Game in particular, to teach values of respect, community, conflict resolution, and teamwork. Their mission was simple: "to develop understanding, trust, and friendship among Arab, Jewish, and Palestinian youth, using the character-based sport of Ultimate as its tool." The hard part was talking parents into sending their kids to a camp where the group would be so mixed, but UP had a couple of things working for it. One was that the kids were naturally attracted to playing this American sport with a bunch of Americans and therefore tended to work their parents hard. Another was that UP, with the help of the ministry and the aid of their Arab director, pitched the idea in Arab and Palestinian schools.

The shocking thing is how well it worked. The pictures and

videos of camp tell a stunning story. A girl in a hijab guarding an Israeli girl, team cheers before games, the games themselves, and a whole lot of old-fashioned camp-style goofing around when they are not playing.

"We have had friendships that stuck," Barkan said. "Arab kids have been in the wedding parties of the Israeli friends they met at camp."

The makeup of the program was 35 percent Israeli Jews, 15 percent Palestinian, 50 percent Arab Israelis. Most of the coaches were Ultimate players from the United States who paid their own way to get to Israel, and more than a couple of them, including Jimmy Levine, were Hostages. Ultimate Peace has been recognized by the United Nations and has expanded beyond the camp itself, with the players and coaches traveling to different cities to put on clinics and raise funds.

You could argue that the peak for the Hostages had been at Regionals in 1981. But it wouldn't be crazy to say that the peak was yet to come, that attaining world peace was right up there with beating the Rude Boys. I had always been a Spirit of the Game cynic, and I still was to some extent, but I couldn't argue with it in this context. I particularly appreciated the fact that Ultimate Peace had grown out of Barkan's intransigence and his efforts to overcome it.

I would like to report that the rest of our talk that night was as high-minded as our discussion of Ultimate Peace. Barkan wasn't the only one who had grown up, after all. Karen was a doctor and had volunteered as the staff doctor at Ultimate Peace for the first six years, and Neal was a doctor, too, one who had gone back to medical school in his thirties after having hung up his cleats. Jeff and I were both teachers. We didn't often drool on trophies anymore.

But while we were clearly capable of high-mindedness, it would be a lie to say that we spent the night talking about profound things. The night went where it always went with these old teammates after exercise and alcohol. We drank late and told stories we'd all heard before. It was just like the old days. In a sport with no external commentators, no coaches, and little TV coverage, we could tell ourselves our own stories about what we had seen and experienced. Not surprisingly, as the night wore on, those stories often starred ourselves.

We returned, as always, to our habitual subject: how great we were.

And we were great, goddamn it.

We really were.

Acknowledgments

Much of the meat of the present book was conceived and written in an insomniac blaze over eight days in the spring of 1998 as I tried to set the oral tradition of the sport I'd been obsessed with to the page. When the proposal for the book didn't sell I was crushed. It isn't just in Ultimate that I have suffered some hard losses, and the book's failure was the equivalent of the Hostage loss in the 1983 Regionals. Both took a long time to get over.

The book's tortuous comeback, through the metaphorical losers' bracket over the course of almost two decades, hinged on the support of Ultimate players, who discovered the essay I had made of the book online and started to spread it out into the world. This gradually gave me the confidence to believe again in *Ultimate Glory* as a book. Then, in the late winter of 2015, Dennis "Cribber" Warsen and Dave Blau, old rivals from New York, New York, asked me for creative input on their film, *Flatball,* a history of Ultimate. I was both impressed by the story that Dennis was telling and reinspired to tell my own. Not long after that the Olympic Committee announced that they were considering Ultimate as an Olympic sport, and suddenly Ultimate was hot. In a happy coincidence I had just signed on with my new agent, Peter Steinberg, who greeted the project with great enthusiasm. I was worried that once again publishers would ask "Is that the thing you do with dogs?" but Peter quelled my fears. We had long been friends but now I got to see, and be dazzled by, his professionalism as he, in short order, edited the manuscript, kept my spirits up, and sold the book.

Steve Mooney is a model of consistent dedication and, despite the flak he has taken over the years from me, the Hostages, and certain New Yorkers, I hope he sees that he is in many ways the book's hero. In the opposite corner is the other man who lent this book his life, Ken Dobyns. When we spoke he was, as always, honest, blunt, and articulate. Obsession has long been both the subject and method of my work and I've never encountered someone so wonderfully obsessed as Ken was as a young man. Though I did not focus as much on Ken's partner in crime, Pat King, his insights and ideas and written tributes to players and teams were indispensable.

Tom Kennedy, the father of California Ultimate, couldn't have been more gracious, taking me into his home and sharing his photos, writing, and memories. Keay Nakae pointed me toward Tom in a long interview he gave me after attending a reading I gave in New York. Thanks to Harvard teammates Simon Long, Jon Epstein, Charlie Bliss, Emmit Thomas, Stuart Gross, Peter Sanborn, and Bennet Goldberg. And thanks to Nathan Salwen: there should be a statue of him built next to the Harvard fields. A more recent Harvard grad, Aidan Shapiro-Leighton, has helped me usher the book toward publication and get it out to current Ultimate players.

Thanks to the Hostages, starting with David Barkan, our leader back then and the founder of Ultimate Peace. If there is a warts-and-all aspect to my portrait of Barkan as a young man, I hope it is clear that it is tinged with love and admiration, or, as I sang at his wedding, "I got you, Dave." I'm less worried about offending Steve "Gus" Gustafson, since I'm not sure it's possible. Let me just say thanks and also this: like Jack London, I'll always take a superb meteor over a steady planet, and for two years when Boston was the sport's hotbed there was no question who the most superb of the meteors was. I've mentioned all the Hostages by name in the dedication, but for interviews and specific help, thanks to Jeff Sandler, Karen Bayle, Eileen Everett, Paul Turner, Bill MacAvoy, Adam Phillips, Jim Levine, and Mark Honerkamp. On the Rude Boy side thanks to Chris Heye, Phil "Guido" Adams, Jim Herrick, John Mooney, and Finlay Waugh. Thanks also to recent Boston players Mike Zalisk and David Reshef, who spoke to me after their lost in the semis at Nationals in 2015.

Among the many great Boston women players, I owe special thanks to good friends Heather Morris and Liz Swann. My writing about the founding of women's Ultimate owes much to my interview with Suzanne Fields, who played a crucial role in those early days. Thanks to Gloria LustPhillips, who made me laugh while helping me understand the history of Lady Godiva.

Thanks to Dan Weiss, for help giving me a fuller picture of both the New York dynasty and Flying Circus, and to Ron "Ronar" Oliner, who caught many of the goals Dan threw. For helping me understand the early days of Ultimate at Columbia High School and beyond, thanks to Irv Kalb, David Leiwant, Jim Pistrang, Jon Cohn, and Mark Epstein. While the interviews with early players were vital to the book, it was also important to have the steady baseline of research that came before me to riff off of. Thank you to Pasquale Anthony Leonardo, Adam Zagoria, and Joe Seidler for creating *Ultimate: The First Four Decades*, a comprehensive and well-researched history of the sport.

In Boston I need to thank Eric Zaslow, Jeff Brown, Mike Cooper, and Paul Sackley. A special thank-you needs to go out to Jim Parinella, who has been there all the way on this project and who kept my stories in line, and John Axon, who was always a great teammate and accompanied me to Nationals in 2015. At Nationals that year we had the pleasure of interviewing Beau Kittredge, who was that tournament's MVP. Will Deaver, of USA Ultimate, also took time out from a busy weekend to give me a full state-of-the-game report. The women on Boston's winning team, Brute Squad, also took a break from their jubilation to talk to me. And thanks to Carl Seville, who described the joy of seeing his daughter, Paula, win Nationals.

I owe a special thanks to Bob Pease, who for many years played the Moons role in Colorado. Thanks, too, to Jimmy Mickle, who won with Colorado in college and club during the same year, and sat down and talked to me about more recent teams. I made too many good friends in Boulder and I know I will leave out some names, though I tried to list a few back on **page 301**. Thanks to Phil Lohre, Mike Morrissey, Mark Karger, Dave Smith, and Randy "Hall-o-Fame" Ricks for taking the time out for interviews. Thanks to Gary Foreman and the whole Old and In the Way gang for letting me play along in Florida, and for Charlie Lian, who got me back in shape. And a special thanks to Dave "Buzzy" Ellsworth, both for the interview and for being there on the field with me from about second grade on.

Over the years I've learned that once you think you've finished a book the work has just begun. I have been very lucky, over the last couple of years, to have a great researcher in Doug Diesenhaus, and this time he helped me, among other things, organize and get permissions for the photographs in the book. Like Ultimate players, the photographers from my time went unheralded and unrecognized, and it is with great pride that I get to present the work of Stuart Berringer, Dan Hyslop, Karl Cook, Mark Honerkamp, Rick Collins, Mark Epstein, Ellise Fuchs, and Toby Green. And thanks to UltiPhotos and Kevin Leclaire, Jolie Lang, and Paul Andris.

My experience with Riverhead Books has been delightful, from brainstorming with Katie Freeman about ways to wake the world to Frisbee to working with the uber-efficient Kevin Murphy. Most of all, I need to thank my editor, Courtney Young, who took something that was rough, wild, and going in many directions and helped shape and structure it, beautifully tempering my instincts toward excess. With a light touch and a sharp mind, she gently ushered me, after some resistance, in a direction that has led to a tighter, stronger and better book. My deep thanks for that.

As always I end by thanking the two who make me me. Hadley and Nina, for ever and always.